# GAMBLING

*Readers in Social Problems*

DONALD R. CRESSEY, CONSULTING EDITOR

UNIVERSITY OF CALIFORNIA, SANTA BARBARA

# GAMBLING

EDITED BY

## ROBERT D. HERMAN

POMONA COLLEGE

J. & J. HARPER EDITIONS
HARPER & ROW, PUBLISHERS
NEW YORK AND EVANSTON

FIRST J. & J. HARPER EDITION 1969

*Printed on long-life, acid-free paper, with reinforced bindings*

LIBRARY OF CONGRESS CATALOG CARD NUMBER: 67-12549

# CONTENTS

364,17208
H55

36675

# PART IV / GAMBLING, CRIME,
# AND PUBLIC POLICY

# PREFACE

THIS BOOK includes some selections because they explore the social and psychological meanings of gambling itself, others because they present major arguments in the debates on public policy and the regulation of gambling, and still others, taken from the popular literature, because they describe some of the profoundly personal, living issues in gambling.

Gambling is made up of activities with rich symbolic content, hence some of the most intriguing analyses of the subject have been made by anthropologists and psychoanalysts (and characteristic examples of their writings are included in Part Three, "Gambling as a Pathology"). The reader may make his own evaluation of the utility of the psychoanalytic view, but he should be aware that the largest proportion of the serious literature on gambling considers it pathological, a manifestation of sickness or weakness either in the individual or the social order. Such writings tend to emphasize the common elements in different forms of gambling, they usually show greater interest in players than games, they are more conscious of losers than winners, and they are preoccupied with bizarre rather than with conventional modes of gambling behavior.

Of course, it may also be said that in *most* discussions of gambling commanding the public's general attention, its negative features are given prominence. For example, we hear, among other warnings, that the flow of money from individual bettors to owners of certain gambling establishments is often diverted into political channels, with serious consequences for the entire society. Or we are told that gambling is intimately related to certain types of criminal activity (see Part Four in this book). These views are currently being given wide publicity as voters in several states are drawn into debates on the desirability of extending gambling opportunities to larger markets by liberalizing laws on lotteries, card games, and off-track betting on horse races.

Thus gambling is often presented to the public as a specific social problem, a source of tension, and a stimulus to deviancy.

Whether the questions raised are phrased in terms of economics, morality, or individual compulsion, the general debate has largely failed to encourage systematic efforts by serious students of human behavior to collect and analyze empirical data about gambling practices and institutions. Thus in the large sociological literature on social problems, gambling is rarely given more than passing treatment.

However, when the subject is changed from gambling-in-particular to games-in-general, social scientists and the general public both have learned to profit from a more balanced point of view. It has become a commonplace to say that games are vital elements of culture. Children's games, rather than being thought of as trivial, harmful, or irrelevant in the socialization process, are seen as necessary learning mechanisms, as engaging models of the "real" world, as both fun and functional. Furthermore, it appears useful to interpret interpersonal relationships of all sorts—of adults as well as of children—as "games people play." (See Eric Berne's book by that title, N.Y., Grove Press, 1964.) By making such interpretations, whole new dimensions of social behavior are brought to light, important elements of mutual influence are revealed, and consequences of many interpersonal encounters are more efficiently predicted. In short, we have learned to appreciate that games should be constructively analyzed, openly studied, and carefully evaluated.

Although it is correct to say that the question of "legalizing" gambling has not inspired studies equal to those of games-in-general, several selections in Parts One and Two which define the subcultural contexts of gambling also identify some of its functional advantages as well as its disadvantages. These are in marked contrast to the more conventional strictures (of Part Four), which are included here because they represent views of important public officials or church spokesmen.

The editor, then, does not agree, in the usual sense, with all of the authors whose works are represented here, but he is anxious to thank them for their contributions, which help to continue the wider discussion of gambling.

ROBERT D. HERMAN

# PART I

# Forms of Gambling

THIS SECTION examines the meanings of selected different forms of gambling by emphasizing the social contexts from which the players are recruited and in which the "action" occurs.

Drake and Cayton discuss the "policy" business in the selection taken from their lengthy work on the Negro ghetto ("Bronzeville") of Chicago. Whyte probes some of the subtle dimensions of racketeering in his detailed study of Boston gangs. Together with Zola's article on lower-class tavern life, these analyses offer the reader an unusual view of the social system of illegal gambling.

Frazier interprets compulsive poker playing in a chapter from his famous analysis of the Negro middle class. Rosten has written an interesting book about the occupations and preoccupations of Hollywood folk, including, in this selection, their interests in horse racing.

# "Policy": Poor Man's Roulette

### ST. CLAIR DRAKE AND HORACE CAYTON

Almost as numerous as the churches (and more evenly distributed) are Bronzeville's 500 odd "policy stations," in any one of which a person may place a bet that certain numbers will be announced as lucky by one of fifteen or sixteen "policy companies." Policy is a lottery game.[1] It is also a "protected business," operating in defiance of Illinois State Statute No. 413, but under the benevolent patronage of the city political machine. In order to keep up a semblance of respect for the law, about half the stations are "fronted" by legitimate businesses. Most of the others can be easily recognized by the initiated, sometimes by a light over a basement entrance, again by a sign on a window or door: "OPEN"—"4-11-44"— "DOING BUSINESS"—"ALL BOOKS."

A knowing observer can also spot a policy station by the constantly moving stream of customers going in and coming out carrying "drawings"—the slips on which the winning numbers are printed. (Figure 1.) These slips are distributed three times a day, and at busy stations long queues form as people come to place new bets, collect their winnings, or inquire about results. The unwary person who stands too close to the door of a policy station at certain hours is likely to be hit by the small roll of policy slips—the drawings— which are flung from a speeding car by the "pick-up men" as they hasten from shop to shop carrying the latest numbers.

TWO LEGGED BOOK                    ONE LEGGED BOOK

| ROYAL PALM<br>c867½ MN | | |
|---|---|---|
| 40 | | 56 |
| 50 | | 7 |
| 4 | | 26 |
| 2 | | 11 |
| 7 | | 22 |
| 77 | BOTH | 52 |
| 47 | | 50 |
| 12 | | 44 |
| 39 | | 15 |
| 66 | | 61 |
| 17 | | 62 |
| 45 | | 27 |

IOWA
c277½ MN

1st Six { 72, 29, 56, 28, 30, 38 }

2nd Six { 8, 59, 2, 53, 4, 6 }

1st Cap } 72, 29
2nd Cap } 56, 28, 30, 38
3rd Cap } 8, 59, 2
4th Cap } 53, 4, 6

Figure 1. Policy "Drawings" or "Slips"[a]

[a] For explanation of the terms used in this figure, see footnote on p. 251.

Bronzeville places its bets in one or more of thirty "pools" known colloquially as "books." These pools have distinctive names, such as Monte Carlo, Bronx, Royal Palm, Harlem, Interstate, North and South, East and West. (If you're unlucky in one book today, you may shift to another tomorrow.) The policy slips in Figure 1 are announcements of the winning numbers in Royal Palm and Iowa books for a midnight drawing. The Royal Palm, with twenty-four numbers, is knowns as a "two-legged book." The Iowa, with twelve numbers, is a "one-legged book."

If a policy addict had gone to a station between noon and midnight on the day of these particular drawings and said, "I want to put a dime on number 56 in the Iowa book," his lucky guess that this number might appear at midnight would have made him the winner of fifty cents. Playing a single number in this fashion is known as playing a "day number."

The most popular "play" in Bronzeville is the "gig." In this case, the player would have guessed at three numbers that might "fall"—for instance, 72-59-4. For his dime he then would have received $20. (The odds against guessing three numbers out of twelve are 76,076 to 1!) Policy players often "saddle their gigs" by investing an additional dime in a bet that at least *two* of the numbers will appear.[2] Then, if the whole gig is lost, the player may still salvage something. The reward for a saddle is a dollar to the dime. To guess on the appearance of four numbers is to play a "Horse." The winner receives $40, but the odds against such a winning are 1,426,425. A five-number bet—a "Jack"—pays $200 for a dime.

Winning numbers are listed three times daily, after selection at a public "drawing." The places where the drawings are made are known as the "wheels." These "wheels" are scattered about the community at strategic spots.[3] The drawings are made from a small drum-shaped container in which 78 capsules or balls, numbered consecutively, are placed. After each turn of the drum, a ball is pulled and its number read aloud. As they are called, a printer sets the numbers and locks them into a special printing press. As soon as the last number is drawn, the press rolls out the policy slips, which are then distributed all over Bronzeville.

In "normal" times, when the "heat is off," a wheel is a beehive of activity, day and night.[4] It is run by a corps of well-trained white-collar experts. Usually, several hundred persons are present to watch, and sometimes the crowd includes a co-operative policeman or two. Many of the onlookers are "walking writers," some 2,000 of whom were canvassing Bronzeville in 1938, writing up plays for a 20 per cent commission on the amount played.

Just before the wheel begins to turn, the walking writers arrive, straighten up their books, turn in duplicate slips, and fraternize with one another. Some wheels provide chairs with writing arms; a few even have a lunch counter. All have a "bouncer" or "overlook man" to keep order, to hurry the writers along so they will have the bets recorded before the drawing is made, and to enforce silence during the process. A drawing has been described by an observer as follows:

"Up and down the aisle, a large, dark man (I learned later that he was a prize-fighter) walked to and fro. He shouted continuously, 'All right, get them in, folks. Get those books in.' A large sign in front of the room read: ALL BOOKS MUST BE IN FIFTEEN MINUTES BEFORE PULLING TIME. PULLING TIME, 1:30.

"The overlook man looked in our direction and said, 'Baby, is that your chair? If not, you'll have to go downstairs. We don't want any confusion about the chairs. You know how crowded it is here.'

"By this time it was nearly 1:15 A.M. and the barker continued to prod the writers. 'Let's get them in, folks!' Everyone seemed in a jocular mood. Then suddenly there was a deep silence. At 1:40 a syndicate official stepped to the office window. A small wooden barrel fixed horizontally on an axle was placed in front of him. He set it spinning, and when it stopped a young lady put in her hand and pulled out a small pellet of paper, which she handed to the man. He opened it and, walking close to the microphone of the public address system, called out a number. A young man and the young lady pulled numbers alternately, 24 times for the North and South book and the same number of times for the East and West book.

"The people were rapt. The silence was broken by happy ejaculations or almost inaudible sighs as people saw that they had hit or just missed by a small margin. When the last number had been called, a sudden rushing noise arose, as people began to form in line at the printing press in the back of the room. In less than five minutes, the slips had been printed and were being distributed in the streets. Pick-up men were speeding through the Black Belt carrying the news of the latest winning numbers."

At the policy stations throughout the community, the players reach avidly for the slips to see if they have "caught." There are intense little groups discussing the close margins by which they have missed. Occasionally one can hear the rejoicing cry of a winner. A conversation is in progress on a street corner.

"Yes, maybe the jinx is on us, huh?"

"This 9-9-29 [Death Row] is playing right well. It saddled last night and again this morning. The same with the Nigger Baby Row, too—13-32-50."

"Oh, I missed on that Death Row. I don't play it because it made me miss my mother's name once. Man, I would have had good money. You see, my mother is dead and I dreamed about her. Instead of playing her name, I played the Death Row, and missed out because her name fell out in the first sixes. Wheeee, I would have been a rich man."

Suddenly, a shout: "I caught on my son's name, 'Henry'! It's out in the last sixes in the North and South, 27-31-33. Wonder why I didn't put some *real* money on it? Well, anyway, I caught $5.75 and that's better than nothing. Then, with these saddles, I think I'll clear about $6. Not bad for a dollar. It'll help out a lot at home."

## "POLICY"—A CULT

As is evident from the conversations quoted above, policy is not only a business—it is also a cult. It has a hold on its devotees which is stronger than the concrete gains from an occasional winning would warrant. It has an element of mystery and anticipation. It has developed an esoteric language. It organizes, to some extent, the daily lives of the participants. And, as in all cults, it has developed a group of functionaries and subsidiary businesses dealing in supplies.

Just any number will not do for a "gig." People want "hot" numbers. Numbers and combinations of numbers derived from "lucky" situations are much more powerful, have more of what the anthropologists call *mana,* than ordinary run-of-the-mill, garden-variety numbers. Lucky numbers may be obtained from the license plates of a car involved in an accident; from hymns announced at a church service; from streetcar transfers; from newspapers; or by asking a child. ("Children are lucky, you know, and are the best ones to give you winning gigs.")

Indispensible to the inveterate policy player is his "dream book," valuable for translating both dreams and "significant" occurrences into "gigs." The five most popular dream books in 1938 and 1939 were *The Three Witches, The Gypsy Witch, The Japanese Fate, Aunt Della's,* and *Aunt Sally's.* The gigs range from Abdomen (28-33-54) to Young (51-52-77), with a word like Accident subdivided into "to see" (4-31-50) and "to be in" (1-37-50). Boy's names range from Aaron (12-17-48) to Zephaniah (16-21-33); women's names from Ada (7-2-50) to Zenobia (46-47-53).

Many persons use the dream book not only for the interpretation of dreams, but also for the translation of personal experiences and public occurrences into numerical expressions. It is said that following the death of Will Rogers, the plays were so heavy on 7-10-11 (William) that some policy syndicate members sent out notices not to accept plays of over fifty cents. Some dream books contain numbers for the primary biological functions, and where the book does not have them, they are generally known by the initiated. (For instance, numbers for urine, dung, or copulation are not printed in books read in polite society; but everybody knows them.) One writer, advising another on how to hold down a job in a station, indicated the function of the dream-book symbolism:

"What you need to know is what each common thing and common name plays for. Sometimes a player forgets his book or can't remember. Some of the old-time writers get so good they can write poems with gigs, they know the meaning of the numbers so well. Incidentally, you mustn't bat an eye at the plays when they give 'em to you. You know some darkies think it's cute to play some of the dirty gigs when a pretty 'chick' is the writer. But a good writer doesn't let it feaze her an inch."

A middle-aged woman who has been writing policy for years said to an interviewer on the sources of gigs:

"Well, some play by hunches, dreams, or numbers on a car or transfer ticket. Some go to Spiritualists. They are obtained for the most part, though, from dreams and hunches. You watch the 'book' your dream falls in most and play in that 'book.' Some people are lucky and some are not. Some people believe in burning different incenses for luck. They claim it gives them success. My dreams are good in the Harlem and the Bronx.

The Spiritualists referred to are not, as a rule, pastors of churches (although some few Spiritualist pastors do actually give out numbers), but "spiritual advisers," who may or may not conduct actual church services. A few spiritual advisers who also conduct worship services frankly admitted that they give out gigs. One explained the manner thus:

"As far as literature is concerned, I don't believe these people read anything but policy slips. There are policy stations all around here, but you can't blame the people for trying to better their condition to the best of their knowledge. The whole thing is just this—there is so much sin that we can't be surprised at what happens.

"I have done good for a lot of people and they never forget what I do for them. When the spirit comes to me, whatever it tells me I do that. If it says pray, I do that. To give numbers is no sin because the people have to live, and to try to win a little money. That is no harm. Knowledge will have to come from God and no man can do the job if he is not in possession of that knowledge. That power I have. On many occasions God comes to me in a dream. That dream I will play in policy and catch it. Then, I invest the money wisely. That is all there is to it. But you have to live free from sin to do this."

This minister is an atypical Spiritualist preacher, however. He is on the border line between a minister and a "spiritual adviser" such as MADAM WILLIAMS, "Your Friend and Adviser," who advertises special meetings every Wednesday, Friday, and Sunday evening and who has "advised thousands in their personal problems with complete satisfaction." The Madam offers "advice on all affairs of life, love, health, domestic and financial conditions." She advertises LUCKY NUMBERS FREE—11 HITS IN 3 DAYS. She makes no charge, but lifts a silver offering announced as twenty-five cents! There are several hundred such advisers in Bronzeville.

Somewhat closer to a purely commercial enterprise is the establishment of PROFESSOR EDWARD LOWE, ASTRO-NUMEROLO- GIST. The Professor, Texas born and bred, sells gigs ranging in price from ten cents to $3, the latter guaranteed or money back. Professor Lowe asserts that his "gift" came from his mother, that he has studied "the science of the Zodiac," and that "some of the most intelligent people in the city of Chicago are in sympathy with the work that I engage in." In a bookstall outside of his store, the Professor displays his own magnum opus, the *Key to Numerology,* side by side with *Albertus Magnus, The Sixth and Seventh Book of Moses, White and Black Art for Man and Beast, The Book of For- bidden Knowledge,* and others of the same general type. Displayed too are Adam and Eve Roots, Policy Player's Oil for 50 cents, Genuine Live Lodestone, and the Lucky Oil of Mystery.

Occasionally, the magico-religious and the commercial en- terprise are combined, as in the case of Doctor Pryor who has his Japo Oriental Company on the first floor and King Solomon's Temple of Religious Science in the basement. The latter teaches "The Fellowship of God and the Brotherhood of Man," while the former sells adjuncts to the faith—Sacred and Lucky Powders, Holy Oriental Oil, Oriental Controlling Oil, John the Conqueror Oil, and Dr. Pryor's Holy Floor Wash and House Spray Oil. The Floor Wash and House Spray is guaranteed to "rent houses, draw crowds, and eliminate the evil works of the Devil." The Doctor insists that he is "The World's Greatest Psychoanalyst," and his gifts range from "changing love to hate" to giving out gigs.

He advises his clients to distinguish carefully between "dreams" and "visions"; and between dreams induced by "overindulgence in food, drink, unhappiness, exercise, and worry" and dreams in which "the Good Spirit appears." He also gives some advice on how to play policy:

"I've put out a book designed to give accurately the number following or pertaining to any dream one may have of any consequence. I tell them to stay on their numbers and don't change them too often. Do not play too many different gigs. Put all your energy on one set and wait. Do not be too impatient and jump from gig to gig. They're all in the wheel."

As an added impetus to buy some oil or roots, the Doctor further advises his clients:

"Why many persons are not successful in games or financial enterprises is because they are crossed with the evil influences and bad wishes of someone else. Before one can be successful this condition must be removed. Believe it or not, success cannot and will not come in unhealthy homes. The word jinx means the evil works of a would-be friend, a representative of the Devil. I advise them to search themselves, find out what the trouble is, and get rid of it. *All advice is free.*"

But the Doctor "makes his" from the sale of "jinx-removal candles" and efficacious oils. If you seek his help he leads you to the temple in the basement and places you in front of the elaborate altar, where a rack of candles burns and a colored glass bowl contains oil and water. You drop your coin into the water, letting your fingers touch the liquid. Then you light your candle and the Doctor places it in the rack. If you don't "catch" on the next gig, there is always the suspicion that you were not "purified" sufficiently or didn't burn enough "jinx-removal candles." So you return for more.

# The Racketeer in the Social Setting

### WILLIAM FOOTE WHYTE

The strength of the racketeer rests primarily upon his control of gambling activities. In our middle-class society gambling is a disreputable activity. In Italy, as in many European countries, gambling is taken for granted, and the state promotes its own lotteries. Protestants tend to identify law and morality and therefore to consider illegal acts as immoral. The Catholic church makes no such identification. Gambling is a temporal matter. The state has the right to forbid it, but the legal prohibition does not make it immoral. According to the church, gambling is immoral only when the gambler cheats, uses money which is not his own, or deprives his dependents of what is needed for their maintenance. Recognizing that it often involves such deprivation and that it tends to be associated with immoral activities, the church looks with suspicion upon gambling; but that is quite different from an outright moral ban.

The common Cornerville attitude toward gambling was expressed to me in this way by a corner boy:

Suppose I'm a rich man, and I like to follow the horses. When they're running in Crighton, I can go out there and bet my money. When they're in Florida in the winter, I can go down there and play them. That's all legal. That's all right. But suppose I'm a poor man. In the summer I go out to Crighton. In the winter I can't afford to go to Florida, but I still want to play them. I don't lose interest just because they're in Florida. Is it immoral for me to bet them in a horse room? Why should it be immoral for me if it ain't for the rich man?

Cornerville people have quite a different attitude toward

robbery and murder. They draw a sharp line between respectable and nonrespectable illegal activities. Gambling is respectable.

Gambling plays an important role in the lives of Cornerville people. Whatever game the corner boys play, they nearly always bet on the outcome. When there is nothing at stake, the game is not considered a real contest. This does not mean that the financial element is all-important. I have frequently heard men say that the honor of winning was much more important than the money at stake. The corner boys consider playing for money the real test of skill, and, unless a man performs well when money is at stake, he is not considered a good competitor. This helps to fix the positions of individuals· and groups in relation to one another. Suppose that Team X challenges Team Y, which is generally considered to be the superior team. Team Y accepts on condition that a designated sum of money is wagered. If the sum is large and the members of Team X are not confident of the outcome, they may refuse to put up the stakes. In this case, the contest will not take place, and Team Y will continue to be regarded as the superior team.

In individual and team competitions the corner boys organize their own gambling. If they wish to play the horse or dog races or the numbers, they cannot handle the situation in the same informal way. It is here that the racketeer comes in. He organizes gambling as a business.

The corner boy knows very well that, in playing the number pool or betting on the horses, he will lose on the average. For him the financial incentive is not the only one. He enjoys studying the horse-racing lore and matching his skill at selecting winners against that of his friends. There is no skill involved in playing the numbers, yet people develop attachments to their "steady numbers," and they enjoy discussing their experiences with the numbers.

A corner boy who saved his nickels and dimes would have more money in the long run than if he bet them on the numbers, but he could not pursue this course without disagreeable social consequences. The corner boy who has money is expected to help his friends. The free spender is popular and respected. Saving, therefore, is not a real alternative to gambling on the numbers. The small change would be dissipated in one way or another, whereas the large amounts occasionally won have real meaning for the corner boy. The sixty dollars that comes from a ten-cent three-number hit is used to pay off debts, to buy an outfit of clothes, to treat his friends, to give some money to his parents, and to gamble again.

The racketeer conducts activities which lend themselves particularly to the extension of his social influence. In retail trade, price and quality of goods have some influence upon sales, but the odds paid on winning numbers and horses are exactly the same throughout Cornerville. Personal ties and personal trust are, then, the only factors which influence the customers to place their bets with one agent instead of another. The corner boy wants to give his business to a friend, and close ties are established between the agent and his customers. Those on a higher level in the organization have risen to their positions through forming the same sort of relations of friendship and trust with the Cornerville people. These relations continue to exist, though in somewhat modified form. T. S., for example, cannot have close relations with all those who do business with his organization, but he spends much of his time in Cornerville, and, when he is there, he hangs on a certain corner, or in a certain barbershop, and has his "coffee-and" in a certain restaurant like any of the corner boys. Although he lives outside the district, he has not cut himself off socially from the corner boys as have most successful business and professional men.

Organized gambling activities tend to place a number of the corner boys in a position of dependence upon the racketeers. It is part of the code of the man who makes a profession of gambling that he give back some of his winnings to the losers who are "cleaned out." I know one crap-game holder who used to take home all his days' earnings to his mother. He came to be regarded as "a cheap no-good" fellow, and, had his associates in promoting the game not abided by the code in quite a liberal manner, he would have lost his customers.

In Cornerville the racketeers are known as free spenders and liberal patrons of local enterprises. They spend money in local stores. They patronize the activities of the corner boys with purchases of blocks of tickets to dances and with other contributions.

One young man in a legitimate business said of T. S. and his associates:

> These gangsters are the finest fellows you want to meet. They'll do a lot for you, Bill. You go up to them and say, "I haven't eaten for four days, and I haven't got a place to sleep," and they'll give you something. Now you go up to a businessman, one of the respected members of the community, and ask him. He throws you right out of the office.

This pattern of action is substantially the same for all racketeers. While the generosity of outlaws is a theme as old as time, it is important to understand it in this case not as a peculiar personality trait but as an important aspect of the racketeer's adjustment to his society.

Generosity creates obligations which are recognized by its recipients. Beyond the group of "parasites" who are completely dependent upon his support, there are a large number of corner boys who are at some time or other beholden to the racketeer for money lent to them or spent upon them.

The racketeer's power is seen in clearer perspective when he is compared with some of his possible competitors for influence. Legitimate business and professional men are usually considered the leading members of the community. There are a number of prosperous business and professional men who grew up in the district and still have their stores or offices in Cornerville, but most of them have made their homes in less congested and more socially desirable sections. They spend many of their working hours in Cornerville, but they have little time and usually little inclination to "hang with the boys." Even those few who have continued to live in Cornerville tend to be limited socially by the nature of their activities. A storekeeper must remain in his store and wait for the customers to come to him. He must rely upon the steady trade of his circle of friends and acquaintances, and yet he cannot afford to become too intimate with the corner boys. In fact, sometimes one hears it said that a man failed in business because he had too many friends—because too much of the business of these friends was on a credit basis. If a man is too closely tied to the corner boys, he will have difficulty in refusing them credit, whereas if he avoids becoming involved with them he may still have their business if his products are good, his prices reasonable, and his location central to their activities. However, in the latter case, he will not have the influence of the man who is "one of the boys."

Many stores are dependent upon the numbers business, and the storekeepers thus become a part of the racket organization. Numbers are sold in all kinds of stores, but they are most commonly found in small variety stores, barbershops, lunchrooms, and poolrooms. It is significant that these are places which are used as hangouts by the corner boys. The boys are friendly with the owner of the store, and the owner depends for much of his income upon his numbers business. In such circumstances the influence of the racketeer needs no further explanation.

While the Cornerville rackets are organized around gambling, local racketeers have a number of other interests. Some still deal in bootleg liquor, underselling the legal product by evading the government tax. However, this business is insignificant compared with the prohibition traffic, and there are many racketeers who have nothing to do with it. At times certain men in the organization have furnished strikebreakers to industry, but this work has been sporadic. At present there are no houses of prostitution in Cornerville. The dope traffic is little in evidence in the district, though some local men have been arrested and sentenced on dope charges. There may be a tie-up between the racket syndicate and these businesses. "The Boss" who organized the liquor monopoly also controlled the Eastern City dope traffic. However, there is no evidence that any Cornerville racketeers up to and including the 50 per cent men have business interests in prostitution or dope.

There are in Cornerville some small gangs indulging in holdups and burglaries. While some prominent racketeers be-

gan their careers in this line, they have discontinued such
activities since becoming established in the more secure
and respectable field of gambling. Some agents occasionally
participate in holdups, but this is discouraged by those
prominent in the organization. It is bad business for the
racketeers to have their subordinates get in trouble with the
police any more than is necessary in the operation of the
rackets. The hoidup men usually operate independently with
a few associates. Some of them are friendly with racketeers
and seek their help when in trouble with the law. While the
racketeers look down upon holdup men, there are informal
relations existing between them.

If they exist at all, protection rackets preying upon legitimate Eastern City businesses have certainly not been organized to the extent found in other cities. Some years ago
in Cornerville the racketeers forced all the bakeries to pay
them protection, but the racket was short lived. On another
occasion in a near-by city, racketeers attempted to set up
control of the poultry market, but the murder of a well-known
local businessman and member of the American Legion upset
their plans at the outset.

In all their activities, legal or illegal, the racketeers perform the important function of providing employment for a
large number of men. Most of the employees have no background of experience and skill to prepare them for jobs in
private industry. Furthermore, it is widely believed in Cornerville, and not without considerable evidence, that a Cornerville Italian is discriminated against when he applies for a
job. The corner boys do not fit into the socially approved
economic organization, and in the depression the rackets provided them with jobs which were difficult to find by other
means.

The racketeers also provide investment capital for new
enterprises. One story will serve as an example. Tom Leonardi
was a young Cornerville man who worked for a large corporation. Tom learned the business well and saw opportunities
for profits if he started out for himself. Without any capital
to back him, he began selling the product among his friends.
He built up a small trade, but he needed capital to expand

his operations. City investment bankers would hardly be interested in backing an unknown young Italian who was entering into competition with firmly intrenched corporations. Tom approached several Italian racketeers, and they agreed to invest. With their capital, he was able to buy the plant and equipment necessary for the expansion of his business. At the same time his board of directors pushed sales with enthusiasm—which sometimes led to coercion. Today the business is firmly established, and certain "tough" sales methods of earlier years are less in evidence. The company produces a product of excellent quality and seems likely to enjoy a long and prosperous existence. The evidence indicates that Tom Leonardi had superior business ability, and yet, had it not been for the support of his racketeer friends, he would still be struggling to get ahead. This is not an isolated example. The support of racket capital has helped a number of able men to rise to positions otherwise unattainable.

Racket capital in Eastern City has been invested in a large number of legitimate enterprises. It is most in evidence in the production and sale of liquor, in finance companies, in night clubs and restaurants, in race tracks, and in sports promotion.

From the racketeer's standpoint there are several advantages to having legitimate business interests. Profitable investments are welcomed for obvious reasons. Even unprofitable interests serve as convenient "fronts" for the illegal activities.

The promotion of prize fights is an uncertain and frequently unprofitable business. I understand that the racketeer most prominent in this line cleared a profit of less than a hundred dollars on the operations of a recent year. Nevertheless, he and his associates considered it well worth the trouble.

They pass out the tickets to certain police officers and businessmen. Suppose they send ten tickets to a certain officer every time there is a fight. He uses them and passes them out among his friends. Sometime if they need a favor from him, he is supposed to do it for them. That's why it's good business. . . . And then they pass out tickets to all their numbers writers—to show their appreciation.

It appears that one of the chief incentives for entering legitimate business is the hope of becoming "respectable," as the following story indicates. Joe the Wolf started out as a bodyguard for a prominent gang leader. He had frequent clashes with the law. Once, when a gangster was shot, Joe the Wolf was caught running away from the scene of the crime. He was tried for murder and acquitted. For some time after that Joe was picked up by the police whenever a gang murder had been committed. He complained that he was being hounded. His activities were changing. He made money in the numbers and acquired some legitimate business interests. He played up the respectable side of his career and discouraged the use of his nickname. He refused to allow his daughter to go out with racketeers. She married a man of a respectable family who was engaged in a legitimate business. The elaborate wedding reception attracted a large gathering, including many local businessmen and prominent politicians. Newspaper accounts of the affair described the bride's father as a "well-known sportsman." Although Joseph Lupo is still known to the corner boys as Joe the Wolf, he has traveled far toward respectability since his early days.

The rackets function in Cornerville as legitimate business functions elsewhere. The racketeer patterns his activity after the businessman and even strives to gain respectability so that he may become accepted by society at large as he is accepted in Cornerville.

# Observations on Gambling in a Lower-Class Setting

*IRVING KENNETH ZOLA*

## INTRODUCTION

Studies in gambling have often focused on matters of individual pathology[1] and yet, on a number of psychological dimensions, no significant differences have been found between gamblers and non-gamblers.[2] Part of the explanation for this lack of difference is the fact that so widespread an activity as gambling can be "many things to many people."[3] Another reason is that while recognized as one of our major social problems, gambling also constitutes a major American paradox, fluctuating as it does between tolerance and condemnation, with a very thin line drawn between legal and illegal forms.[4] It seems obvious that to exist in this state of limbo, gambling must serve important social and psychological functions. This report is an attempt to delineate some functions of one form of gambling as it occurs in a small lower-class residential community.

## THE SETTING

East Side was a small working-class area within a large New England city. Successive waves of immigrants once flooded the streets, but in recent years the population had become more stable, predominantly Italian with smaller seg-

Reprinted with permission of Irving Kenneth Zola and The Society for the Study of Social Problems from *Social Problems*, Vol. 10, No. 4 (Spring, 1963), 353–361. Mr. Zola is now on the faculty of Brandeis University.

ments of Eastern European Jews and Poles. As part of an
anthropological field team, the observer spent several months
in East Side, becoming a habitué of meeting places, bars, and
taverns and participating actively with several sub-groups. His
identity and role were, however, unknown to the community.
Most of the observations on gambling were made at Hoff's
Place, one of many taverns along the main street of East Side.
It was a bar and grill frequented mostly by Italians and Poles
who were either present or former residents of the immediate
neighborhood. At Hoff's one type of gambling predominated:
off-track betting where wagers are made with a "bookie" or
"bookmaker." Though the men spent much of the day here,
virtually all over thirty were married and relatively few were
unemployed. Some were on vacation or on their day off. Some
worked nearby, drove delivery trucks or taxis and dropped
in and out while ostensibly working. Others worked on split
shifts and visited between them. Still others had jobs which
ended early in the day or started very late.

One of the first observations made of Hoff's was the dissociation of the bar from other spheres of the men's social life.
Violent reactions often greeted any invasion or intrusion.

One wife became concerned when her husband did not return
for supper and so she called and asked the bartender about his
whereabouts. Although he knew he gruffly denied any knowledge.
Whereupon she burst into tears, pleading with him, "Please don't
tell him I called, 'cause he would beat the shit out of me if he
knew."

"One day my mother sent me after my father. It was gettin'
late. When he came home was he mad! He kicked her all the way
down Lawrence Street and back and said to her, 'Don't you never
send anyone after me here. No buts, anything can wait till I get
here.' And she never did it again."

A further distinction was made between gambling and other
spheres of economic activity. A man was not expected to
share his profits with his family and was thought a "damn
fool" if he even told them of his winnings. The fact that
most gambling activities take place in a context institutionally
defined as "recreation" helps to emphasize this dissociation
from ordinary utilitarian activities.[5]

## A GROUP IN PROCESS

The men at Hoff's, however, did not constitute a group in the formal sense. Regardless of when in the day one entered, the men in the bar seemed only to be whiling away their time drinking, barely taking notice of one another. On any day the pattern would be quite similar.

In the first booth, Hal reads the Morning Telegraph while Sammy naps in a corner. Behind them Smiley studies the Star Racing Section and Silvio looks at Phil's Armstrong. Phil, the bookie, sits at the bar going over his slips. Beside him Nick stares blankly at the wall and not two stools away Johnnie and Joe sip beer without speaking. Further down the bar sits an unidentified man and next to him stands Al, the bartender, gazing aimlessly out the window as he washes glasses.

Ten minutes before the start of each race, however, this changed. Men who were outside came in and those previously silent began to talk.

"Do you think he's got a chance?"
"I don't like the jockey."
"He likes muddy tracks."
"He's long overdue."
"They've been keeping him for this one."

Some of the remarks were addressed to one's neighbor, some to no one in particular. The bookie began to take bets. Gradually, the conversation became more agitated.

"Get your bets in while you can," kids Phil. Silvio turns and hands him five dollars while Smiley shakes his head, "He'll never win." Sal laughs, "Here Phil, a bean on the nose, number seven, a 'sure thing.'" "I'm the one who's got that," roars Al, reaching into his pocket and taking out a twenty-dollar bill. "Twenty thousand on number one. C'mon Irv, stick with me." "Uh, uh," I answer, "You're bad news, I like Principio." Meanwhile Phil proceeds gingerly down the bar as others turn and bet, rise from their booths or motion him toward them.

Some last minute bets or changes were made and then the race began. If the race was broadcast, a group formed near the radio. The cheering was restrained and muffled.

"See, look what's happening."
"Why is the jockey holding him back?"
"Just watch him finish with a spurt."

Regardless of whether the race was broadcast, the announce-
ment of the winner always led to the same discussion. All
attention focused on the winners.

"How did you figure it?"
"How come you picked her?"
"How did you know?"

And their answers . . .

"I've noticed that jockey . . ."
"Did you see that weight shift? Well . . ."
"I figure they've been saving him . . ."
"His last time out, he . . ."

If no one picked the winning horse, the discussion was still
the same, but more philosophical and not as prolonged. Within five minutes, however, it was quiet again.

Al is back washing glasses. Silvio and Smiley return each to a
separate booth. Hal goes outside and Sammy goes back to sleep.
Joe and Johnnie leave but Paul and Charlie replace them at the
bar sipping beer without speaking. Nick studies the chart for the
next race. Sal stands at the door looking at the sky and Phil, slips
of paper in his hand, walks slowly toward the phone.

Once more they appeared to be strangers . . . until the next
race.

Yet gambling is more than a mode of communication. It
creates a bond between the men—a bond which defines in-
siders and outsiders. This function of gambling first became
apparent when a newcomer arrived at Hoff's.

Joe did not live in East Side, though he was distantly related
to one of the bookies. He worked on a nearby construction gang
and gradually began to patronize Hoff's. At every opportunity, he
would come in, order a drink, and sit at the bar or in one of the
empty booths. Although he was through work at 4:00 P.M., he
often remained until 5:00 or 6:00. When he offered to buy someone a drink, he was gently, but firmly refused. All he gained was
an occasional nod; until, in an off-hand manner, he asked questions
about the races, horses, odds, and ways to bet. At first he bet the
choices of others and then finally his own. Only when he started

betting did others being to interact with him, respond more than monosyllabically, and "allow" him to join them as they sat at the bar or in the booths.

For the younger residents of East Side, gambling seemed a way of preparing them for later adulthood. A number of teenagers always hung around Hoff's; and, although they were not allowed in the bar to drink, they were welcome to place bets. It was during such times that they first initiated conversation with the younger men (19–21)—a preliminary step in "anticipatory socialization."

Thus, even though someone might appear at the same time every day, or the same day every week, this was insufficient to designate one a "member," a "regular," or an "insider." At Hoff's, this was accomplished only by off-track betting—an activity which served as the entrance fee, defining membership and initiating newcomers.

## THE PRESERVATION OF
## GROUP ATTACHMENT

Three observations made by Devereux in his analysis of gambling and the social structure are relevant here: (1) Although the making of a wager polarizes the field and artificially creates the gambler's bond of interest in the event, it does not follow that winning money is the dominant motivational force; (2) many gamblers go to great lengths to deny their emotional involvement in specific events; (3) the importance and relevance of competition to gambling varies with the social context in which it occurs.[6] Each of these observations were found to hold true for Hoff's, but here in East Side, they have yet a secondary function. In de-emphasizing emotionality, monetary gain, and competition, not only were several basic sources of hostility often emanating from gambling eliminated but, at the same time, attachment to the "group at Hoff's" was thereby reaffirmed.

While the excitement accompanying any sporting event was present, it was restrained. The extremes of overexcitement and depression were both negatively sanctioned. On more than one occasion, a person who went "over the line" when he won was called "nuts" or told to stop "acting like a jerk"; or if one persisted in bemoaning his "hard luck," he too was reprimanded. Even overconcern during a race or contest was regarded with skepticism.

Donnie was disturbed about the ball game—he had bet $10 on the outcome. He would get up, pace back and forth, sit down again. Each time he asked questions about the ability of the players or the manager. "Do you think he knows what he's doing?" As he returned to his seat once more, Mario shook his head indicating Donnie. He commented on his nervousness, adding, "After all, it's only money."

While these men cared when they lost, such depression was remarkably short-lived, perhaps until post-time of the next race. Little systematic effort was made to retain one's winnings. These men never stopped while ahead, nor reduced or even maintained the size of their bets after having won. If a person was ahead at the end of the day, it was more likely because there were no more races than through any conscious effort to accumulate profits. At Hoff's, there was no prototype of the conservative gambler who quit while ahead. People who did were disliked, and not only by the bookies. Instead of admiring them, the regulars shook their heads and called them "cheap bastards." One would have to increase the bet continually in order to gain any substantial amount of money, and yet there is still the problem of a stopping or cutting-off point. The following legend is illustrative of this:

Bob was relating the experiences of an old East Sider. "I know a guy who won a $100,000. First here and then he wanted to gamble so badly he flew to New York and then back here and kept losing till he had nothing." "Yeah," added Spike, "it could happen. You lost twenty G's and figure you've still got eighty, so you take another shot, and finally you've got nothing."

Thus, if no limit, no matter how theoretical, exists then monetary gain *per se* becomes an indefinite goal and one impossible of attainment. Finally, individual competition was almost non-existent. Within the group itself, members were not explicitly compared with one another as being better or worse players. In part to salve the wounds of defeat, and to share the fruits of victory, there was the common practice of mutual treats where the winner paid for the drinks of his closer acquaintances.

Particularly striking was the shift of competition from within the group to "the system." There was continual talk of "beating the system," "cracking the system," "not letting the system beat you." While this ostensibly referred to the scheme or principle governing the results of races, the actual hostility was more often expressed against the agent of that system —the bookie. The group complained that "he can't be hit" or dubbed him "the undertaker," and alluded to how they would "like to bury him . . . in an avalanche of losses."

Joe told of one bookie. "Why, you know why that son-of-a-bitch makes more money than anyone else? It's because all the bettors hate his guts, so they make all bets with him, even 'hot tips' just in the hope they'll break him."

"Remember the time that 'Happy' bet 20-20-0 on a long shot and won. Do you remember Sam's face. I thought he would bust a gut."

"Well, I took care of that bookie. I bet $5 on the fifth and kept betting it all on each race. By the eighth, he had to close up shop."

In this situation, the bookie served a dual function. As the personification of the system they were trying to beat, he facilitated the shifting of competition from within the group to outside the group; and by serving as the target for their hostility, he also became an integrating force of the group— their scape-goat.

Thus the de-emphasis on thrill, money, and competition not only prevented the individual member from becoming too involved with his own personal success and failure; it also made him more dependent on the group and reinforced his attachment to it and the rewards which it alone can bestow— prestige and group recognition. To understand these rewards, it is necessary to examine their dispensation.

## SYSTEMS OF BETTING AND THE PRESTIGE HIERARCHY

As depicted in the opening illustration, at Hoff's all available attention and admiration was focused on those men who had chosen winners. Everyone clustered about them, prodded them to reveal the basis of their choice, praised them on their good judgment, and regarded their subsequent opinions highly. Rewarding someone in this manner assumes that he has *done* something to merit such an action. Not all types of gambling warrant such behavior. In the "numbers" or "policy game" where full rein is given to hunches, omens, dreams, and where a person may have his own special number and play it day after day, year after year, no one is congratulated on his ability if he wins, nor asked to explain the rational basis for his choice; he is rather congratulated on his good fortune or luck. In short, methods of selection and the social rewards for winning reflect a conception of the numbers as a game of chance, whose outcome is beyond human control and comprehension, explainable only in terms of luck, fortune or fate.[7]

The methods and social rewards of off-track betting reflect a different assumption, i.e., the existence of an underlying order, a principle which can be figured out and mastered by a skilled observer.[8] While segments of the larger society deny this in their educational and legal attempts to eliminate gambling, there is hardly a single major newspaper which does not publish the opinions of at least one professional racing expert. As a rule, the latter not only names his choices but gives his reasoning. This was similar to the behavior of the bettors at Hoff's, who consulted with the winners or joined in a general discussion to explain the results, to figure out why it happened or what factors had not been sufficiently considered.

Not all criteria for making decisions were equally regarded. Basically, there were two positively valued modes, one subtype of these, and one devalued mode. Generally, an individual was characterized by his reliance on a particular mode, though it was possible that he might use more than one method on any given day. The four systems were differentiated not only by their basis of selection but also by the degree, amount, and quality of attention and recognition the group bestowed on the successful user of such methods.

Handicapping, the method which elicited the highest respect, was based on some pragmatic system of integration of available information such as past performances of horses and jockeys, weight shifts, post position, track conditions, etc. Using any available factual data, there was an attempt to *figure out* one's choice. Calling an individual a "handicapper" was the highest compliment that could be paid. When someone wanted information about a particular horse or race, the "handicappers" were the ones to whom questions were directed. Moreover, their opinions were solicited even though their total losses might actually outweigh their gains.

At one time, I hit upon a system of betting a number of horses in combination. For three straight days, I won the daily double and in the next five days, at least one of my choices won while the other finished second or third. Each of these bets, however, was only for fifty cents and thus the net profit on each day was between five and ten dollars and after the first three days I lost. For this eight-day period I was operating at a loss, and yet for the next few weeks I was consulted by other bettors and kidded by the bookies as being "too good." One even joked about barring me.

Thus, it seems apparent that the "handicapper" gains and retains prestige not because of monetary profits or a preponderance of winners, but because he has demonstrated some technique or skill enabling him to select winners or at least come close.

The "hot tip" was the second positively valued mode. It was based on the use of "inside information," facts about the horses not published or known to the general public. Though the knowledge was supposedly secret, "hot tipsters" usually revealed its possession. For only in so doing could they be acknowledged by the group. While the method of selection is a rational one, the distinguishing feature is *access* to information and not the exercise of any particular skill. This fact was recognized by the men at Hoff's and though they would ask tipsters, "Got anything hot?," "Any inside dope?," their seeking of advice would not usually go beyond this. Nor were the personal choices of such men given undue weight or consideration unless they had also achieved some recognition as handicappers.

The "hedge" is more complex and seems to be a subtype

of the above two methods. One or more of the following statements usually introduced the "hedge."

"You saw me give that to Spike and Angelo and the others and I told them it would win and then I go and bet on another. Whatta dope!"

"I couldn't decide which one of these would win so I didn't bet any."

"I had him [the winning horse] but I had to do an errand before I got here so I arrived too late to bet."

"Remember how I figured it out at home and picked number three to win but then I came here and saw the Armstrong so I bet the six. If only I hadn't seen 'the Arm.'"

The groundwork was usually laid before the race and the sequence was often as follows:

Before: "I like Ocean Rock but Principio is long overdue and that blasted Pilot's Express is always a threat with Hobbes aboard."

After: The fact that he bet Ocean Rock is ignored. "See, what did I tell you, that son-of-a-bitch Hobbes brought him in. I told you that would happen."

These remarks not only covered the bettor if his choice did not win, but also communicated to the group, "See, I also picked the winner, even though I didn't play it." For the most part, it succeeded. The group listened to the "hedgers," included them in the discussion of the results, and so allowed them to share to some extent the rewards of picking a winner. Considering their verbalization, it also seems likely that acceptance hinged on the presumption that the basis of their "unbet" choice was really handicapping or a "hot tip."

At the bottom of this prestige ladder was the hunch or random choice bet—lowest because it embodied a denial of the rationality which underlies the concept of "system" and hence "figuring out" of race results. Although "hunch betting" was chided as a "woman's bet," it was difficult to ignore if it produced a winner. Congratulations might be offered, but the reasoning behind the choice was never seriously solicited nor was future advice sought. The underlying attitude toward this technique was best shown when it produced a loser.

Jack bet on a dog called Cerullo because it was the name of a local hockey player. When it finished second, he was furious. "Damn it, that's what happens when you only have a bean [a dollar] —if I'd had more, I'd have bet him for second too." He barely uttered this when his friends began to tease him. "Say Mickey Mantle is running in the third and Williams in the ninth." They harped on the "why" of his bet. Jack fought back, shouting, "You wouldn't act that way if the shoe was on the other foot." But this only encouraged them. They continued berating him till he began to sulk and finally walked out.

Only in "hunch" betting and only when it lost did such hostility occur in the group.

## THE FUNCTIONAL ASPECTS AND SATISFACTIONS OF BETTING

A rational-cognitive dimension seems to pervade these methods of selection. Since the races were considered capable of human understanding, this emphasis on rationality reflected and manifested the idea of understanding. By using these methods, the players were "beating the system." The "system," which they frequently mentioned, referred to more than a principle underlying the races but rather to life or fate. Miller claims that many lower-class individuals feel that their lives are subject to a set of forces over which they have relatively little control and that furthermore this world view is associated with a conception of the ultimate futility of direct effort towards a goal.[9] Gambling can help deny this futility, as illustrated by the response of one "regular."

Joe continually talked about "hitting it big." Today was no exception as he spoke of just missing a $1000 double. I looked at him quizzically, "You know you always talk about your ship coming in. Do you ever think it will?" Startled, he raised his head and without looking at me, muttered, "No . . . but what else have I got besides this?" [betting on the races].

By "beating the system," outsmarting it by rational means, these men demonstrated they *can* exercise control and that for a brief moment they *can* control their fate. Off-track betting is thus a kind of escape. It denies the vagaries of life and gives these men a chance to regulate it. At Hoff's, there was an emphasis on rewards rather than punishments, on how much can be gained rather than lost. One was rewarded by increased attention and recognition when he won but never punished or ignored when he lost except when the very structure of the group was threatened. "Hunch" betting was just such a threat because it not only denied the concept of an underlying order but also was a way of admitting defeat, of granting that everything *was* beyond one's control.

Recognition was the supreme reward of the winner. By competing against the system rather than against themselves, however, recognition was no longer a scarce commodity, for theoretically there was no limit to the number of winners. Thus, wherever possible success and recognition were shared, whether by extending the definition of winners in the acceptance of "hedgers" or sharing the fruits of victory by "mutual treats." One regular revealed the meaning of being a winner when amid the talk and praise of his selection, he yelled, "What do you think I am, a nobody?" It was a statement so appealing that it was taken up as a byword and used over and over again by the group. In some ways, it was an insightful joke, for in picking the winner and becoming the center of attention, the winner leaves the realm of the nobody for the realm of the somebody.

## CONCLUSION

Although betting doubtless serves many idiosyncratic needs, much of its structure, function, and persistence can only be understood by an examination of the social context in which it occurs. Gambling offers these men more than a means of recreation, just as Hoff's offers them more than a place to drink. Though such betting may produce neither recreation nor monetary gain, this does not necessarily mean that it is a sterile, non-productive, or even dysfunctional activity. As many observers have pointed out, these men are aware of the major goals and values of middle-class society but are either unwilling[10] or incapable of achieving them by the use of the ordinary methods.[11] However, as recent empirical[12] and theoretical[13] literature has demonstrated, deviance may be more than a symptom of dysfunctional structures. For these men, gambling may be a way of harnessing or channeling their otherwise destructive frustrations. Instead of lashing out at society, they lash out at "the system." In this sense, gambling may be an activity which helps reinforce and preserve some of the major values of the larger social system. At Hoff's, they *can* "achieve" and *can* gain recognition for their accomplishments—by exercising skill or knowledge in the selection of horses.

Moreover, these goals of achievement and recognition can be aspired to with few of the conventional risks. In the society at large, one's success or failure alters and affects one's whole way of life while here it is completely incidental to it —a reflection of the isolation of gambling from other spheres of life. Here there is an emphasis on rewards rather than punishments, on gains rather than losses, on being a "somebody" and not a "nobody." For these men, gambling, or at least off-track betting, is not simply the flight, the withdrawal, or the escape as so often claimed. By making success and recognition possible, it allows the players to function in the larger society without suffering the consequences of the realization that they indeed have little else.

This paper is necessarily limited by the way the observations were made and thus depicts only one small but significant slice of the social context of gambling—the relation of bettors to one another. Unfortunately little was known of the lives of these men outside this particular setting, so no explanation is possible of how or why the groups at such places as Hoff's originated nor of the origins of gambling in general. As with so many other phenomena, the sources or causes have long faded into the background and may even be unimportant. This report is but a single case study—an attempt to delineate some of the possible reasons for the persistence of gambling and some of the functions it may presently serve. Whether similar observations hold for dif-

ferent settings[14] and for different types of gambling will have
to be settled by further empirical and more systematic investigations.

# Playing Seriously

### E. FRANKLIN FRAZIER

For a large section of the black bourgeoisie, their activities
as members of "society" are their most serious or often their
only serious preoccupation. Their preoccupation with "society"
has its roots in the traditions of the Negro community in the
United States. As we have seen above, in their position of
house servants during slavery, Negroes acquired from their
white masters notions of what constituted "social" life or
"society." After emancipation they continued in the role of
personal servants, and therefore saw the white man only
in his home or when he was engaged in recreation. They
never saw the white man at work in the shop or factory and
when he engaged in the serious matter of business. As
a consequence they devoted much time and much of their
meager resources to attempting to carry on a form of "social"
life similar to the whites'. For many Negroes, it appears that
"social" life became identified with the condition of freedom.
"Social" life among the masses of Negroes was a free and
spontaneous expression of their desire to escape from the
restraints of work and routine. But for those who set themselves apart as Negro "society," "social" life became a more
formalized activity. Among the Negro elite as well as
among the masses, "social" life acquired a significance that
it did not have among white Americans.

The great significance which "social" life has for Negroes has been due to their exclusion from participation in American life. The numerous "social" clubs and other forms of voluntary associations which have existed among them provided a form of participation that compensated for their rejection by the white community. At the same time these various "social" clubs have been a part of the struggle of Negroes for status within their segregated communities. The elite, who have set themselves apart as Negro "society" and have attempted to maintain an exclusive "social" life, have been extremely conscious of their inferior status in American life. For them "social" life has not only provided a form of participation; it has represented an effort to achieve identification with upper-class whites by imitating as far as possible the behavior of white "society."

The exclusion of middle-class Negroes from participation in the general life of the American community has affected their entire outlook on life. It has meant that whites did not take Negroes seriously; that whites did not regard the activities of Negroes as of any real consequence in American life. It has tended to encourage a spirit of irresponsibility or an attitude of "play" or make-believe among them. Consequently, Negroes have "played" at conducting their schools, at running their businesses, and at practicing their professions. The spirit of play or make-believe has tended to distort or vitiate the ends of their most serious activities. For example, in a number of cities where Negro doctors have been excluded from joining the white professional associations, they have set up "reading societies," supposedly to offset such exclusion. But, on the whole, these "reading societies" have turned out to be "social" clubs for drinking and playing poker. Playing, then, has become the one activity which the Negro may take seriously.

In fact, great importance is attached to "Negro society" in the Negro press because it is a serious preoccupation among the black bourgeoisie. One can get some notion of its importance from an editorial in the September, 1953, number of *Ebony* entitled "Is Negro Society Phony?" The editorial asserts that those who say that Negro "society" is a pretense are envious of those who have been accepted by "society." It goes on to show that members of American white "society" have achieved entrance in the same manner as the members of Negro "society." Then the editorial points out that people like Dr. Bunche, Louis Armstrong, Marian Anderson, Mary McCleod Bethune and Joe Louis have won their places in Negro "society" by achievement. The article concludes with the statement that brains rather than blood should be the basis for admission to Negro "society" and that if this is made the basis of acceptance, then Negro youth will seek recognition by Negro "society." It seemingly never occurred to the writer of the editorial that Negroes with brains would prefer not to seek escape in the world of make-believe of the black bourgeoisie.

The exaggerated importance which the black bourgeoisie attaches to "society" is revealed in the emphasis placed by the Negro press upon the "social" aspects of events concerning Negroes. When it was announced recently that a Negro businessman had been named a member of the American delegation to the United Nations, it was stated in a leading Negro publication that he was invading the "glittering international UN scene—the most exclusive and powerful *social* set in the world." The news item added that the nominee had "already made plans to acquire new formal wear" and that he was preparing his wardrobe for his entrance into the United Nations. In fact, generally when white middle-class people have sought the co-operation of the black bourgeoisie in some serious community project, they have found it difficult unless it could be interpreted as a "social" event. For example, such liberal middle-class white groups as the League of Women Voters and League of Women Shoppers have constantly complained that they could not interest middle-class Negro women. On the other hand, let us take the following account of an interracial group of women who raised money for the fight against infantile paralysis. There appeared in the February 25, 1954, issue of *Jet*, under the section labeled "People Are Talking About," the statement that $1,500 was raised by a group of fifteen white and colored "society" women who wore over $500,000 worth of furs and gowns.

Anyone who achieves any distinction in any field may become a "socialite" in the Negro press. It is not simply that, as a Negro journalist stated, "anybody not in the criminal class can get a 'personal' or 'social' note in the Negro paper." This suggests only a small-town attitude which may be found among any people. In making a "socialite" of a Negro, the Negro press is attributing to him or to her the highest conceivable status and recognition. For example, when a Negro anthropologist, who never attended "social" functions, gave a lecture in Chicago, the account in the Negro press referred to him as a "socialite." Consequently, one learns in the Negro press that wives of gamblers, policemen, waiters, college professors, doctors, lawyers, petty civil servants, and public school teachers are all "socialites"—often when their husbands are not so designated. It should be pointed out, however, that being called a "socialite" in the Negro press is generally regarded as a high compliment by the members of the black bourgeoisie, whatever may be their occupations.

As a consequence of the prestige of "society," many Negro professional men and women take more seriously their recreation than their professions. Once the writer heard a Negro doctor who was prominent "socially" say that he would rather lose a patient than have his favorite baseball team lose a game. This was an extreme expression of the relative value of professional men and women take more seriously their recrea-geoisie. At the same time, it is indicative of the value which many Negro professional men and women, including college professors, place upon sports. Except when they are talking within the narrow field of their professions, their conversations are generally limited to sports—baseball and football. They follow religiously the scores of the various teams and the achievements of all the players. For hours they listen to the radio accounts of sports and watch baseball and football games on television. They become learned in the comments of sportswriters. Often they make long journeys in order to see their favorite teams—white or Negro—play baseball and football games. Although they may pretend to appreciate "cultural" things, this class as a whole has no real appreciation of art, literature, or music. One reads, for example, under what "People Are Talking About" in the September 2, 1954, issue of *Jet*, that a "wealthy" Negro doctor in Detroit is planning to install a "Hammond organ" on his "luxurious yacht." The decor of their homes reveals the most atrocious and childish tastes. Expensive editions of books are bought for decoration and left unread. The black bourgeoisie, especially the section which forms Negro "society," scarcely ever read books for recreation. Consequently, their conversation is trivial and exhibits a childish view of the world.

The prominent role of sports in the "serious playing" of Negro "society" stems partly from certain traditions in the Negro community. It reflects to some extent the traditions of the "gentlemen" who engaged in no serious work. But in addition, preoccupation of Negro "society" with sports is related to its preoccupation with gambling, especially poker. This latter preoccupation is especially significant because it is related to the religious outlook of the black bourgeoisie, especially Negro "society."

## FROM CHURCH TO CHANCE

The black bourgeoisie cannot escape completely from the religious traditions of the Negro masses, since many of those who are achieving middle-class status have come from the masses. They are often haunted by the fears and beliefs which were instilled in them during their childhood. However, they are glad to escape from the prohibitions which the Baptists and Methodists placed upon dancing, card playing, and gambling. They want to escape from the concern of the Baptists and Methodists with sin and death and salvation. The middle-class Negro is like the "suburban agnostic" with whom Mary Kingsley compared the missionary-made African, who keeps the idea of the immortality of the soul and a future heaven but discards the unpleasant idea of hell. The middle-class Negro will tell you that he believes in a Supreme Being.

some vague entity who runs the universe, and the immortality
of the soul, but he does not believe in hell because he thinks
that man has his hell on earth. As a rule, the black bourgeoisie do not give themselves to reflection on these matters.
They are regarded as impractical and unpleasant questions
which should be left to a few "queer" Negroes, who should
spend their time more profitably in making money. An outstanding educated Negro minister, who is a sort of a mystic,
was generally regarded with amusement by the black bourgeoisie, and he sought a more congenial audience in an interracial church and as a visiting preacher in white colleges.

When the middle-class Negro abandons the traditional
religion of his ancestors, he seldom adopts a new philosophical
orientation in regard to existence and the world about him.
Since he is as isolated intellectually as he is socially in the
American environment, he knows nothing of humanistic
philosophy and he rejects materialism because of his prej-
udices based upon ignorance. Negro intellectuals have nothing to offer him, since they have never developed a social
philosophy, except perhaps a crude and unsophisticated op-
portunism. Therefore, as a rule, the middle-class Negro is the
prey of all forms of spiritualism. He avoids the fantastic ex-
travagances of Father Divine's cult, partly because lower-
class Negroes are associated with it. He concedes, however,
that Father Divine "does some good" because his followers
are "honest and faithful domestic servants." Nevertheless, the
black bourgeoisie are interested in "psychic" phenomena because, according to them, "scientists do not know everything."
Therefore, the little reading in which they indulge is often
concerned with "faith healing" and popular accounts of
"psychic" phenomena. In some cities it has become a fad
for members of Negro "society" to make a novena though they
are not Catholics, and they have reported that this religious
exercise has resulted in their securing a dress or mink coat
which they have always desired.

Without the traditional religion of the Negro and a philosophy to give them an orientation towards life, the black
bourgeoisie, especially the element among them known as
Negro "society," have often become the worshippers of the

God of Chance. This new faith or dependence upon chance finds its extreme expression in their preoccupation with gambling, including the "numbers" (the illegal lotteries in American cities), betting on horses, and more especially poker. At one time the black bourgeoisie regarded the "numbers" as a lower-class form of gambling and restricted themselves to betting on horses. Likewise, playing poker was formerly regarded by them as a pastime for the sporting element among Negroes. But with the emergence of the new Negro "society," playing the "numbers" has become respectable. This is not strange, since some members of "society" derive their incomes from the "numbers." Therefore, it is not unusual for Negro professional men and their wives to play the "numbers" daily. Even the wives of Negro college professors are sometimes "writers" or collectors of "numbers" for the "numbers racket."

But poker has become the most important form of recreation for members of "society" among the black bourgeoisie. In fact, poker is more than a form of recreation; it is the one absorbing interest of Negro "society." It is the chief subject of conversation. Negro "society" women talk over the telephone for hours on the last poker game. According to an article in *Ebony*, March, 1953, the bane of many "society" editors is that "social" affairs turn into poker games, though the latter "can be exciting" when the stakes involve "homes, lots, and automobiles." Even a chance encounter of members of Negro "society" will lead to a poker game. Moreover, poker has tended to level all social barriers among Negroes. At the richly furnished homes of Negro doctors, chauffeurs, waiters, and gasoline station attendants gather with college professors to play poker. So important has poker become among the black bourgeoisie that the measure of a man has become the amount of stakes which he can place at a poker game.

In many cities of the United States, the black bourgeoisie usually spend their weekends in which might be called "poker marathons" or "poker orgies" which last sometimes from Friday night until Monday morning. Some poker players who still have old-fashioned religious ideas may leave the poker table long enough to go to church, because, as they say, they believe in God. But usually most of them, being refreshed with food, remain throughout the "marathon." Some college professors boast of leaving the poker table and going directly to lecture to their classes on Monday. Likewise, Negro surgeons have been heard to boast of leaving the poker table and going directly to perform an operation. Because of their devotion to poker, some middle-class Negroes form groups and journey periodically from city to city in order to engage in these gambling orgies. News of these orgies, with details emphasizing the high stakes played are the main topic of conversation among Negro "society." The importance of poker may be measured by the fact that some middle-class Negroes assert that poker is the one thing in life that prevents them from going crazy. Therefore, the role of poker as a "religious" force in the lives of the black bourgeoisie can not be discounted.

The activities of Negro "society" are an extreme expression of the world of make-believe.

# The Adoration of the Nag

### LEO ROSTEN

No one who has been in Hollywood can have failed to be startled by the horse-racing fever which possesses the movie colony; a study of Hollywood which neglected to comment on the role of horses, gambling, and race tracks would be derelict in its duty and incomplete in its insights. The offices, commissaries, stages, and dining-rooms of Hollywood echo

Reprinted by permission of Leo Rosten from *Hollywood: The Movie Colony, The Movie Makers* by Leo C. Rosten, New York, Harcourt, Brace & World, 1941, pp. 212–223.

with knowing tips and detailed genealogies, with debates, wagers, analyses, and grave references to a dozen dope sheets and racing forms. The more devoted votaries of the turf place wagers all year round, on horses they do not know, running in places they have never visited, in races they never see.

So "natural" has the cult of horses and the obsession with the race track become in Hollywood that the *Hollywood Reporter* and *Daily Variety* regularly print racing charts and bulletins in their pages—as if these represented legitimate news about the motion picture industry. It is difficult to imagine an oil or automobile trade journal giving unabashed space to items on the animal kingdom, but "Today's Santa Anita Consensus" is a customary feature in Hollywood's trade papers during the racing season. In one issue of *Daily Variety*, "Doc Baker's Selections" was featured in a box on page 1, a column called "Stalling Around Santa Anita" was on page 2, the "Chatter" column was full of racing items, and half of page 8 was dedicated to racing dope and tips. Even the movie reviews in trade papers occasionally bear testimony to the power of the equine: "Two entries from the Burbank celluloid stables ran in the money. . . . Breezing home several lengths ahead of the field was *Torrid Zone,* followed by *Flight Angels.*" Some anonymous wit once summarized Hollywood's daily life as a span "from track to Troc."

No one knows the size of the toll which the "sport of kings" takes from the movie makers each year. In the first nineteen days of a recent racing season in California, thirty-nine places were won by thirty horses owned by picture people. In one Santa Anita Handicap no less than twenty-seven of the 107 horses nominated belonged to members of the film colony. Movie stars, producers, directors, and agents are active in the business affairs and operation of the Santa Anita, Del Mar, and Inglewood race tracks. They turn out in generous numbers for the races each day; they own stables and horse farms; they hire expert trainers, caretakers, and grooms; they send their thoroughbreds to perform on various tracks throughout the land; they import stallions from England and South America; they go by special train and plane to such rites as the Kentucky Derby or the Saratoga Springs Handicap;

they place sizable wagers, from their offices or at the track; they follow the hardly cosmic contests of Santa Anita, Hialeah Park, Narragansett, and Churchill Downs with an intensity which transcends recreation and passes into fanaticism. The time, attention, telephone bills, and sheer distraction-cost which go into Hollywood's adoration of the nag represent a hidden drain on the exchequer and the process of movie making.

It is no secret that studios' telephone bills shoot up fantastically during the racing season. On some sound stages there is a daily letdown of activity after 3:30 P.M., during the racing season, so that the talented and costly persons assembled can get the racing results. One movie executive said: "No one can work Saturday afternoon: if they're not at the track, their mind is. And if it's not the horses, it's the football games." During a conference with labor leaders, one studio representative showed a surprising sympathy for the idea of a five-day week; the illusion of liberalism was dispelled by his confession that he favored a five-day working week because as long as there were races, Saturday mornings were wasted at the studios anyway.

Every company in Hollywood has initiated stern drives designed to cut down the use of studio telephones for calling bookies, laying bets, or getting the latest racing results. This resulted in the wholesale introduction of radios, and orders had to be issued to cope with this crisis. Some fanatics had private telephones on their desks wired directly to bookie offices; the phones were finally removed by official fiat. Hollywood's gossip columns are sprinkled with tidbits such as this: "An important picture was held up for three hours the other afternoon because one of its important players did not show back after lunch. The player had gone over to a bookie joint to hear the running of the fourth race at Narrangansett and was caught in a raid."

One movie star bets as high as $15,000 on a big race; one producer established himself as a one-man "winter book" on the Kentucky Derby and took $20,000 worth of bets from colleagues at his studio; one executive rises early during the racing season and goes to his office after several hours at his stable watching his horses work out. "Shooting schedules are often arranged to let stars spend afternoons at the track."

The wide influence of Hollywood's passion for horseflesh is seen in such curios as the Motion Picture Democratic Committee's recommendations for the 1939 Los Angeles primary elections, which were printed as a racing form! Under each nominee's name were parenthetical comments, of which a few are worth preserving for posterity:

1st District..............................Oscar C. Leach
(A Tough Liberal in a Muddy Race)
2nd District............................Norris J. Nelson
(The Best Man to Beat the Worst Man)
3rd District........................No recommendation
(This Race Should Be Scratched)
15th District...............................Fred Reaves
(A Great Handicapper)

It is said that Groucho Marx once appeared in the offices of an executive at the MGM studio dressed in a jockey's uniform because, he said, "This is the only way you can get to see a producer these days." The story may be apocryphal, but the point is well taken. It is wearying to recall the time and emotion which adults in the movie colony devote to discussing the speed with which four-legged animals can traverse an elliptical course.

The Nirvana of a goodly share of the movie makers is Santa Anita, some fifteen miles from Hollywood, one of the most beautiful and lucrative temples to racing in the world. The following facts offer some idea of Santa Anita's stature:

The annual $100,000 Santa Anita Handicap is the richest race in the universe; there is a $50,000 Derby and a $25,000 San Juan Capistrano prize as well.

The lowest Santa Anita purse is $1,500; there is at least one $2,000 stake a day; every Saturday there is a $10,000 prize.

In 1939, $1,425,000 was spent by the horsemen and their stable staffs.

The total purse in 1939 was $917,000 unequaled anywhere in horse circles.

In the short fifty-three-day season, $36,656,590 was handled through the 304 betting windows.

The State of California annually collects $1,500,000 in taxes from Santa Anita.

Santa Anita is also famed for the fact that during its first season (1934), so much money was taken in that the officials of the organization took the unprecedented step of reducing their share of the intake. The length of the season has been reduced on three occasions, and yet the golden tide goes higher.

Santa Anita was born in the mind of Hal Roach, the whilom director and producer of the "Our Gang" comedies, who approached some four hundred people to invest in the stock. Many movie people were on the favored list, but only Bing Crosby, W. S. Van Dyke, and Henry King invested. Wealthy Californians in Los Angeles, Pasadena, and San Francisco came to the rescue and bought into the enterprise. Mr. Roach became the president of the organization.

The glorified race track opened in 1934 with an elegant clubhouse for members, twenty-five beautiful rooms, and twenty bars. The opposition to horse racing from Los Angeles merchants, reformers, and church groups has never abated. But the hotel, apartment, and restaurant people share in the bonanza when thousands arrive from all over America to attend the season. No other race track has so celebrated a clientele. "On an afternoon in the Turf Club, the exclusive section atop the clubhouse, I have seen Warner Baxter, the Walt Disneys, the Fred Astaires, the George Burnses, Cecil B. DeMille, Cary Grant, Spencer Tracy, Joan Crawford, Pat O'Brien, Victor McLaglen, Basil Rathbone, Frank Capra, Florence Rice, Rupert Hughes, and dozens of others." These names scarcely begin to do justice to Hollywood's representation.

Del Mar, eighty miles from Los Angeles, is another race track in which the movie people figure prominently. Bing Crosby is president, guiding spirit, and chief owner of this shrine (in addition to his heavy holdings in Santa Anita); Pat O'Brien is vice-president.

The Hollywood Park Turf Club at Inglewood, a suburb of Los Angeles, was organized by Harry M. Warner, who pledged collateral for a $1,000,000 loan from the Bank of America and later lent the corporation $250,000 to pay off pressing debts; Jack L. Warner was made chairman of the board. The Hollywood Park track paid a twenty percent dividend for the first two years, added another ten percent in the third year, has repaid its original stockholders seventy percent of their outlay, has paid an excess profits tax of $500,000, and started the 1941 season with $100,000 in the bank and nary a debt or tax obligation outstanding.

The publicity which linked Hollywood, horses, and the race track boomeranged, of course, and a movement of abnegation began when the picture people became more sensitive to public reaction. Hal Roach resigned the presidency of Santa Anita, Jack L. Warner resigned as chairman of the board of Hollywood Park, movie directors Raoul Walsh and Alfred E. Green withdrew from the same board, and other film figures began to play down both their horses and their race-track investments.

The horse owners in Hollywood are a proud legion. The biggest and most famed are Bing Crosby, L. B. Mayer, and H. M. Warner, and the roster includes William LeBaron, Raoul Walsh, Mervyn LeRoy, Spencer Tracy, David Butler, Howard Hawks, Barbara Stanwyck, Robert Taylor, John Considine, Jr., George Raft, Zeppo Marx, Errol Flynn, J. Walter Ruben, Lynne Overman, Myron Selznick, Don Ameche, John Cromwell, Robert Riskin, Joe E. Brown (who paid $20,000 for a South American horse), and William Goetz.

Bing Crosby was one of the first and remains the most famous of Hollywood's horse owners. He owns a formidable stable and with the son of the owner of the celebrated Seabiscuit, possesses a profitable animal named Ligaroti. (Mr. Crosby is an energetic golfer, fisherman, tennis player, and ice-skater as well; he promotes one of the leading golf tournaments in the land.) Louis B. Mayer, a late convert, has plunged into racing with characteristic vigor, now owns over eighty horses and a stable estimated at almost half a million dollars, and nominated seven horses for the Santa Anita Handicap of 1939. The Warners and Mervyn LeRoy jointly own a fine stable and practice track at the Warner Calabasas ranch, where some thirty thoroughbreds are groomed in faultless surroundings.

Some of the movie people maintain that their horses are

simply a business investment, bred and raced for profit; this makes it possible to deduct the expenses for horses and stables from taxable income as a "business loss." One of the rationalizations which is used to defend the great cost of a racing stable is that "the government would take most of our money anyway."

It is also suggested that those whose hearts are on the turf are motivated simply by a love of horses. This is not convincing; affection does not require competitive testing. Those who love their families are not in the habit of racing their wives or betting on their children. We do, of course, "groom" our wives and show glee over Johnny's report cards; but we have not yet invented institutions for pitting our loved ones against each other as a candid end in itself.

The movie people who own stables and wager substantial sums on selected animals have created new outlets for their competitive impulses. When Mr. Crosby's mare noses out Mr. Roach's mare, for example, Mr. Crosby wins *personal* kudos—even though he neither ran the race nor rode the beast. Mr. Roach, in turn, suffers a rebuff which pleases not only Mr. Crosby, but all the other horse owners, bettors, or general antagonists of Mr. Roach. Mr. Crosby has demonstrated a symbolic superiority over Mr. Roach, and over all the other proprietors whose quadruped chattels sweated to win the contest. The element of vicarious aggression involved here, as well as the competitive joys and the demonstration of superiority, should not go unnoticed. (The verb "beat" refers to physical blows as well as to victory in contest.)

It is also suggested that Hollywood's mania for horses is an innocent one which harms nobody, and that racing is a commendable pastime which refreshes the soul and does not interfere with work. The influence of the equine on the spiritual poses a problem beyond this writer's province; but it is foolish, on the face of it, to assert that a daily preoccupation with horses does not interfere with the production of movies. Grave economic and administrative burdens are involved when shooting schedules are arranged so that the favored can spend the afternoon at the races, and there is no evidence that a studio's personnel are improving their skill or attend-

ing to their chores by sitting at Santa Anita during working
hours for which they are being reimbursed. The business of
movie making suffers when the minds of movie makers are
on the track or the stables. There are executive offices in
Hollywood in which radios are turned on to catch the "fifth
at Inglewood," in which bets are placed all afternoon, in
which there is more concern over a horse's rheumatism or
the condition of the track than over the day's shooting
schedule. It is a well-known fact in the movie colony that
the fanatical engrossment in racing presents serious hin-
drances to movie production during the racing season. Hollywood's output suffers from the conflict—especially in the
upper ranks—between the duties of creation and the echo of
the race track.

Psychologically, racing represents an artificial crisis which
imparts fresh excitement to jaded spirits. "It's a shot in the
arm," one of Hollywood's leading horse addicts explained
to this writer. "It's the only thing that can take my mind off my
troubles. I tried golf, but I'd be thinking of my work in the
middle of a stroke. I tried bridge, but my doctor advised me
to get more sleep and get out in the open. There's nothing
like the races."

Racing is more than a recreation in Hollywood; it is a
new show window in which screen celebrities can appear
and in which they can win social favor. Horses and aristocracy
go hand in hand; the cultivated affection for thoroughbreds
is allied to the struggle for prestige. Isabel Dodge Sloane, like
certain movie magnates, was "frightened of horses and unable
to ride" but "she nevertheless [maintained] a magnificent
stable, hoping to usurp the crown of Mrs. Payne Whitney as
the first lady of the turf of the Republic." And Oliver Belmont,
one of the social lions of his day, considered his stables the
most important part of his estate.

At the races, as at the opera, those who attend to see also
attend to be seen. At Santa Anita, which has been expertly
publicized, much of the populace comes to see the stars as
well as the horses. Hollywood's actors, in turn, can scarcely
resist the conspicuousness of the setting. Once the stars and
producers have, by their patronage, put the seal of station on

racing as a top-drawer avocation, attention is focused, the imitative process begins to operate, and soon half of the studios are making hopeful phone calls to bookies.

The races bring a distinguished and cosmopolitan set to Hollywood, and this has strengthened the ties between Hollywood and the scions of the East. The Whitneys, du Ponts, Vanderbilts, and Donahues come to California for the racing season, and participate in the social gaieties of the circles which revolve around the turf. The Los Angeles Turf Club Ball, which closes the Santa Anita "meeting" each year, is a brilliant fête which compares favorably to the more glittering social events of the nation; it is a meeting ground for Hollywood, Pasadena, and Southampton.

There is another aspect to the role of the races in Hollywood—gambling. The popularity of gambling in the United States as a whole suggests that it is more than a marginal phase of our civilization.† Gambling is an integral part of our culture, and it rests upon potent sanctions. Business is itself a species of gambling; business negotiations are contests backed by wagers; investments are gambles on unpredictable future events. In 1835 the percipient Alexis de Tocqueville wrote:

> This perpetual change which goes on in the United States, these frequent vicissitudes of fortune, accompanied by such unforeseen fluctuations in private and in public wealth, serve to keep the minds of the citizens in a perpetual state of feverish agitation, which admirably invigorates their exertions, and keeps them in a state of excitement above the ordinary level of mankind. The whole life of an American is passed like a game of chance, a revolutionary crisis, or a battle.

Hollywood's people are geared to an industry which is especially subject to sudden changes—which is, in fact, a highly organized attempt to guess what the public will want and when. "Making movies is like shooting dice all day," said a producer. It is not surprising that the profession is implemented by forms of recreation which offer new tensions to those who thrive on them.

Gambling, apart from the sums wagered on horses, has attracted distinguished disciples in Hollywood. For years the

Clover Club on Sunset Boulevard, and the Dunes in Palm Springs, catered to that part of the movie colony which enjoys roulette and other games of chance. Tia Juana, just across the Mexican border, Agua Caliente, and the great hotel at Ensenada used to be patronized heavily by film folk devoted to gambling and races, until the Mexican government abolished gambling. *

Poker is particularly popular in the top circles of the movie colony. Hollywood's trade papers carry a heavy amount of gossip on poker games and losses. At one Santa Monica home, $15,000 has often changed hands in an evening of card play. There is no reason to be alarmed at the figure; no one of those who sat around the bitter table earned less than $2,500 a week. Joe Schenck, Hollywood's biggest and best liked gambler, suffered gambling losses of $30,905 in one day, and his losses for one year (1937) totaled $64,894.15. In another year he lost over $20,000 (including $12,190 to Herbert Bayard Swope, $4,711 to Harpo Marx, $2,400 to Darryl Zanuck) and won $15,000 in election bets. In one painful experience, Chico Marx lost around $7,000 and found it necessary to borrow $3,000 to make good his debt.

But there is no evidence that Hollywood's stakes have ever scaled the heights of those games, famed in the annals of New York, where James Buchanan Brady won $180,000 in a night, or where "Bet-a-Million" Gates, in concert with coffee tycoons, coke barons, and sulphur giants, exchanged $750,000 in a night between them. The movie colony cannot produce gamblers like the Donahue who, according to *Fortune*, has lost $900,000 at the gambling tables in Florida.

Gambling is a violation of our moral creed, which rests on the axiom that property and power are *earned*, not won. But the rich have generally given gambling wide license in their ranks. For the rich are familiar with wealth which is derived not from skill, thrift, and virtue—the cardinal middle-class virtues—but via sheer luck—inheritance, "contacts," nepotism, or lucky investments. The fortunes of the rich are in greater or lesser measure testimonials to the role of good luck, and it is not surprising that they try to court the factor more widely.

In Hollywood, where careers are made overnight, where success can depend upon a profile or a voice, where the accident of contacts, relatives, or the omnipotent "break" are in evidence, luck is a prime attribute of living. Where the pursuit of luck can be joined to the augmentation of prestige, and where it offers opportunities for personal triumph at the expense of others, then one sees the full flowering of the sport of kings—or aces.

# PART II

# The Gambling
# Enterprise

THE "BUSINESS" side of horse racing is considered in John McDonald's article taken from *Fortune* magazine. A review by the editors of *East Europe* journal shows that some of the issues being confronted in Soviet countries are similar to those faced by Americans. Geoffrey Gorer, a British anthropologist, has written perceptively about both England and America, and, in the article included here, he analyzes gambling in Britain in terms unlike those of most public commentators. This editor's article is a sociological study of the gambling behavior at the Hollywood Park race track.

# Sport of Kings, Bums, and Businessmen

## JOHN MCDONALD

"When a race is to be run by such horses as these, and perhaps by others which, in like manner, according to their breed are strong for carriage and vigorous for the course, the people raise a shout and order the common horses to be withdrawn to another part of the field. The jockeys, who are boys expert in the management of horses, which they regulate by means of curb bridles, sometimes by threes and sometimes by twos, as the match is made, prepare themselves for the contest. Their chief aim is to prevent a competitor from getting before them. The horses too, after their manner, are eager for the race; their limbs tremble, and impatient of delay they cannot stand still; upon the signal being given they stretch out their limbs, hurry on the course, and are borne along with unremitting speed. The riders, inspired with the love of praise and the hope of victory, clap spurs to their flying horses, lashing them with whips, and inciting them by their shouts." John Stow's translation from the Latin of Thomas à Becket's clerk, William Fitzstephen (c. 1174).

In January, 1960, about eight hundred years after the spirited description above—the first known report on horse races in England—they were off and running before thousands of U.S. fans in the pink splendor of Hialeah, Florida, in the eighty-eight-year-old Fair Grounds on Gentilly Boulevard in New Orleans, at Santa Anita, under Los Angeles' San Gabriel Mountains, and at other racecourses across the palm-tree belt. In February they were running at Hot Springs, Arkansas, and with snow still on the ground they were running at Bowie, Maryland, and within the city limits of New York. On Memorial Day, 70,992 fans turned up at New York's sleek and

Reprinted from the August 1960 issue of *Fortune Magazine* by special permission; © 1960 Time Inc.

53

capacious new Aqueduct racetrack, 50,447 at New Jersey's compact Garden State Park, 63,957 at L.A.'s flowery Hollywood Park, and about 230,000 more at sixteen other tracks around the country; records for attendance and betting were being broken everywhere. Now in deep summer the leading three-year-olds-and-upward are pretty well classified, and of all the horses being saddled—among strolling crowds under the trees at Saratoga, in the foothills of the Adirondacks, at Washington Park in Homewood, on the outskirts of Chicago, and at Del Mar, beside the surf near San Diego—the two-year-old newcomers inspire a special interest. In the autumn great handicaps will again test and sort out the older horses, and then many of the horses go south and west for the winter season and the renewal of the cycle of spectacles that has captivated sporting audiences for thousands of years.

But in the U.S. today, racing is more than a sport. It is a big business and a fat tax source, and these facts have some profound implications for the sport itself. They have meant a new era for U.S. racing—an era those in the sport see as one of revolution.

It is, in fact, only the second revolution in the sport since that first chronicled race in England eight hundred years ago. The first set of changes began in the seventeenth and early eighteenth centuries, in the reigns of James I, Charles II, and Queen Anne. Racing was organized with royal patronage: in time the thoroughbred was produced by breeding the fastest to the fastest, and the wager between competing owners was formalized in the stake race. Breeding, racing, and betting were thus formally joined into the structure of a vast and intricate game. The second great change began to materialize in the U.S. less than thirty years ago, when the tracks and the states in large numbers first took a share of the "handle"—i.e., of the total amount bet. It would be an oversimplification to say that this in itself made horse racing an entertainment business, but the business aspect emerged much more sharply when racing became an impressive instrument for raising state tax revenue.

Racing today may be thought of as a private industry operating under state regulation. Horsemen often talk as if they feared the business would swallow the sport and the taxing agent would swallow both. Thus far, racing has managed to keep its essential charm, and indeed it has a broader base in participation and a larger public than it had in earlier times; and yet, paradoxically, the vast expansion of interest in racing, and in the handle, threatens some of the traditions on which this most traditional of sports has rested.

The raw figures of thoroughbred racing's recent expansion are impressive. The attendance, estimated at 8,500,000 in 1940, rose to 33,543,900 in 1959. In the same period the handle soared from about $400 million to $2,439,168,200. The twenty-four racing states collected $186,579,600 in racing taxes in 1959, and this figure represents roughly half of the total "take," i.e., half of the percentage that is taken out of the betting pool before the winners are paid off. (The take varies from 12 per cent in Delaware to 17 per cent in Maine, and the state's share of the take varies too.) The rest goes to the tracks, which are ordinarily private corporations, although some of them are set up on a nonprofit basis.

All together, the thoroughbred industry—that is, horse racing exclusive of harness and quarter horse racing—today has a capital investment estimated at $2 billion. About half of this investment is in ninety-eight racetracks, $700 million is in breeding farms, $200 million is in breeding stock, and $150 million is in horses actively racing. In 1960 the industry employs about 50,000 people, who will take down a payroll of about $250 million; these figures do not take account of such related industries as farming, printing, publishing, food catering, Totalisator machines, etc. In 1959 some 25,000 horses participated in some 32,000 races, and the tracks paid the owners $85,068,000 in purses.

In years past, racing was a sport that belonged to kings, bums, bookies, touts, and others of deep and reckless imagination. Now the dominant figures are often businessmen and those who manage the affairs of racing are coming to seem like executives and trained professionals. And now racing has a mass following; its attendance in 1959 exceeded that of professional baseball by two million, automobile racing by five million, and college football by 14 million. And the sport, which was pilloried for centuries by disapproving Puritans, has attained respectability. Just fifty years ago U.S. racing was almost extinguished. Governor Hughes closed down racing in New York, its leading state, and for two years the sport continued only in Maryland and Kentucky, and in a minor way in Colorado, Montana, and Washington. Racing fought uphill against forces similar to those that supported prohibition, and for a while it seemed doubtful that its wealthy, socially prominent, and politically influential friends could keep it alive. Through the 1920's it thrived in New York, Maryland, Kentucky, Illinois, Louisiana, and Florida, but still had no real national following.

What saved racing was pari-mutuel betting, the arrangement by which the bettors weigh their judgments against one another in a pool. The pari-mutuels helped racing to become respectable because they got the bookmakers out and at the same time enabled the government to get in—i.e., the machines offered a handy means for the states to meter the betting and take a cut. Conceived in Paris in 1865, pari-mutuel was adopted by Churchill Downs at Louisville, Kentucky, in 1908, after bookmaking there was outlawed. It became more practical when it was mechanized in the late 1920's, and before 1933 it was in use in six states. In the 1930's more tax-hungry states eyed the mutuels and in one legislature after another the need for revenue was the decisive argument of the city representatives, who generally favored the legalizing of tracks, against the rural representatives, who generally opposed it. New York favored private legal bookmakers until 1940, when it became the twenty-fourth state to adopt mutuel betting.

The modern racing boom actually began early in World War II. Attempts were made in the name of austerity to close tracks, or at least to prevent the opening of new ones. But the government took the position that racetracks were good for the war effort because they siphoned off money that otherwise would have been chasing scarce goods. Between 1940 and 1946, racing attendance patriotically tripled to about 24 million, and the betting handle quadrupled, to about $1.8 billion.

Thereafter for four years the attendance remained level and the handle declined to $1.3 billion; and then both rose sharply from 1951 through 1953. Some of this rise can be attributed to television; millions who had never seen a horse race became fans of Alfred Gwynne Vanderbilt's Native Dancer, whose gray coat could be seen clearly on television screens. Since 1953 thoroughbred racing has expanded slowly, and not all of the expansion reflects a real rise in the number of fans. Some of the increased attendance is accounted for by tracks that have lengthened their seasons. And much of the expansion in betting comes from these longer seasons, and from increases in the number of races on a day's program.

In 1941, just before the racing boom began, the great American racing writer Salvator (pseudonym of John Hervey°) recalled that: "With these great changes there has come, as was inevitable, a corresponding change in atmosphere. There had been complaints more than twenty-five years ago that racing in America was getting too much the savor of commercialism—the familiar epigram that in England it is a sport, in France an entertainment, and in America a business antedates 1916 by some years. But 'back in them days' even the commercialists and the anti-commercialists hadn't so much as a glimmering of what racing as a business would develop into . . . with the 'handle,' the 'take,' and the percentage for the state the dominant results."

It now appears that Salvator, in 1941, also had no glimmering of what racing as a business was developing into. While the customers multiplied, the group of people who "produce" racing—the breeders, horse owners, trainers, track owners, and racing officials—began to look and act like businessmen, some of them pretty big businessmen at that. Some owners fortunate enough to have top horses were soon capitalizing them at $1 million or more, and syndicating them like pieces of real estate. The venerable American institution of buying and selling horses also looked new in the meshes of modern taxation. But perhaps the most striking change was in racetrack operations.

Some racetracks are nonprofit institutions: a controlling interest in Del Mar, in California, was given to Boys Inc., a

national boys' club, by Clint Murchison and the late Sid
Richardson. Some tracks are nondividend-paying—e.g., all
those run by the New York Racing Association, which is
controlled by trustees named by the gilt-edged Jockey Club.
But most tracks are public corporations very much interested
in profits for the stockholders; and racetrack stocks have
had a considerable over-the-counter boom. Tracks make
money out of admissions, concessions, and, above all, their
share of the betting handle. All track operators today arrange
races that will attract betting. In the long past—when betting
was a side activity that brought no income to track or state—
it was enough just to arrange good contests.

Perhaps the most noticeable change today in racetrack
policy and plant design is the "California influence." Since
racing was renewed in California in 1933, after a long lapse,
two of its southern tracks have generally led in attendance
and betting—and in establishing atmosphere of community
respectability. Hollywood Park and Santa Anita were designed for the comfort and convenience of a large number
of customers. Hollywood, especially, is a "customer's track."
After a fire in 1949, it was rebuilt to give the customers
plenty of space to move around in, for racing crowds are
always in motion—to the rail, to the eating and drinking concessions, to the benches to study the form sheets, to the betting windows, back to the rail or seat. The man who designed
Hollywood was Arthur Froehlich, who had been a designer of
shopping centers and knew how to build for moving crowds.
The results at Hollywood were so successful that Froehlich
was pressed into service at Laurel, Maryland, Garden State,
New Jersey, Woodbine, Canada, and Caracas, Venezuela.
The managers of Roosevelt Raceway (harness track) in New
York had Froehlich rebuild their plant in 1957. The California
influence came resoundingly to New York thoroughbred racing when the N.Y.R.A. then engaged Mr. Froehlich to design its spacious and efficient new racing plant, Aqueduct
(capacity 80,000). This track is breaking attendance and
betting records in its first year (which ends next month),
attesting to its efficiency in handling big-city crowds, although
a customer at the "Big A" can hear wistful talk about the

design of the old charmers—tracks like Belmont, Saratoga, and Keeneland.

The new, businesslike look of racing should not be over-stated, of course. Many of the owners who have come into racing since World War II are in it not for profit or tax benefit but because they love the old sport and its world. To many Americans, horse racing still symbolizes the spirit of high society, as it did in the nineteenth and early-twentieth centuries, though as always, in contrast to Europeans, whose elite attend the races in striped trousers, cutaway coat, and top hat, American males would not be caught dead "dressed" for the races. The delight of racing a horse in their own colors has appeal to many businessmen. And they are pleased to see their names intermingled in the racing programs with old names—Whitney, Widener, Ryan, du Pont, Phipps, Headley, Bostwick, Field, Gerry, Jeffords, Vanderbilt, Morris, Haggin—names associated with racing for as many as three generations*

Threads of the very old racing tradition in the U.S. turned up again this year when the Howell Jacksons of Virginia (and General Motors) last spring won the one-mile classic "1,000 Guineas," and the Epsom Oaks at a mile and a half, two of the most prized races in England, with their filly, Never Too Late; the horse was foaled at Claiborne Farm, Kentucky, and may be the best three-year-old filly in Europe. The Jacksons' racing silks, maroon with a maroon cap, are the oldest registered colors in the U.S. and came down from General William Harding who registered them with the Nashville Jockey Club in 1825.

Another pleasant feature of the new era is the increasing difficulty of fixing races. The efficient, businesslike track managements today are concerned with assuring their customers of a fair game, and work closely with the Thoroughbred Racing Protective Bureau, run by a former FBI man, Spencer Drayton. The tracks have set up control procedures that almost automatically exclude the "ringer" and doped horse. Carefully selected and trained stewards, with the help of complete motion pictures of each race, taken from several angles, are a formidable threat to unfair racing. The improvement is due in part to these better control procedures and good management and also, perhaps, to a change in incentives.

In former times in the U.S. (and to this day in England), purses were on the whole too small to come anywhere near supporting even the winners in the sport. In an effort to make it pay, the owners used to bet heavily on their horses when they looked good, and trained their horses most carefully for races on which they intended to bet. The bets were taken by licensed bookmakers who paid odds that were agreed on at the time of the bet and could not be changed; after one or two big bets on a horse, the bookmakers might drop its odds for the next bettor, thus performing a kind of arbitrage (and hedging their own risks). John D. Hertz, the founder of Hertz Drive-Ur-Self Corp. and Yellow Cab, had a stable in the era of the big bet (his silks are yellow and black, like his cabs), and in his memoirs he tells a story that suggests a lot about the way things used to be. At Saratoga in 1927, Hertz bought a two-year-old in training, who became quite a horse. Named Reigh Count, he won the Kentucky Derby in 1928, and was the best three-year-old that year. (Later he sired the very great Count Fleet.) One sunny September Saturday in 1928, Hertz and his friends bet enough on Reigh Count at Belmont Park to knock his odds on the bookmaker's blackboards down to less than even money—despite the fact that Harry Payne Whitney had walked into the betting ring and laid $50,000 to win on Victorian, his own horse in that race. Reigh Count won and Hertz took home so much money that it disturbed him. He resolved never to bet big again, a resolution he says he kept except in two races Reigh Count ran in England the following year (one of which he won).

Hertz and Whitney, of course, were real sportsmen, sporting in the bet as well as in the racing of their horses. But not all stables were run by men like them, and with some owners trying to make a go of it by means of betting alone, there was an incentive to try to improve the odds by controlling a horse's form, that is by holding him back for a race or two when he might have been ready to win. With the big bet so important, there was also a problem about bookmakers. Even though they were, in the main, honest, the problem was that *dis-*

*honest* bookmakers were able to attract big bets on a horse they intended somehow to prevent from winning. Crooked gamblers were always trying to get at racing; some did, and gave racing a bad name. All these problems were diminished as the era of the big bet receded in the U.S., and stable owners began to concentrate on purses. This brought respectability to the sport, and made it more attractive to businessmen, with some spectacular effects.

The new "purse economy" has raised the incomes, and the capital values, of the big winners far beyond what was possible in the betting economy. A large number of purses ran from $50,000 to as high as $280,000. Consider some modern success stories:

Isaac Blumberg, an immigrant who is a retired machinery manufacturer, two years ago paid $10,500 at the Lexington sales and got Venetian Way, winner of this year's Kentucky Derby, and winner by mid-year of $316,322. Leonard Fruchtman, a steel fabricator from Toledo, paid $2,500 to the Gaines brothers of Walton, Kentucky, and got Bally Ache, who was second in the Derby, first in the Preakness and New Jersey Derby, and by mid-year a winner of $742,522. At present, the all-time money-winning record is held by Round Table, whom Travis Kerr bought when the horse was a three-year-old in 1957. Kerr, who is vice chairman of the board of Kerr-McGee Oil Industries (his brother, U.S. Senator Robert S. Kerr of Oklahoma, is chairman), bought the horse for $175,000 from A. B. (Bull) Hancock, a top Kentucky breeder, and steered him cleverly through a long handicap career during which he won a record $1,749,869 in purses; he is now at stud at high fees.

The transition from a betting to a purse economy, coupled with high income-tax rates, has created a new kind of financial problem for the owners of big money winners. The purses are taxable as income; so are the stud fees for a stallion, and these run as high as $10,000 for each of the thirty-five or more services he performs in a year. Rather than pay the taxes on this income, the owner may prefer to sell the horse and take a capital gain. The most likely buyer these days is a syndicate, which divides the horse into "shares," usually about thirty-five. (An owner who is fond of a horse, but feels obliged to sell it for tax reasons, often compromises by buying some shares of the syndicate for himself.) Syndicates have paid over $1 million for horses, with part of the return on this investment expected to come during the horse's short racing life and an additional return coming from a long stud life (say, ten to fifteen years). Of course, horses are fragile and break down easily; and insurance premiums on a horse in training run to 3½ per cent of his insured value per year. Most of the big syndication sales have been made when the horse goes to stud.

Texas oilman Ralph Lowe's Gallant Man, one of the greatest horses in recent years, was syndicated at stud for $1,333,333. Tom Fool, handicap champion of 1953, was syndicated for $1,750,000. Bally Ache was syndicated by Fruchtman for a reported $1,250,000. John Galbreath, the real-estate man, is one of the very few big buyers who have taken on big horse properties singlehandedly. He paid $2 million for Swaps, the great champion from California, and he imported the undefeated Italian and European champion, Ribot, on a five-year lease for which he paid $1,350,000. How much sense do such prices make? In general, the prices make sense when the horses "prove out"—i.e., when the great horses prove that they can pass on their greatness.

Owners come into the sport mainly in one of three ways: by buying an active racehorse; by buying a yearling, which is the commonest way; or by buying one or more mares and breeding their own horses. However they get into racing, there is no substitute for being lucky.

A stranger walked into the stable office of trainer "Maje" Odom at Belmont Park a few years ago, introduced himself as Leroy Hetzel, owner of a company that distributes electrical equipment, and inquired: "How do I get into racing?" Odom eyed him and said, "You don't really want to do that, do you?" He did. Odom told him that there were impending yearling sales at Keeneland in Lexington, Kentucky, and at Saratoga, New York. Hetzel said Saratoga was closer, and asked if Odom would help him pick out a yearling. Odom agreed, and said he could be found at Barn 60 in

Saratoga almost any day in August. Hetzel found him, and bought a yearling filly for $5,000. The following spring the filly, named Countess Jane, won two big races in New York —the Fashion Stakes and the Rosedale Stake—and, as Mrs. Hetzel says, "We were hooked."

Jack Dreyfus, head of the Dreyfus Fund, has had a taste of good and bad luck as an owner. He once came to admire the late Louis B. Mayer's fine mare Bellesoeur. The mare got a colt, Beau Gar, by Count Fleet, and Dreyfus bought a quarter-interest in the colt. The colt was injured, and never showed his potential, but Dreyfus still liked him, and bought out the other partners. As it happened he paid one of the partners with $7,000 in Polaroid stock, which later got to be worth $230,000. Then he sent Beau Gar to stud, rented mares for him, and developed a substantial breeding and racing establishment. His best product so far is Beau Purple, a three-year-old who had a couple of good races last spring, suddenly became a Derby hopeful, went to Louisville, and won the Derby Trial in fast time. But in the Trial Beau Purple received an injury that prevented Dreyfus from starting the horse in the Derby. Now he is looking hopefully at next year's crop.

How well do the owners make out in the new purse economy? There are some 25,000 horses in the U.S. competing for $85 million in purses, which in the aggregate is just about enough to pay for their upkeep—but not enough, in general, to recover all the owner's capital costs. And so racing is scarcely a good commercial proposition, except to a minority that is very good at it, or very lucky, or in a high tax bracket. In effect, a substantial amount of racing is "subsidized" by a large number of small owners—they constitute perhaps a third of all the owners—who come in for the fun, lose, and leave; and by a small number of large owners who are in the game to stay and take losses (and income-tax deductions) when they have to. It is clear that the high passion of man to associate himself with the myth of greatness in a race-horse (like the low passion to back a winner) is not exactly reducible to ordinary business concepts. And yet the new economy of racing has brought pressures on owners that force them, increasingly, to give more attention to the business of racing than to the sport itself. Look at some of these pressures.

The owner has paid, say, $10,000 in July or August in a gamble on a pretty good yearling prospect. He boards it at a farm for, say $100 a month for seven to ten months, and then sends it to a track in the hands of a public trainer. At the big tracks the cost of keeping the horse in training ranges around $400 or $500 a month. Unless he is one of racing's real "patrons," the owner naturally wants to get his money out as soon as he can, and he finds that the tracks are only too eager to cooperate with him. He races the horse as often as possible when it is a two-year-old. For the really good two-year-olds, the U.S. tracks hold out the bait of eight stake races with purses of $100,000 or more, and plenty of other good two-year-old stakes from $10,000 up. Top two-year-olds have, in fact, earned over $350,000, and even a fairly good one can earn a lot more than its cost and keep. But for the owner who wants a high-grade three-year-old (the "classic" year) and up, overracing the two-year-old is a bad idea; it may result in physical unsoundness of one kind or another. Many owners find it just about impossible to exercise the restraint necessary to develop a horse gradually.

The owner is also under considerable pressure to put a higher value on speed than on stamina, because most of the races offered are at sprint and middle-distance lengths—i.e., from six furlongs to one mile and a quarter. A one-mile horse can make a good living. A two-mile horse will have trouble finding races. And so most U.S. owners go for speed horses. Only a few owners, like the retired Boston banker Joseph E. O'Connell, seek stamina and race their two-year-olds lightly. O'Connell won two recent mile-and-a-half Belmont Stakes, one with Cavan in 1958 and the other this year with Celtic Ash. He bought both of them abroad as yearlings.

It is not surprising that stamina in racehorses is found more often abroad than in the U.S. Even in England, where there is a tendency to speed, the classics range up to their Derby at a mile and a half and the St. Leger at a mile and three-quarters. And France really goes for staying power in a horse. In April and May there are four classics for French-breds at up to one mile and five-sixteenths, followed by the big four classics that are the pleasure of Paris in the spring, ranging from a mile and five-sixteenths race up to the Grand Prix de Paris, late in June, at a mile and seven-eighths. A 1956 study of selected race meetings in the U.S., England, and France in *The Blood-Horse*, a Kentucky journal of distinction, edited by racing's brilliant and severest critic, J. A. Estes, showed that only 5 per cent of U.S. races and 50 per cent of English races were at more than one mile and a quarter, while 76 per cent of French races were at more than one mile and a quarter. In other words, most French racing starts where ours stops. French breeders at the racetrack prove out horses with stamina and breed their best mares to the colts that win these long-distance tests. This is the classical standard, based on the "improvement of the breed" that serious racing men have always insisted is the real object of horse racing.

It is widely agreed by race-horse owners and racetrack operators that distance racing is more interesting than sprints, that the drama in racing is seeing whether horses can go on and on to longer distances, and that this is the public preference. However, there are some large difficulties in the way of giving the public what it wants. One difficulty is in the realm of biology: it is a fact that the thoroughbred breed has a tendency to retrogress, especially in the quality of staying power, which is much harder to breed than sheer sprinting speed. This tends to create a shortage of distance horses, and the shortage is reflected in the design of most U.S. races. It works this way:

In the course of racing, horses grade themselves into the conventional pyramid shape, with a small number of good ones at the top and a large number of poor ones at the bottom. The races are also graded, of course, so as to bring horses of a similar class together and to make for equal contests.

The top races are the classics, the weight-for-age races, and the great handicaps in which the best horses are held down by extra weight in order to produce an even contest. Below these kinds of superior races are the so-called "allowance" races, which are designed to bring out good horses under various conditions; and the races for "maidens" (those that have never won a race). Finally, at the base of the pyramid, there are the claiming races, in which all the horses entered are, in effect, put up for sale at a stipulated price level; any such horse may be bought before the race and possession taken of it after it runs. The point is to bring together horses of similar quality—or lack of quality. Prices on claiming races range from $1,000 to $35,000, but most are around $2,000 or $5,000. Claiming races are increasingly the racetrack's bread and butter; even at the best tracks they occupy about two-thirds of the program. Claiming races are more likely to be short distances, mainly six-furlong sprints, because racetrack managers know that these are the easiest kind to fill. And this is the crux of the problem.

The amount of betting on each race, the main source of revenue to the track and the state, is believed by racetrack operators to be influenced by the number of horses in the race. With fewer horses, the betting payoffs are lower, especially for "place" and "show"; the bettors are dissatisfied; they bet less; and track and state take in less revenue. And so most racetracks insist on large fields; they will cancel a good race, with quality horses, if the field is small, and will substitute a claiming race with a larger number of horses. For the same reason, they will cancel a claiming race at a long distance when it doesn't fill, and substitute a sprint race that will fill.

Thus at most tracks the betting market—the handle—tends to determine the quality of most races, and with distance horses and quality horses in short supply, and sprinters and claimers in long supply, the cheaper races predominate. A trend is established that affects not only the horses active at the time, but the future generations being bred by owners and professional breeders.

Even the U.S. classics are affected by this situation. U.S. racing was at one time at distances longer even than present French racing. Salvator, the champion of 1889, raced *up to four miles!* The Arlington Classic, at a mile and a quarter until 1952, is today a mile. The American Derby, once at a mile and a half, was reduced to a mile and a quarter in 1928, to a mile and three-sixteenths in 1951, and settled on a mile and an eighth in 1958. These two races, both at Chicago tracks, were once the ranking classics after the Triple Crown (the Derby, Preakness, and Belmont Stakes). Marge Everett, the efficient manager-proprietor of the two Chicago tracks, was asked by *Fortune* why she did not make the American Derby a mile and five-eighths, that is, longer than the Belmont Stakes. She replied candidly, "It would be a match race." And indeed it might. Even the Belmont Stakes can seldom be won any longer by an American horse. Three of the last four winners were imported from Europe.

There are countertendencies in spots in the U.S. New York has a massive stakes program of high quality. Delaware has a pretty and specialized program of filly and mare stakes. Eugene Mori's Garden State has the plutocratic mile-and-one-sixteenth autumn test for two-year-olds, which has brought together the best at this age. Hollywood Park is valiantly sticking with its mile-and-five-eighths Sunset Handicap. Laurel has a unique mile-and-a-half Washington, D.C., international race that has even attracted some Soviet horses.

In sum, then, the case may be put this way. The track operators want races with a lot of horses, in order to raise the handle. The betting demand, in effect, is for whatever kinds of horses are in good supply. These happen to be two-year-olds, speed horses, and, in general, horses of lower quality. And because they are in demand, their supply is most readily renewed. The spiral is downward.

How real is the danger that the loss in quality will react on the business of racing? Over the past twenty years, the attendance at racing has grown 300 per cent. Over the past seven years, it has grown only 15 per cent. During this same period the number of racing days increased by 25 per cent. (New York thoroughbred racing suffered especially in this period because of the new competition from the rapidly growing night harness racing; however, both attendance and betting in New York are likely to be up a bit more sharply this year because of Aqueduct.) These figures suggest that the existing racing public is being more heavily cultivated and

exploited, but that the number of real fans is not increasing—
and may actually be declining.

The French success in preserving classic racing may offer
a clue to Americans looking for a way to arrest the downward
trend of our racing. French racing is entrusted by the government to nonprofit racing societies that have a rank and responsibility comparable to, say, the French Academy, or the
Comédie Française; free of direct economic pressure, the
societies watch over the sport and zealously guard its classical
style. To be sure, their circumstances, and perhaps their taste,
are different from ours. The supporters of French racing
are a homogeneous community, concentrated in a small world
around Paris; in the U.S., by contrast, there is no one racing
community, only some millions of fans spread all over the
continent, going to tracks that compete against all the other
tracks for the horses available and that are regulated by
twenty-four different state legislatures. Since racing is cen-
trally directed in France, the sport can be protected against
the economic pressures and tax interests that beset it in the
U.S.—where no one state could reform the sport even if it
wanted to. U.S. racetracks, however, have a rudimentary national body in the Thoroughbred Racing Association which
was founded originally to defend racing in wartime and
which has made a good name for itself with its protective
bureau. John W. Hanes, chairman of the New York Racing
Association, has proposed a national body combining all
branches of the sport and the business. Such a body might
be able to formulate standards for the sport against the pressure of the betting handle and perhaps educate the state
legislatures in the preservation of their golden egg.

Almost seventy-five years ago, the authors of the authorita-
tive *Badminton Library* volume on racing, published in London, wrote with alarm about the revolution they detected in
the sport. "Of all the changes wrought upon the turf by
modern requirements," they said, "few have been more re-
markable or more potent in their influence than those which
have resulted from the introduction of gate-money meetings;
and since the first institution of racing, no such signal

revolution is recorded as the system now so extensively pursued of enclosing race courses . . ."

First the fence, then the admission ticket, and then the tote, and the revolution was complete. In a sense, modern racing has always been divided between Salvator's "commercialists," who are concerned essentially with racetrack and state tax interests, and the "anti-commercialists," who are concerned with the sport itself. Over the years, the former have usually carried the day. It is a testimony to the vitality of racing that, even in this intensely commercial era, it has remained a sport fit for kings.

# The Jackpot:
# Gambling in the Soviet Bloc

Chance and risk have by no means been eliminated from the fortunes of men in Communist society—as the careers of any number of the current leaders in the Soviet bloc attest. But while hazarding all on a shrewd or lucky estimate is apparently an acceptable feature of political life under Communism, as an economic method it is generally looked down upon. In fact, financial "speculation," whose grossest expression is gambling, is considered by Communist doctrine to be the root and branch of capitalist instability and injustice, and is accorded no place in the rational and just society in which the only permissible source of income is work.

Organized gambling, in the form of State lotteries as well as sports pools, racetrack betting, etc., functioned freely and legally in most European countries before the war. The Communist regimes upon coming to power in Eastern Europe after

Reprinted by permission of the Free Europe Committee from *East Europe*, vol. 10 (February 1961), 3–7.

the war suppressed and condemned all forms of gambling. But by 1957, pragmatic (mainly financial) considerations had led all of them to reintroduce legal betting on a grand scale.

The two basic forms of legal gambling in the Soviet bloc are the State lottery and the sports—mainly soccer—pools (betting on the results of team matches). In addition, there are "numbers games" which, where they exist, are evidently the most popular of the offerings. In Hungary this game, called Lotto, was organized by the Kadar regime early in 1957, just after the Revolt. The method consists of a public drawing of five numbers from 1 to 90, the winners being those who have previously picked at least two of the numbers drawn. Similar to this is the Polish Toto-Lotek, which requires picking six numbers from some 99 printed on a ticket. Toto-Lotek is run by a State gambling syndicate called Totalizator Sportowy, which was set up by a December 1955 government decree, originally to conduct the soccer pools. Today there are branches of the syndicate in almost every Polish provincial district, separate from the State Lottery Monopoly, but all of course under State control.[1]

Organizations, institutions and commercial enterprises also run small lotteries. These require a permit from the State. Typical are the Book Lotteries which provide substantial prizes and claim that "every ticket wins," because those which are not drawn can be redeemed at face value for books at the State store.

## LOTTERIES AND POOLS

The State lotteries and the soccer pools function more or less according to the standard European models. There are some forms, however, which, if they cannot be called precisely "Socialist," are a departure from normal capitalist practice. One of these is the lottery on savings accounts in lieu of regular interest. Under this system in Poland, the depositor chooses the kind of account he wants to have according to the prize he wishes to gamble for.

The system was introduced by the Communist regime in

Czechoslovakia at the beginning of 1954 (three years earlier than the State lottery and sports pools were revived), and within the first six weeks one hundred thousand depositors had put more than 50 million *koruny* into the savings accounts. There are two annual drawings for twenty-five prizes, the first amounting to double the deposit in the winning account, two equalling the deposit, and 22 equal to half the deposit. Winnings are tax free. The draw is arranged so that there is one "pay-off" for every 40 accounts.

The betting introduced by the Communist regimes caught on like fire in dry hay and is now a virtual rage in Eastern Europe. When the first Communist-sponsored sports pool got under way in Czechoslovakia in 1956,[2] the press reported that it had at once become "the popular pastime of hundreds of thousands of citizens"; and the necessity for extending the betting hours at the post office because of the lengthy waiting in line was stressed. When Lotto was introduced in Hungary, public interest was said to have exceeded all regime expectations, and the supply of tickets gave out before the closing date. The average sale of Lotto tickets in 1960 was over four million a month, the equivalent of one ticket a week for every two persons in Hungary (based on total population figures).

## ODDS—AND ENDS

The reasons for this ubiquitous enthusiasm are not hard to find. Betting introduces excitement, diversion and hope into the tedium and austerity of ordinary day-to-day life in the Soviet bloc. Where living standards are low, opportunities for radical improvement few, and many pleasures and comforts hard to come by quite apart from the difficulty of paying for them, the "little man's" best hope is for a windfall. (This, of course, is precisely the kind of thinking which the Communists try in theory to extirpate from their society.) And the pay-offs in Communist-organized gambling games are not negligible. Not only are there dazzlingly large cash awards (in Polish Toto-Lotek, an initial investment of 10 *zloty* can win as much as one million *zloty*; the first prize at a recent book lottery in Hungary was 25,000 *forint*, which is the average two-year income of a skilled worker). In addition, many of the prizes are in amenities which are in short supply and cannot be obtained without a long wait or some sort of favored status: cars, excursions abroad, above all, apartments.

In the Bulgarian State lottery, for example, 60 percent of the pay-off is in cash, 40 percent in goods and trips. A representative list of the prizes awarded in monthly drawings would be as follows:[3]

| *In articles* | *Excursions* |
|---|---|
| 1 "Moscowitch" car | 1—Sofia-Prague-Budapest |
| 1 "Volga" car | 1—Sofia-Kishinev-Moscow |
| 1 two-room apartment in Sofia, boulevard Mihailov | 1—Sofia-Kiev-Moscow |
| 1 two-room apartment in Sofia in the Stalin complex | 1—Sofia-Dresden-Potsdam |
| 1 sewing machine | *Cash* |
| Motorcycles, bicycles, watches, cameras, radios | 1 prize of 20,000 leva[4] |
| 2 cooking stoves | 4 prizes of 1,000 leva each |
| 1 TV set | 9 prizes of 400 leva each |
| 1 lot of land for villa in v. Pancherevo, Sofia district | 3 prizes of 200 leva each |
| | several of 100 leva each |

Apartments are probably the most valued prizes, and as such are being increasingly included. Cooperative apartments awarded as prizes in Hungary are located in so-called Lotto Housing Projects financed partly by the Lotto fund. These projects are now under construction in Budapest and the provincial cities. At a Hungarian Lotto drawing on October 7, 1960, the first prizes were two two-room apartments, one one-room apartment, one two-room family house, and a car.

## EXCESSES

Thus it is that—in the words of the Warsaw paper *Slowo Powszechne,* December 14, 1958—"the numbers games have become a national institution, a social phenomenon which with each succeeding Sunday is becoming more and more a set habit of millions of citizens. Each year, several score of them join the ranks of millionaires, while a more or less equal number go behind bars because they were unlucky with the money they 'borrowed' from their places of employment. . . . "

The East European Communist regimes, and (alleged) public opinion, are distinctly ambivalent toward this particular "institution." Only the Kadar regime expresses no misgivings openly and promotes Lotto and other gambling games with unrestrained zest through the press and radio.

In Poland, however, the regime press began sometime ago to refer to gambling as a "national disease"—in the same category as alchoholism—although it had earlier supported gambling as a source of revenue for the State coffers. *Slowo Powszechne*, December 14, 1958, said that public opinion in Poland is divided into three camps on the subject: "one demanding a radical move totally to eliminate the numbers games; the second—equally radical—maintaining that gambling is completely harmless and there should be no limit on the prizes; and the third, which believes that people who want to play should be allowed to do so, but that the amount of prizes should be limited, so that after the initial period of widespread participation, the number of players will drop to a harmless level. Today it can be said that the victorious group are the 'maximalists,' who called for a liberal attitude which would permit the majority of citizens to gamble until they lost their proverbial shirt." (Currently there is a one-million zloty "ceiling" on a single win at Toto Lotek.)

The Czechoslovak regime has lately been taking a markedly dim view of the gambling craze which, of course, it initially instigated. The argument against the betting is that it distracts the masses from more "socially useful" activity, such as work, and lures the weak into crime and ruin.

## SPORTS WEEK

A letter from a reader in Slovakia, printed in *Praca* (Bratislava), January 8, 1958, described the situation in his office. He professed astonishment over the way his office colleagues "manage to squander office time over Sportka and Sazka.

Such a 'sports week' begins as early as Monday morning, when there is a great debate over the previous week's wins and losses. From Tuesday to Thursday tickets are hunted for. No one is satisfied with filling out two or three forms, but takes at least ten. It goes without saying that he does not fill them out in five minutes; moreover, he has to consult with the other bettors. Whole collectives are formed to bet because two heads are better than one and at the same time the risk is smaller. All this at the expense of working time. On Thursday and Friday the bettors have to make an 'official' trip to the city which they extend according to the length of the line which their co-bettors have already formed at the counter. Then they spend Sunday yearning for the results, and on Monday the whole merry-go-round begins again with the same tension and passion. Thus week after week, month after month go by. If the 'sports hours' were computed over the year, it would look very bad. It is fortunate that such a state of affairs prevails only in our office. Elsewhere they certainly give preference to their work over the betting in Sportka. Or does anyone else have other experiences?"

According to figures published in the Czechoslovak press, more than 3 billion *koruny* has gone into the sports pools since they began four years ago. *Mlada Fronta* (Prague), August 3, 1960, apparently in some embarrassment at the size of the sums involved, said: "Let us not be misled by these figures. The foundations of our wealth lie not in 'chance,' but in the fruits of planning and work. Let us therefore consider the sports pools merely a harmless diversion. . . . "

Inevitably, perhaps, excesses, rackets and crime have arisen in connection with the betting. *Vecerni Praha* (Prague), January 24, 1958, complained that not only does the "little man" try to change the numbers on the lottery tickets with an ink pencil but so does the chief of the Sazka Control Department (he was sentenced to four years in jail). The pernicious effects of addiction were described in the case of Josef Migl, who stole material from the factory where he was employed, sold it to a private plumber, and spent the money on Sportka and Sazka. The sums he asked for the stolen material were "ridiculously small," since his only concern was to get enough to pay for the pool ticket. Migl did not win, but was sentenced to two years in prison.

A case which created something of a sensation in Czechoslovakia in 1960 involved a group of prominent persons, among them leading athletes, who were convicted of fraudulent "manipulation" of the results used in the Sazka sports pool during the 1957–58 season. Last December, the Polish radio reported a similar case in which employees of the Cracow branch of Totalizator Sportowy were accused of attempting to obtain for themselves the first (one million *zloty*) prize by falsifying the results of a Toto-Lotek drawing. The leading defendant, a Totalizator inspector from Warsaw, was sentenced to six years in prison and a 10,000 *zloty* fine. (Radio Warsaw, December 17, 1960.)

Reportedly there is a flourishing black market in the Soviet bloc in winning tickets on the betting games, which can be used as a "cover" for income acquired illegally (through theft or graft). Thus, in Hungary, winning Lotto tickets worth 30–40,000 *forint* can be sold on the black market for an additional 6,000 *forint*.

## THE TAKE

While the Communist regimes stand to lose something of their ideological purity by the promotion of gambling, this is evidently outweighed by their financial interest in it. Organized gambling is a not inconsiderable source of revenue to the State, and its reintroduction in the Soviet bloc in 1957 was clearly as a means of "voluntary taxation" of the population in a more palatable form than the forced "peace loans" of the Stalin era, which were then being dropped.

As a general rule, the State takes 50 percent of the price of Lotto and Toto tickets. The State also receives 20 percent of the take of other lotteries, such as the book lottery (although exemptions are granted). A further income for the State is derived from taxes imposed on the winnings (e.g., in Hungary, 20 percent on everything over 20 *forint*). In theory, the State income from the sports pools constitutes a major part of the State subsidy of sports (and thus people are encouraged to "support the national sports" by betting). In Hungary part of the State profit from Lotto is earmarked for housing. There is, of course, no check or public accounting of the State's use of these funds, nor any visible popular concern with it (although in Poland it has been questioned whether revenue from gambling should not be put to more useful purposes than the financing of sports). In general it appears that organized gambling is one of the least questioned functions of the current governments in Eastern Europe.


# In Britain, Gambling Is a
# Growth Industry


With stable New Hampshire veering off into a state lottery venture, and Mayor Robert F. Wagner's proposal for legalized off-track betting going on New York City ballots in November, gambling ranks as a hot political—and revenue-raising—issue in the U.S.

As the arguments pile up, governmental authorities turn for guidance to Britain, with its reputation (at least pre-Profumo) for staidness and balance. Though many other countries have lotteries, the British through long experience have acquired a relatively cool and unemotional attitude toward gambling. So both New York State and New York City (the state has final say on Wagner's proposal) have sent emissaries to study Britain's methods.

Perhaps to the surprise of many, gambling today in solid, serious Britain is big business, with some giant bookmaking and pools operators, organized as public or private companies, taking in well over $100 million a year each. So successful

Reprinted with permission of the editors of *Business Week* (September 14, 1963), 29–31.

have they been that they have branched out with investments in clothing manufacture and retail chain stores.

## STAKE

With the start of the British soccer season late last month, the betting fever is on again in earnest. Lured by the prospect of winning up to $420,000 with the "investment" of a farthing —one-fourth of a British penny—millions of Britons stake an average 70¢ a week on the big football (soccer) pools.

No one knows just how much is laid out in a year by gambling Britons, from the lord who lost $445,000 one evening at the chemin de fer tables of a London club to the lowly "punter" (British for low-stakes bettor). In the past 12 months, punters laid out $200 million on the pools, another $100 million on their competitor, fixed-odds football betting. Besides that, there are betting on the races, bingo, the gaming clubs. Estimates of the total run from $2 billion to $4 billion and on up. A New York committee concluded that the British spend on gambling 65% of what they budget for defense.

Chancellor of the Exchequer Reginald Maudling points out that most of this money is bet over and over. He figures the gambling public is probably not out of pocket more than $280 million a year.

## LEGAL PUSH

This doesn't seem too startling to Britons because it's nothing new. Good Queen Bess herself—Elizabeth the First—sponsored a lottery. Some exclusive West End clubs have kept a "betting book" for generations.

It has taken the affluent age, and the Betting and Gaming Act of 1960, though, to make gambling big business. On-track and on-credit race betting and football pools were already legal, but the act legalized off-track cash betting, chemin de fer, and—more or less by oversight—other forms of gaming such as bingo.

Since the act took effect on Jan. 1, 1961, nearly 14,000

licensed betting offices have opened. Bingo for cash prizes is carried on in 400 to 500 commercial establishments, including elaborate ones of the Rank Organization in former movie palaces. As for the gaming clubs that flourish everywhere, the government has been using ads in an effort to register them and make a tally.

## BIG-TIMERS

The government, of course, gets its bite in the form of revenue from licenses, gambling taxes (33 1/3% on football pools, 10% on greyhound totalisator betting, but nothing on gamblers' winnings), and income and profits taxes.

Probably the two heaviest contributors in the last category are the William Hill group, the "world's biggest bookmakers," and Littlewoods, biggest pools operator.

Hill, now organized like any self-respecting big business in a publicly held holding company, Holders Investment Trust, Ltd., has a total annual gambling turnover of around $112 million—some $70 million in racing bets, the rest in fixed-odds football coupons.

William Hill, still group chairman, started as an on-track bookmaker.

In 1939, the war curtailed racing. Inspired by the success of the football pools (where stakes are pooled and "dividends" determined by the total stakes and numbers of winners), Hill devised the fixed-odds system. The "punter" gets fixed odds (up to 100,000-to-1) for correctly selecting any of several variations of home wins, away wins, and ties. In 1939, Hill took in Lionel Barber, an accountant, to help run the business.

## GROWTH STORY

It was after the war that Hill's fixed-odds system really took hold. Since then, Hill's has been the tale of a growth company. Until 1954, the various companies were owned 80% by Hill, 20% by Barber. In that year they acquired Holders, sold the other companies to it.

So far, the only diversification has been acquisition of debretta, ltd. (fancifully spelled without capitals), a North Ireland children's wear manufacturer.

Though Barber insists "we are businessmen, not gamblers," there's a risk, as in most growth industries. In last winter's bitter weather, for example, there were two months without racing or football. Pretax group profits of $4.5 million in the year ended July 31, 1961, fell to $1.7 million the following year. Latest figures haven't been announced, but there's a loss of $1.7 million on football alone. In the last year or so, Holders stock has dropped from $4.20 to $1.68 on the market.

## BANKER

There are a few other large bookmakers. But most bookies have few shops, little backing.

The Hill organization, with $3.6 million cash at last report, does a sizable commission business in hedging other bookies' bets.

## PROFITS IN POOLS

Unlike Hill, all of the pools operators are private companies. Littlewoods, owned by the Moores brothers, is oldest and biggest, with about 50% of the business. Vernons gets about 30%.

The pools got their big push after the war, with the invention of the "treble chance," in which odds against success are so huge that the wins are correspondingly enormous. Since 1957, Littlewoods alone has had 28 winners of more than $280,000 11 over $560,000. The largest: a cool $840,000.

Littlewoods, as a private company, doesn't have to report profit, but it does have to report total pool stakes—145 million in the bumper year of 1960–61, $117 million for the year just ended. The Moores brothers' private company is thought to take about 3% of gross stakes.

The Moores have also gone in for diversification. In the

1930s they developed a mail order business and later a chain of retail shops. Selling mainly clothing, the Littlewoods shops now rank third among British retail chains.

The government has its own modest toe in the gambling pool, with its Premium Savings Bonds, on which the 4½% interest all goes into a pool for monthly prizes—totaling $43 million last year.

# British Life—It's a Gamble

## GEOFFREY GORER

More than two years have gone by since Britain's Betting and Gaming Act changed the law of the land. Since then—if the anti-gambling factions are to be believed—the country has been gripped by betting fever; but the truth of the matter is that reliable statistics are hard to come by. The figures put out by reformers are intended as propaganda and are thus tendentious. They should not be taken too seriously by the representatives of New York State and City concerned with the effects of legalizing off-track gambling in Britain.

Anybody with experience of British life would probably agree that the vast majority of adult British men and women are, and have long been, petty gamblers, while a relatively small minority are addictive gamblers, sacrificing most of their energy and waking thoughts and financial resources to their passion. On the other side, there is another minority, again probably small, which is passionately opposed to gambling on what it considers to be religious or ethical grounds.

It is hard to find passages in the Scriptures which specifically condemn gambling—although there are passages con-

demning usury or the taking of interest on money loaned!
This puritan minority, probably chiefly nonconformist in its
religion and chiefly middle-class, is both energetic and vocal,
providing most of the scarifying figures which suggest that
a large proportion of British money is squandered on gambling.

But even if these figures are accurate—and there is little
reason to suppose they are better than guesstimates—they are,
intentionally or not, grossly misleading. They take no account
of the gambler's winnings. Suppose, for example, a man
gambles £1 a week on the football pools with a 5-to-1 chance
of winning and wins once every five weeks. You can then
calculate that the man is spending £52 a year on gambling.
This will be the sum he has put into the pools and the amount
which will be quoted in the anti-gambling figures.

But in point of fact, he has a revolving sum of £6, and if
the odds are correctly calculated, he will have the same
amount of money at the end of the year as he had at the
beginning. The odds, of course, are *not* correctly calculated
but favor the bookmaker and, even more, the pools promoter;
but for the majority of the British working classes, this picture
of a relatively small sum in continuous circulation is a closer
approximation to the facts than the picture of 10 per cent of
workers' wages being squandered weekly.

The Betting Act was really a piece of egalitarian law-
making, another piece of "welfare-state" legislation. Off-
track gambling for credit has been legal in England for
generations; it was only cash gambling that was formerly
forbidden. This meant that the middle and upper classes, who
were credit-worthy, could gamble as much as they wished,
while the working classes, who were not credit-worthy, found
it more difficult. Nevertheless, the working classes still managed to gamble continuously. Every street (nearly), every pub,
every factory had its bookie's clerk or commission agent—
technically a criminal and liable to be apprehended by the
police. All who had dealings with him were touching the
fringes of the criminal underworld (as were those who dealt
with bootleggers during Prohibition).

The Betting Act took these subcriminal transactions out of

the underworld into the light of day and at once there appeared to be a great increase in petty betting. But the analogy with Prohibition is very close. Are there any reliable figures on whether drinking increased in the United States after Prohibition was repealed in 1933?

As far as the literary evidence goes, the English have been constant gamblers for at least two centuries. In the 18th century, the upper classes spent much of their leisure in gambling, the ladies chiefly in various card or table games in which they were often joined by the gentlemen who, by themselves, gambled on various sporting events—horse racing, pugilistic competitions and the like. The peasantry and urban working classes not only participated in these gentlemanly amusements but also organized their own contests with animals: cockfights, dogfights, whippet races, pigeon races and so on. Such contests, whether between animals or humans, were all considered sporting, and the British have prided themselves for generations on the fact that, compared with most foreigners, they were both better sportsmen and better "sports."

A "good sport" is knowledgeable about, and participates in, at least the majority of contests of which he is made aware. A "good sport" will take a "sporting chance" with his money, and will demonstrate his sportsmanship by showing neither regret at losing nor elation at winning his wagers. A "poor sport" usually refuses to gamble at all. Or if he does do so, his response to the outcome is unseemly.

Even though England is now one of the most urban countries in the world, this rustic attitude to sportsmanship and sporting events is still a basic ingredient in British gambling. Most of the bets are placed on horses, greyhounds or football teams. Nearly every office, every factory, every social club runs a sweepstake on the two most important horse races of the year—the Derby for flat racing and the Grand National for steeplechasing. It is only the occasional eccentric —I am one—who does not take a chance on these two races.

In many large factories there is a permanent football-pool permutation organization, a kind of workers' syndicate which covers some of the tens of thousands of different football-result combinations possible each week by a complicated system of mathematics. The organizer of such a factory pool has an unofficial position analogous to that of a union shop steward, giving nearly all his time to collecting the stakes, calculating the permutations and distributing the winnings. He will receive very adequate compensation from the pools company concerned for the business he brings.

Compared with other societies in which gambling is widespread, the British are generally less inclined to gamble on their own skills or on the operation of pure luck. It is rare for card games to be played for more than token stakes (except among the richer business classes).

In pubs, cribbage, whist or rummy are the most common games. They are as likely to be played for drinks as for pennies. The same is true of darts and ten-pin bowling in those regions where it is played. I have never seen the British play craps, save for occasional individuals who have been in constant contact with Americans, while the National Premium Bond "lottery" seems to excite minimal interest.

The casino games—roulette, *chemin-de-fer* and the like—are played for very high stakes on occasions, but the players are almost entirely confined to the British equivalent of cafe society. Before currency restrictions were imposed in 1939, they gambled in a similar way in the European casinos; from the end of the war until the passing of the Betting Act, there was widespread evasion of the anti-gaming laws in this small section of British society, with "floating" *chemin-de-fer* games analogous to the "floating" crap games described by Damon Runyon in New York.

Besides their attraction for addicted gamblers, such games supply an opportunity for the socially ambitious newly rich to mingle on equal terms with their social superiors. Serious gambling, like most other forms of socially disapproved-of pleasures, tends to override class differences.

The only gambling game of pure luck which is widespread in Britain is bingo—and its Army equivalent, "housey-housey." Bingo players are predominantly middle-aged housewives, who traditionally have no knowledge of or interest in sport. Housey-housey is mostly played in wartime, when sporting events are suspended, or by troops in peacetime garrisons out of touch with daily sporting events and unable to contact professional bookmakers.

For British men in civilian life and, increasingly, for British women, gambling is a technique for demonstrating their continued interest in, and knowledge of, "sport." It is an important component in maintaining the national delusion that Britain (with Belgium, the most crowded country in the world) is predominantly rural. During the darkest days of World War II, a nation of town dwellers sang pathetically:

> There'll always be an England
> While there's a country lane . . .

The race course on the other side of the hedge, as seldom visited by its devotees as the lane itself, carries the same message, preserves the same delusion.

Sporting events, together with the weather, television programs and, for many men, gardening, also supply safe subjects of conversation for a nation tongue-tied with shyness. "Sports" can spend easy conversational hours discussing yesterday's and tomorrow's runners or soccer matches without saying anything they will be sorry for later, without making personal remarks, getting emotionally involved or allowing an awkward silence to mar the conviviality of social life. A spot of gambling makes the whole world kin.

Theoretically, it should be possible to maintain this interest in sport without gambling. (There is very little gambling connected with cricket, one of the most rural and, for the mass of the population, one of the least popular sports.) One could, in theory, follow the fortunes of one's favorite horse or football team without backing one's fancy with money, but a bet does increase the personal involvement.

And the real satisfaction sought by habitual British gamblers is what they typically refer to as "the thrill" of learning the results of their gamble: a momentary climactic excitement without undertones of guilt or danger, a pure and controllable analogue to a physical orgasm.

The results of horse races and football matches are announced in special editions of the evening papers and are regularly broadcast by radio and television. Ticking off one's successes or failures is frequently accompanied by the increase in heartbeat, involuntary sweating and other vaso-muscular changes which also accompany the act of love. Although it certainly cannot be demonstrated at the moment, I would tend to interpret continuous petty betting as a sign of an unsatisfactory sex life.

Another component of addictive petty betting is, perhaps, the fact that for many British children money is a token of love. Often, British children do not earn their allowance, as do many Americans, by performing chores suitable to their years and getting paid for them. They are given weekly pocket money by their parents (the withholding of pocket money is one of the most usual punishments for childhood misdemeanors) and occasional "tips" by other adults. Money, in the experience of many British children, is therefore for "fun"—for self-indulgence after the necessities of life have been attended to. In the great majority of cases, I would hazard that the money used for petty gambling is "fun" money, and that a win is the equivalent of an unexpected "tip" from a benevolent uncle.

But although the average British gambler plays only with a few shillings a week, they add up to very big business indeed for the bookmakers and pool promoters who cater to the national passion. And another beneficiary is the British General Post Office, for stakes in the football pools have to be placed in money orders, obtainable only from branch post offices, and sent by mail. It may be only coincidence, for the figures are impossible to disentangle from the published accounts, but I see a connection between the business brought to the Post Office by gamblers and the undoubted fact that Britain is one of the very few countries in the Western world where mail delivery is as rapid and as frequent as it was a generation ago.

Again, it may be only coincidence, but when the weather prevented football matches from being played in the early months of 1963, the British Broadcasting Corporation (which is rather closely associated with the Postmaster General) arranged for "notional" matches to be decided on television by experts and celebrities. Bets were placed as usual and winnings paid out, so that the flow of postal money orders and mailed entries never dried up. Neither snow nor ice . . .

British gambling is not only a source of big business but also of big crime. The Betting Act did away in great part with the petty crimes of street betting (though one hears that in respectable areas where housewives dislike going openly to the licensed betting shops, daily tradesmen such as bakers and milkmen will still oblige), but the fact that betting winnings are untaxed attracts the unscrupulous.

British newspapers have recently carried accounts of gangs arranging for the doping of race horses or the bribing of football players, and there have been ugly stories of thugs employed by bookmakers to frighten their rivals off race courses, or to destroy rival betting-shops with hand grenades.

The only gambling tax is one levied on bets placed through the totalizator (the pari-mutuel). What is left of the British nonconformist conscience feels it is repugnant that the state should profit from gaming. Under the present British tax system, the only way that a person without capital can acquire capital is through gambling. With progressive rates of income tax, not even the cleverest, the most inventive or the most industrious man or woman in Britain can accumulate in a lifetime of hard work the capital which football-pool winners are announced as winning every week throughout the season. Some skill is involved but football pools are still basically a form of lottery. There are many reported instances of people with little or no knowledge of the game finding a lucky combination which rewarded them with six-figure winnings.

Neither political party is willing to deal with the problem. Labor speakers wax indignant about the capital gains made by speculators in property and the like and threaten punitive taxation—although it is a rare tycoon who makes as much in a year as pools winners do in a week. They castigate the Conservative Government for having produced "the bingo state," but they have made no proposals whatsoever for dealing with the untaxed capital gains of gambling.

The reason may be that there is almost certainly a higher

proportion of regular gamblers in the working classes than in the middle classes and to interfere with or tax their winnings would diminish the pleasure of their daily or weekly "little thrill." Worse still, it might bring into question the Briton's self image of a nation of sportsmen and of "good sports." No political party which had realistic hopes of achieving power would dare take such risks.

# Gambling as Work:
# A Sociological Study of the
# Race Track

## ROBERT D. HERMAN

This article examines a single type of gambling institution, the large, commercial horse race track. Three comments are in order concerning the social relevance of horse racing in comparison with alternative gambling enterprises. First, horse race gambling is an enormous industry. Almost $4 billion was wagered legally and openly at race tracks in the United States in 1963. Fifty-seven million persons attended horse races that year,[1] a greater number than the total for major league baseball, professional football, and collegiate football combined.[2] No estimates of the size of *illegal* horse playing are trustworthy, but one which is often cited states that $16.50 is wagered "off track" on horses for every dollar wagered legally.[3]

Second, in contrast to Nevada-style casinos, most of which are removed from major population centers and have the

Written especially for this volume. The research for this report was supported by the National Institute of Mental Health, Grant #MH 08040–01.

general features of resorts, race tracks are primarily identi-
fiable with conventional urban culture. They are normally
located well within the physical embrace of the metropolis
itself. For example, "Aqueduct" (the largest race track in the
New York area) enjoys the benefits of its own station on a
subway line.[4] Los Angeles has two major tracks, both located
within a few minutes travel time from the center of the city.
In fact, of the ten largest cities in the United States, only
Houston has no horse race track within half an hour's reach.
While the racing industry often celebrates its connections with
the elegance of old Saratoga and the romance of the blue
grass, it is clear that the realities of modern horse racing
bring it closer to the model of the supermarket than to that
of the vacation spa or the county fair.

Third, many precise data of interest to students of social
behavior are readily available without dependency upon
questionable and troublesome detective work. A variety of
records are kept (and many are published) both because state
governments have economic interests in the revenues of track
operations and because tracks have almost no reason to hide
their records—but every reason to encourage publicity. Exact
tabs are maintained on attendance and wagering, even to the
point of recording where and when every bet is made. In
contrast, there is no way of computing, from the data available
to the public, exact amounts wagered in casinos or card
parlors. Of course casinos appear to do a very impressive
business, but the size of that business is harder to pin down
in exact terms. The Nevada Gaming Commission says that the
reported gross revenue (taxes) from all gambling establishments in that state in 1963 was $260 million.[5] Still, the
amounts actually wagered in that state remain unknown.
While it is tempting to focus attention on the more bizarre
and colorful world of casinos, the present study is an attempt
to appreciate the more routine case of the "local neighborhood race track."[6]

The data for this study were collected in Los Angeles in
1962 and 1963 at Hollywood Park. Although it is one of the
largest tracks in the United States (Santa Anita, across town
is slightly smaller), Hollywood Park may be considered "typi-

cal" of major thoroughbred race tracks. This study should be considered to apply primarily to gambling behavior at thoroughbred races, which presently account for 74 percent of all wagering on horses in this country. Attendance figures, total amounts wagered, and a few other statistics are published in city newspapers and do not require special collection techniques. Some of the details of these figures are recorded by the management of the track for administrative purposes, and I am indebted to the Hollywood Turf Club for access to them. The management also cooperated in giving me and my student assistant the run of the entire establishment in order to make direct observations of patrons' gambling behavior supplemented by the spending of long hours simply counting the numbers of people of each sex as they appeared in various betting lines, as they came through track entrances, or as they purchased programs, tip sheets, or *Racing Forms*. Also included in this study were large numbers of structured and unstructured interviews. Our observations in general became relatively more quantitative as we learned more about the business.

## THE SETTING

For the reader who is unfamiliar with a typical commercial horse race track, this may serve as a guided tour. The physical layout is functional and direct. The running track itself is usually an oval a mile in circumference with a grandstand situated along one side. Horses are walked to the track from nearby stables shortly before the races in which they are to run; they then parade in front of the crowd to the starting gate whose position may be varied to permit races of from ¾-mile (requiring about 1 minute, 12 seconds) to 1-½ miles (2 minutes, 24 seconds). An afternoon of racing consists of nine races spaced about one-half hour apart. Significantly, there is no prepared entertainment between races.

Exhibited in front of the crowd, in the infield, is a "tote" board, a large scoreboard showing, among other things, the payoff amounts for the first three horses in the preceding race and the "odds" against each horse entered in the following race. The odds are actually the payoff prices determined by the relative amounts wagered on each horse. Because these odds change as betting proceeds (betting on one race starts within a few minutes after the conclusion of the preceding one but increases in volume as the starting time approaches), the tote board commands the thoughtful attention of a majority of the crowd.

A major race track draws its patrons from a socio-economic cross-section of the city, a fact that is reflected in the division of the grandstand into three or four stratified zones. The largest is a section (for which the term "Grandstand" is usually reserved) that includes a large ramp for standees. At Hollywood Park, 77 percent of the crowd is accommodated within this area. An area, usually called the "Clubhouse" offers somewhat more elbow room and better conveniences for its patrons, but it seems primarily to serve to segregate the $1.00-extra customers from the crush of the main crowd. Twenty percent of the total attendance is contained in the Clubhouse. A more luxurious and expensive area, called the "Private Turf Club" contains 3-½ percent of the total crowd—but they bet about 10 percent of the money!

Almost all members of the Private Turf Club attend the races in the company of friends or family. In contrast, from 35 to 40 percent of the crowd in the Grandstand attend as loners, while 33 to 35 percent of the Clubhouse attendees are loners. On Saturdays and holidays when the size of the total crowd almost doubles that of ordinary weekdays, a somewhat greater proportion of the patrons attend with companions. The loners, although they number considerably less than half the crowd, are a major factor in its appearance. Casual observers are often impressed by the somber, even gloomy, expressions of horse players; win or lose, they seem withdrawn and joyless. However, this atmosphere is largely an artifact of the absence of conversation with companions. Animation normally requires company. It seems heedless to presume, as many commentators have, that some sort of pathology is indicated by the fact that many horse players wear serious expressions.

A more important element in the calm between races is that most patrons are kept quietly but actively engrossed in the demanding tasks of selecting horses on which to bet. Only a small proportion are "hunch" bettors or are willing to act blindly on the advice of public handicappers.[7] Most people indeed *play* the game; in risking their money, they attempt to select their own betting options by the deliberate application of rational criteria. The task is immensely complex, the list of factors which ought to be considered is very large, and the amount of information which is made available is overwhelming. There is so much, in fact, that most or all players must rely on simplifications and rules of thumb.

The most important source of information is a newspaper, the *Daily Racing Form*, purchased by approximately 40 percent of the Grandstand patrons and 60 percent of the Turf Club members. (We estimate that, at Hollywood Park, 89 percent of *Racing Form* purchasers are men, although two-thirds of the attendees are men.) This document provides three main types of material: (1) A few pages contain feature articles about important horses and their owners, trainers, and riders —of interest primarily to box holders and Turf Club members; (2) A couple of pages consist of ordered selections by the *Form's* handicappers along with equivocal comments on horses thought likely to be "in contention"; (3) The largest section, and most important for the individual bettor, is caller simply, "Past Performances." Past Performances are published for horses entered in each of the day's races at the local track and, interestingly, for *other* major race tracks across the country, in spite of the fact that betting on races is illegal (except in Nevada) where one cannot be present in person. Here are tabulated in astonishing detail the racing histories of each horse entered in each race. Among other particulars, the following information is offered *for each horse:* the weight he must carry in the present race, his age, color of his coat, sire, dam, dam's sire, the names of his owner, breeder, and trainer, the amounts of money he has won for his owner in the last two or three years, his speeds for his last few workouts, the dates, locations, and "conditions" of his last dozen races—and then *for each of those races:* his jockey, weight carried, running position rela-

tive to the leader at each quarter of the race including the
finish, the names of the first three horses to finish, the weights
*they* carried, etc.

Of course, a few important considerations receive no comparable publicity. Obscured, for example, are the subtleties
of health and emotion of each horse just before racing and
the trainer's strategy and instructions to the jockey (e.g.,
whether to press for victory under any condition or perhaps
merely to engage the horse in training and exercise). However,
even here, experienced bettors are sometimes able to draw
inferences from clues in the *Form* or elsewhere.[8]

As might be expected, many "textbooks" on uses of the
*Form* and methods of handicapping and betting are available
to the public. These consist mainly of expositions on the as-
serted significance of a relatively limited number of variables
(speed, consistency, post position, experience, etc.). A few
books examine not so much the past performances of the
horses but rather the possible opportunities afforded by the
betting behavior of the crowd (favorites, prices, shifts in odds,
etc.).[9] Yet both types of books are likely to call for the application of considerable skill and effort. One recent volume di-
rects its reads to *memorize* at least two tables, one with 42
cells, the other with 56, to be able to read and understand
the *Racing Form,* and to be able to apply several complicated
rules rapidly and on the spot.[10] More will be said below of
those persons who, with the help of the *Form,* attempt to
make independent choices; but it may be noted here that
gambling at the race track is seen by most participants, and
this writer, to require genuine mental effort. It is therefore
quite unlike gambling in such casino games as craps, roulette,
or slot machines, which depend almost entirely on chance.

## THE "ACTION"

The actual operation of placing bets is simple enough.
Since the 1930s, American race tracks, by state law, have prohibited private bookmakers from operating openly at tracks

and have required that all wagering be pooled and held by the track for subsequent redistribution—the system called pari-mutuel betting. The bettor tells the "seller" (at a window of the desired denomination—$2, $5, $10, $50, $100) the program number of the horse on which he wishes to bet. The clerk presses a key on a machine (a form of cash register) which prints out an appropriately numbered ticket which is taken by the bettor. As the machine issues the ticket, it simultaneously telegraphs that information to a central computing station, which then, in turn, sends new totals and payoff odds information to the tote board in front of the stands. (Payoff information is corrected for the fact that, from each betting pool, the track withdraws about 15 percent of which about half goes to the state as taxes. The proportion to be returned to the winners, then, is 85 percent of the total bet.) Should the bettor's horse subsequently win, the bettor cashes the ticket at another window; both sellers' and cashiers' windows are distributed throughout the plant and are within a few steps of any potential bettor. Marketing studies have shown that virtually every person in attendance bets on at least one race during the afternoon and a majority bet on half the races or more. It seems that almost no one visits the race track merely to watch horses.

In addition to straight, or "Win" bets, other types of wagers may be made. "Place" bets (in the same denominations as Win bets) pay a return if the horse in question finishes either first or second; "Show" bets pay if the horse is first, second, or third. Payoffs for Place and Show bets are smaller in consequence of the lower risk involved. Increasingly race tracks have also provided opportunities for people to bet on more than one race at a time. For example, a "Daily Double" ticket, sold before the first race, is printed with two numbers representing win selections in both the first and second race; thus the risks and the payoffs are greater than for single races. Other more elaborate betting opportunities are presently being introduced at some tracks which account for occasional news items reporting record payoffs when successions of long shots win.

The horse betting behavior of men is different from that of women. This can be seen in Table 1 which shows the proportions of attendees and bettors who are women in three areas of the stands and in four major types of betting situations. (Women tend to avoid risking larger stakes, hence we made no precise counts of the very few women at $10, $50, and $100 windows. The proportions of women who make Place bets are between the figures given for Win and Show.) Notice should be made, for later reference, of the relatively high percentage of women betting at $2 Show windows and

TABLE 1.   Women as Percent of all Attendees and Bettors in Three Areas of Hollywood Park, by Denomination of Bet, 1963

| Total in Attendance | Turf Club 47% | Clubhouse 33% | Grandstand 26% |
|---|---|---|---|
| Denomination of Betting | | | |
| $2 Win | 48% | 30% | 18% |
| $2 Show | 50 | 61 | 34 |
| $5 Win | 31 | 19 | 9 |
| Daily Double [a] | 39 | 29 | 22 |

[a] Two sizes of Daily Double bets are sold, $2 and $10; these data refer to $2 size only.

the relatively low percentage making the more expensive bets. Pari-mutuel clerks and racing habituees are well aware of these differences in gambling behavior, and they are usually accounted for by such explanations as "Women bet defensively," or "Women try to keep from losing, but men try to win." It will be seen that the interpretation presented at the conclusion of this article is an alternative to these propositions.

The socioeconomic identities of race track patrons are difficult to determine accurately, except those of the 3-½ percent of the crowd who are members of the Private Turf Club who are upper-middle class and above. We must distrust responses to interview questions asking respondents to classify themselves, given sensitivities to traditional, critical judgments of gambling shared by an unknown proportion of attendees. Loners, in particular, are often timid about revealing their important affiliations in this context. (It may occur to some readers that identities of gamblers could be traced through income tax records even though these are not normally made available to the public. Tracks make a practice of requiring only winners of very large amounts to sign special income tax reports before collecting, but generalizations from such a sample would be inappropriate.) As an alternative to direct questioning, we exploited the fact that 90 percent of Hollywood Park attendees travel to the track by automobile (in contrast to the heavy bus and rail patronage of tracks in many other cities). By recording the license numbers of a sample of 604 cars entering the parking lot, while also recording the number and sex of the occupants, we were able to identify the street addresses of the owners of the cars (with the assistance of the California Department of Motor Vehicles).

Then census tract maps were used to indicate the socioeconomic characteristics of the neighborhoods in which the owners resided. Table 2 presents a summary of this information. The data from car licenses suggest that Los Angeles neighborhoods of each social rank contribute Hollywood Park attendees in approximate proportion to their percentage in the county. We have no way of determining whether track attendees are truly representative of their own neighborhoods nor can we judge, from these data, whether the proportionate attendance from middle-class areas is a recent development. Devereux believed most horse players were middle-class people. When he studied race tracks in the late 1940s,

. . . The vast throngs that fill the stands at the modern race courses and that pour their money into the pari-mutuel machines . . . are for the most part middle-class laymen, out-groupers from the perspective of the race track society, who still take satisfaction in a day at the races.[10]

It is also known by the management that Hollywood Park's Clubhouse attendance is now increasing at a faster rate than is Grandstand attendance, but this fact may represent either an increasing affluence among attendees generally or an increasing participation in horse playing by more affluent strata of the urban population. In any case, the data in Table 2 show

TABLE 2. Neighborhood Social Rank of Hollywood Park Patrons by Type of Group Attending, Compared with Los Angeles County Population

| Number and Sex of Group | Social Rank[a] | | | | | | Total | % | Mean Rank[b] |
|---|---|---|---|---|---|---|---|---|---|
| | I | II | III | IV | V | VI | | | |
| Lone, Male | 26 | 37 | 63 | 79 | 68 | 36 | 309 | 54.3% | 11.05 |
| Group, Males | 3 | 13 | 15 | 15 | 19 | 9 | 74 | 13.0 | 11.42 |
| Lone, Female | 2 | 5 | 8 | 4 | 8 | 6 | 33 | 5.8 | 11.48 |
| Group, Females | 3 | 7 | 7 | 4 | 6 | 4 | 31 | 5.4 | 10.55 |
| Group, Mixed | 5 | 20 | 23 | 17 | 39 | 18 | 122 | 21.6 | 11.75 |
| Sample Total | 39 | 82 | 116 | 119 | 140 | 73 | 569 [c] | 100.1 | 11.246 |
| Sample % | 6.85 | 14.42 | 20.40 | 20.92 | 24.54 | 12.84 | | | |
| L.A. County % | 5.00 | 12.98 | 24.27 | 21.12 | 22.80 | 13.8 | | | |

County Mean = 11.308

[a] Rank I represents highest status, Rank VI, lowest status. The "Social Rank" index is a composite of three characteristics of census tracts; median family income, percent of population over 24 having completed 1 or more years of college, and percent of employed males in white collar occupations. This index was developed by Meeker for use in the Los Angeles Area. See Marchia Meeker, *Background for Planning* (Los Angeles: Welfare Planning Council, 1964), p. 81.

[b] The six ranks are actually combinations of sixteen levels, ranging from 3 to 18. The Mean Rank column refers to this continuum; a score of 10.5 is on the dividing line between Ranks III and IV.

[c] Original sample, 604. The remainder were eliminated from consideration as having untraceable addresses, address of businesses or auto rental services, or addresses outside Los Angeles County.

that track habituees are correct when they say that racing patrons "come from all over."

## MYTH AND EVIDENCE

Gambling is popularly believed to ensnare its participants in a system involving (a) the reckless expenditure of scarce resources on events of great risk in the naive hope of (b) "making a killing," and gambling is presumed to be (c) an escape from rationality, even where pathological addiction is not at issue. However, an examination of race track data fails to confirm these impressions. In order to clear the way for alternative interpretations, these popular views are considered in the next few paragraphs.

### Recklessness as Heavy Betting on High-Risk Alternatives

1. The evidence is that the larger the amount of a given bet, the more likely it will be wagered on a favorite—the horse with the statistically *smallest* risk. Approximately 50 percent of the money wagered at $100 Win windows is bet on favorites, while about 29 percent of all smaller bets is wagered on favorites. Hollywood Park has two $100 sellers windows which account for 7 percent of the total handle but 16 percent of the total amount bet on favorites.

2. At one point in our investigation, we interviewed 100 men about the way they bet. (These were mostly loners drawn as a quota sample from the Grandstand and Clubhouse areas.) Among the questions asked was, "When you win, do you usually rebet all of your winnings right away or what . . . ?" Eleven percent of the respondents said they rebet all winnings immediately; 3 percent do so eventually; 34 percent rebet a fixed amount or a fixed ratio only; and 41 percent simply answered "No" to the question. If these responses can be believed, it appears that these men (probably the most likely to be "reckless" of anyone at the track) handle their money fairly "conservatively."

3. A relatively small proportion of all bets made costs over

$50. The figures showing the amounts of *money* (not numbers of tickets) wagered by size of bet are presented in Table 3. In interpreting this information, note should be given of the fact that about half of the $100 bets are made by Turf Club members, and it is very doubtful that any substantial part of the remaining large bets are placed by people without financial means. Most people buy reasonably inexpensive tickets.

TABLE 3.   Percent Money Wagered by Denomination of Wager, Hollywood Park, 1963 [a]

| Denomination | Percent Money |
|---|---|
| $100 | 6.7 |
| $ 50 | 14.6 |
| $ 10 | 21.2 |
| $ 5 | 12.5 |
| $ 2 | 22.8 |
| $ 15 [b] | 5.2 |
| $ 6 [b] | 9.4 |
| Daily Double | 7.2 |
| Total | 100.0 |

[a] First 48 days of 1963 program ($126,791,000).
[b] These are "Combination" or "Across the Board" bets in which a single ticket is purchased betting that a given horse will win, *and* place *and* show, the payoff varying with the horse's actual performance.

4. Dividing the total handle for the tracks in the United States by the number of attendees, the average amount wagered per day was found to be $77 in 1964 ($85 at Hollywood Park, California; about $98 at Aqueduct, New York). Even when the disproportionate influence of wealthy bettors is subtracted, the average still seems sizable. However, these figures are misleading when taken out of context because they include both rebet winnings and fresh money. It is possible to compute the minimum amount of fresh money that must be invested by supposing that *all* winnings are immediately reinvested, and under these fictional circumstances, about 25 percent of the total handle would have to be fresh money. It would be more accurate to accept Scarne's estimate that half of the total handle consists of fresh money.[11] When this is further divided by the number of races per day, the average

amount of fresh money wagered per bettor per race turns out
to be about $4.70 at Hollywood Park and $5.45 at Aqueduct.[12]

### *"Making a Killing" as Betting on High-Payoff Choices*

People tend, in fact, to bet on horses whose odds are relatively low with no possibility at all of paying large returns.
At Hollywood Park in 1963, only 6½ percent of the total Win
bets were on winning horses ranking lower than fourth choice
(and even less was wagered on losing horses ranking that low).
Fifty-seven percent of the money was wagered on the first two
public choices—36 percent on favorites alone, a statistically
"proper" amount in terms of winning probabilities.[13] Long
shots capable of rewarding their backers with large payoffs
must, by definition, rarely be selected by bettors. The existence of high-risk, high-payoff alternatives is, of course, a statistical necessity; observers of gambling should not assume
that the fact that some people play long shots means that
the practice is widespread.

### *Escape from Rationality*

The rationality of the betting public may be inferred from
the wisdom of its choices. (Rationality may be considered by
some to apply mainly to the *prior* choice of whether or not to
take any risk at all or even to play a game, an issue touched
upon in the final section of this article. However, once the
game has been chosen by the player, the efficiency of his play
may be treated as a separate index of rationality.) While any
individual race is an exception to the perfect operation of the
rule, data from any large number of races show a perfect
rank-order correlation between the average popularity of
horses and their ability.[14] In other words, for the crowd as a
whole, betting behavior is consistent with actual probabilities
of winning.

In summary, the data suggest that horse playing is more
characteristic of self-control and caution than of recklessness,
more a participant sport than a spectator sport, and, as we
shall argue below, more ritualistic than innovative.

## INTERPRETATION

Several interpretations of gambling have appeared in the sociological literature which consider gambling to be a form of deviancy or a cultural aberration reactive to a context of *deprivation*. Four examples may be identified.

1. An "escape hatch" interpretation of gambling has been proposed by a number of observers. Gambling is thought to provide an "escape from the routine and boredom of modern industrial life in which the sense of creation and the 'instinct of workmanship' has been lost. 'Taking a chance' destroys routine and hence is pleasurable . . ."[15] Bloch goes on to say that the "chance element" is fostered by certain types of social systems, namely those which base status on competitive, pecuniary standards.

2. A related view is that gambling represents a "safety valve." Here ". . . instead of turning against the original source of their deprivations and unfulfilled aspirations, bettors are relieved through gambling of some of their frustrations and, hence, are less likely to attack the existing class structure."[16]

3. Another interpretation is that gambling keeps alive a hope for social betterment among people "who are least capable of fulfilling their mobility aspirations through conventional avenues . . ."[17] (This, by the way, is the only theory mentioned here which has been subjected to tests against quantitative, empirical data.)

4. Zola, in his study of lower-class clients of a tavern bookmaker, proposes that gambling occasionally allows bettors to "beat the system" through rational means and thus permits them to demonstrate to themselves and their associates that "they *can* exercise control and that for a brief moment they *can* control their fate. Off-track betting . . . denies the vagaries of life and gives these men a chance to regulate it."[18]

While these interpretations attempt to place gambling into appropriate social contexts, they treat rather lightly the differences in gambling behavior among various types of players. In the following discussion, we shall distinguish between the actions of middle-class and lower-class men (Grandstand and Clubhouse), middle-class and lower-class women, and upper-class attendees (members of the Turf Club).

### Middle-Class and Lower-Class Men

I have suggested that a primary characteristic of horse play-ing is the intellectual exercise of selecting horses on which to wager. It may not be an overstatement to argue that, for middle- and lower-class men, it is the *central* element in the attraction of gambling. The exchange of money, of course, is essential, but not central. If the acquisition of money were the main goal, then gambling must be judged inefficient in comparison with other ways that are easier, faster, and more certain. The evidence suggests that most horse players concur in such a judgment: they tend to avoid high-risk horses; they do not invest much money per race (although it is not possible to determine from our data how seriously gambling may drain individual financial resources); they admit, when asked, to the uncertainties involved. I suggest that *the function of money,* in the context of the gambling institution, *is primarily to reify the decision-making process.* Money establishes the fact of a decisive act, and in its being lost or returned, it verifies the involvement of the bettor in the "action." Thus the player, even the "little guy," is brought into meaningful association with processes beyond himself. The impression of involvement and participation in events of importance is facilitated by the presence of large numbers of people, the bustle of general activity, the color and drama of the race, and the movement of money. This is why the more important races, measured in terms of purses and quality of horses, attract relatively more wagering. It is difficult to determine the conditions under which money is primarily an end in itself or a means to other ends—undoubtedly it is usually both. In any case, tote boards give prominence to the total amounts of money wagered in addition to information concerning the odds, and in casinos, the raw cash itself is conspicuous everywhere.

Decision-making requires of players that they study the past performance records, ponder the tote board, consider reason-able lines of action, estimate probabilities, risk money, and collect the fruits of their action. Though on a smaller scale, *they emulate traditional, entrepreneurial roles*—weighing alternatives, making decisions, and signalling these decisions by attaching money to them.[20] Gambling is a game. It has many of the social psychological qualities which have been identified in other games by such observers as Piaget and G. H. Mead who point to the socializing and integrative functions of many forms of play. Horse players demonstrate to themselves their self-reliance and rationality by engaging in decision-making games made up primarily of conventional roles. Gambling, by this view, is less dysfunctional than it appears to be to those who judge it solely by standards linked to the production of goods.[21]

But, in indicating the conventional quality of much horse gambling, we have not accounted for its growing attraction for large numbers of middle-class and lower-class men. The answer appears to lie in the fact that opportunities to demonstrate self-reliance, independence, and decision-making ability are less and less available in other roles in which these men are involved. Occupational deprivations are usually assumed to be more acute among lower-class men, but with the development of white-collar industrial bureaucracies and the more recent emergence of automation, middle-class men may also be increasingly separated from traditional sources of self-esteem.[22] If horse playing fills a decision-making void in a social system increasingly unable to supply alternatives, the future of gambling may be hypothesized to follow changes in the supply of alternative devices for affirming personal autonomy.

## Middle-Class and Lower-Class Women

The gambling behavior of women must be explained differently. As shown above, women are more likely to make Show bets and are less likely to study the past performances in the *Racing Form*. It appears that the search for independence through decision-making activities is not the attraction here. A look at some characteristics of Show betting should provide a basis for interpretation.

Show bets pay a return, of some sort, a large percent of the time! Show bets on favorites pay 63 percent of the time—

though in insufficient amounts to be profitable over a large
number of such bets ($2.93 is the average payoff). Even horses
ranking as low as fourth choice pay a return to Show bettors
36 percent of the time.[23] To appreciate the meaning of this,
we may turn to studies of working-class women by Rainwater,
who describes his subjects as leading dull, sparkless, unfulfilled lives in routinized settings bereft of social-emotional rewards but heavy with responsibility.[24] If this is an accurate
picture of even a substantial portion of lower-class women today, we may link their gambling behavior to their particular
deprivations. Thus in attending the races and in playing horses
to Show, women experience frequent "rewards." The rewards
may be small (too small to make up for the losses) and financial (rather than personal), but they can be symbolic and
meaningful nevertheless. Show payoffs are frequent sparks
against a background of dreariness.[25]

But what of *middle*-class women who appear to gamble in
the same manner? As Komarovsky has shown, middle-class
women are brought up to be more dependent than men on the
authority of their parents. "Competitiveness, independence,
dominance, aggressiveness, are all traits felt to be needed by
the future head of the family . . . " while middle-class girls are
sheltered and given fewer opportunities for independent
action.[26] It is to be expected, then, that middle-class women
will gamble in ways consistent with their training. They will
make low-risk (Show) bets and will follow the "authority" of
public handicappers rather than choices based on their own
independent selection. As it happens, their gambling behavior
is roughly similar to that of lower-class women, but for different reasons.

### Private Turf Club Members

These people suffer few of the deprivations just discussed.
As a group, they bet large amounts of money, they are the
prime supporters of favorites, and their gambling occurs in a
setting of conviviality, sociability, and exclusiveness. Both their
gambling behavior and their sociality are consistent with Veblen's notions of "conspicuous leisure" or "conspicuous consumption." "In order to gain and to hold the esteem of men it is not
sufficient merely to possess wealth or power. The wealth or

power must be put in evidence, for esteem is awarded only on evidence."[27] Clearly, heavy wagering in the exclusive gathering of the Turf Club is wealth put in evidence. However, while it is important to spend money lavishly, it is easier and less disruptive to spend it in ways which suggest conformity to the choices of fellow Club members rather than a rejection of them—hence the tendency to support favorites. Furthermore, since conversation with companions precludes all but a relatively superficial examination of the *Racing Form* during the periods between races, the simplest choice available to the Club member is to "play the favorite!" (It is also true that because favorites win more often than other horses, bettors of large stakes may hope to reduce their "down-side risks," to borrow a phrase from Wall Street.)

Thus, difficult decisions, symbolic of independence, are *avoided* by the Club member, they are *irrelevant* to middle-class and lower-class women, and they are *pursued* by middle-class and lower-class men.

## SUMMARY

The functions served by gambling have been described in terms of the social contexts relevant for three different categories of horse players. By an analysis of this sort, the issue of the desirability of gambling for urban society becomes less one of blanket approval or disapproval but rather one of the evaluation of alternatives. What other cultural devices are available to middle-class and lower-class men that can be as effective in bolstering a sense of independence and self-determination and that so compellingly exercise mental skills and rational powers? What else might be done to brighten the lives of working-class women? How else might the wealthy engage in the open consumption of leisure in ways that would be as "harmless"?

In short, commercialized gambling offers to many people efficient means of enhanced self-esteem and gratification in a culture in which satisfactions are increasingly likely to be found in enterprises of consumption rather than production.

# PART III

# Gambling
# as a Pathology

THE SUBJECT of this section is the gambler as an individual, his personality, his unconscious needs and tensions, and his integration—or lack of it—with the conventional social order.

We begin with a selection from Thorstein Veblen's most famous book, *The Theory of the Leisure Class,* first published in 1899. He contends that gambling encourages habits that should be viewed as destructive in an industrial economy.

Edmund Bergler's *Psychology of Gambling* is the most highly regarded book by a contemporary psychoanalyst on the subject of gambling. The selections quoted here are from the first three chapters of that book. Galdston's brief article is included to illustrate another clinician's use of psychiatric theory in handling a particular "case" of compulsive gambling.

Olmsted is a cultural anthropologist with training in psychology. She examines the symbolism in ordinary playing cards in a section taken from her book, *Heads I Win, Tails You Lose.* An article by the late psychologist, Alvin Scodel, provides a critical description of a recently developed method of treating compulsive gamblers, Gamblers Anonymous.

# The Belief in Luck

## THORSTEIN VEBLEN

The gambling propensity is another subsidiary trait of the barbarian temperament. It is a concomitant variation of character of almost universal prevalence among sporting men and among men given to warlike and emulative activities generally. This trait also has a direct economic value. It is recognised to be a hindrance to the highest industrial efficiency of the aggregate in any community where it prevails in an appreciable degree.

The gambling proclivity is doubtfully to be classed as a feature belonging exclusively to the predatory type of human nature. The chief factor in the gambling habit is the belief in luck; and this belief is apparently traceable, at least in its elements, to a stage in human evolution antedating the predatory culture. It may well have been under the predatory culture that the belief in luck was developed into the form in which it is present, as the chief element of the gambling proclivity, in the sporting temperament. It probably owes the specific form under which it occurs in the modern culture to the predatory discipline. But the belief in luck is in substance a habit of more ancient date than the predatory culture. It is one form of the animistic apprehension of things. The belief seems to be a trait carried over in substance from an earlier phase into barbarian culture, and transmuted and transmitted through that culture to a later stage of human development under a specific form imposed by the predatory discipline. But in any case it is to be taken as an archaic trait, inherited from a more or less remote past, more or less incompatible with the requirements of the modern industrial proc-

Reprinted from Thorstein Veblen, *The Theory of the Leisure Class*, New York, The Macmillan Co., 1899, pp. 276–283.

ess, and more or less of a hindrance to the fullest efficiency of
the collective economic life of the present.

While the belief in luck is the basis of the gambling habit,
it is not the only element that enters into the habit of betting.
Betting on the issue of contests of strength and skill proceeds
on a further motive, without which the belief in luck would
scarcely come in as a prominent feature of sporting life. This
further motive is the desire of the anticipated winner, or the
partisan of the anticipated winning side, to heighten his side's
ascendency at the cost of the loser. Not only does the stronger
side score a more signal victory, and the losing side suffer a
more painful and humiliating defeat, in proportion as the
pecuniary gain and loss in the wager is large; although this
alone is a consideration of material weight. But the wager
is commonly laid also with a view, not avowed in words nor
even recognised in set terms *in petto,* to enhancing the chances
of success for the contestant on which it is laid. It is felt that
substance and solicitude expended to this end cannot go for
naught in the issue. There is here a special manifestation of
the instinct of workmanship, backed by an even more manifest
sense that the animistic congruity of things must decide for a
victorious outcome for the side in whose behalf the propensity
inherent in events has been propitiated and fortified by so
much of conative and kinetic urging. This incentive to the
wager expresses itself freely under the form of backing
one's favourite in any contest, and it is unmistakably a predatory feature. It is as ancillary to the predaceous impulse proper
that the belief in luck expresses itself in a wager. So that it
may be set down that in so far as the belief in luck comes to
expression in the form of laying a wager, it is to be accounted
an integral element of the predatory type of character. The
belief is, in its elements, an archaic habit which belongs substantially to early, undifferentiated human nature; but when
this belief is helped out by the predatory emulative impulse,
and so is differentiated into the specific form of the gambling
habit, it is, in this higher-developed and specific form, to be
classed as a trait of the barbarian character.

The belief in luck is a sense of fortuitous necessity in the
sequence of phenomena. In its various mutations and expres-

sions, it is of very serious importance for the economic efficiency of any community in which it prevails to an appreciable extent. So much so as to warrant a more detailed discussion of its origin and content and of the bearing of its various ramifications upon economic structure and function, as well as a discussion of the relation of the leisure class to its growth, differentiation, and persistence. In the developed, integrated form in which it is most readily observed in the barbarian of the predatory culture or in the sporting man of modern communities, the belief comprises at least two distinguishable elements—which are to be taken as two different phases of the same fundamental habit of thought, or as the same psychological factor in two successive phases of its evolution. The fact that these two elements are successive phases of the same general line of growth of belief does not hinder their coexisting in the habits of thought of any given individual. The more primitive form (or the more archaic phase) is an incipient animistic belief, or an animistic sense of relations and things, that imputes a quasi-personal character to facts. To the archaic man all the obtrusive and obviously consequential objects and facts in his environment have a quasi-personal individuality. They are conceived to be possessed of volition, or rather of propensities, which enter into the complex of causes and affect events in an inscrutable manner. The sporting man's sense of luck and chance, or of fortuitous necessity, is an inarticulate or inchoate animism. It applies to objects and situations, often in a very vague way; but it is usually so far defined as to imply the possibility of propitiating, or of deceiving and cajoling, or otherwise disturbing the unfolding of propensities resident in the objects which constitute the apparatus and accessories of any game of skill or chance. There are few sporting men who are not in the habit of wearing charms or talismans to which more or less of efficacy is felt to belong. And the proportion is not much less of those who instinctively dread the "hoodooing" of the contestants or the apparatus engaged in any contest on which they lay a wager; or who feel that the fact of their backing a given contestant or side in the game does and ought to strengthen that side; or to whom the "mascot" which they cultivate means something more than a jest.

In its simple form the belief in luck is this instinctive sense of an inscrutable teleological propensity in objects or situations. Objects or events have a propensity to eventuate in a given end, whether this end or objective point of the sequence is conceived to be fortuitously given or deliberately sought. From this simple animism the belief shades off by insensible gradations into the second, derivative form or phase above referred to, which is a more or less articulate belief in an inscrutable preternatural agency. The preternatural agency works through the visible objects with which it is associated, but is not identified with these objects in point of individuality. The use of the term "preternatural agency" here carries no further implication as to the nature of the agency spoken of as preternatural. This is only a farther development of animistic belief. The preternatural agency is not necessarily conceived to be a personal agent in the full sense, but it is an agency which partakes of the attributes of personality to the extent of somewhat arbitrarily influencing the outcome of any enterprise, and especially of any contest. The pervading belief in the *hamingia or gipta* (*gaefa, auona*) which lends so much colour to the Icelandic sagas specifically, and to early Germanic folk-legends generally, is an illustration of this sense of an extra-physical propensity in the course of events.

In this expression or form of the belief the propensity is scarcely personified, although to a varying extent an individuality is imputed to it; and this individuated propensity is sometimes conceived to yield to circumstances of a spiritual or preternatural character. A well-known and striking exemplification of the belief—in a fairly advanced stage of differentiation and involving an anthropomorphic personification of the preternatural agent appealed to—is afforded by the wager of battle. Here the preternatural agent was conceived to act on request as umpire, and to shape the outcome of the contest in accordance with some stipulated ground of decision, such as the equity or legality of the respective contestants' claims. The like sense of an inscrutable but spiritually necessary tendency in events is still traceable as an obscure element in current popular belief, as shown, for instance, by the well-accredited maxim, "Thrice is he armed who knows his quarrel just,"—a maxim which retains much of its significance for the average unreflecting person even in the civilised communities of to-day. The modern reminiscence of the belief in the *hamingia*, or in the guidance of an unseen hand, which is traceable in the acceptance of this maxim is faint and perhaps uncertain; and it seems in any case to be blended with other psychological moments that are not clearly of an animistic character.

For the purpose in hand it is unnecessary to look more closely into the psychological process or the ethnological line of descent by which the later of these two animistic apprehensions of propensity is derived from the earlier. This question may be of the gravest importance to folk-psychology or to the theory of the evolution of creeds and cults. The same is true of the more fundamental question whether the two are related at all as successive phases in a sequence of development. Reference is here made to the existence of these questions only to remark that the interest of the present discussion does not lie in that direction. So far as concerns economic theory, these two elements or phases of the belief in luck, or in an extracausal trend or propensity in things, are of substantially the same character. They have an economic significance as habits of thought which affect the individual's habitual view of the facts and sequences with which he comes in contact, and which thereby affect the individual's serviceability for the industrial purpose. Therefore, apart from all question of the beauty, worth, or beneficence of any animistic belief, there is place for a discussion of their economic bearing on the serviceability of the individual as an economic factor, and especially as an industrial agent.

It has already been noted in an earlier connection, that in order to attain the highest serviceability in the complex industrial processes of to-day, the individual must be endowed with the aptitude and habit of readily apprehending and relating facts in terms of causal sequence. Both as a whole and in its details, the industrial process is a process of quantitative causation. The "intelligence" demanded of the workman, as well as of the director of an industrial process, is little else than a degree of facility in the apprehension of and adaptation to a quantitatively determined causal sequence. This facility of apprehension and adaptation is what is lacking in stupid workmen, and the growth of this facility is the end sought in their education—so far as their education aims to enhance their industrial efficiency.

In so far as the individual's inherited aptitudes or his training incline him to account for facts and sequences in other terms than those of causation or matter-of-fact, they lower his productive efficiency or industrial usefulness. This lowering of efficiency through a penchant for animistic methods of apprehending facts is especially apparent when taken in the mass—when a given population with an animistic turn is viewed as a whole. The economic drawbacks of animism are more patent and its consequences are more far-reaching under the modern system of large industry than under any other. In the modern industrial communities, industry is, to a constantly increasing extent, being organised in a comprehensive system of organs and functions mutually conditioning one another; and therefore freedom from all bias in the causal apprehension of phenomena grows constantly more requisite to efficiency on the part of the men concerned in industry. Under a system of handicraft an advantage in dexterity, diligence, muscular force, or endurance may, in a very large measure, offset such a bias in the habits of thought of the workmen.

Similarly in agricultural industry of the traditional kind, which closely resembles handicraft in the nature of the demands made upon the workman. In both, the workman is himself the prime mover chiefly depended upon, and the natural forces engaged are in large part apprehended as inscrutable and fortuitous agencies whose working lies beyond the workman's control or discretion. In popular apprehension there is in these forms of industry relatively little of the industrial process left to the fateful swing of a comprehensive mechanical sequence which must be comprehended in terms of causation and to which the operations of industry and the movements of the workmen must be adapted. As industrial methods develop, the virtues of the handicraftsman count for less and less as an offset to scanty intelligence or a halting acceptance of the sequence of cause and effect.

• • •

Through its cumulative effect upon the habitual attitude of the population, even a slight or inconspicuous bias towards accounting for everyday facts by recourse to other ground than that of quantitative causation may work an appreciable lowering of the collective industrial efficiency of a community.

# The Psychology of Gambling

## EDMUND BERGLER

### IS EVERYONE WHO GAMBLES A "GAMBLER"?

Every person in our culture is a potential gambler, either of the harmless or dangerous variety. In certain personalities this dormant tendency can be awakened, so that the latent gambler becomes the actual gambler. This is perhaps a shocking statement, and one that many would like to deny. It can be denied, however, only by blinking at scientific evidence to the contrary.

So far as it is humanly possible, every scientific investigation is unbiased, and free from preconceived notions on the part of the scientist, whose purpose is to describe and explain clinical facts. A scientific investigation may, of course, lead to conclusions which are erroneous, or which are rendered meaningless or obsolete by subsequent discoveries. But—and that "but" is decisive—these errors in judgment are not the result of a priori opinion on the part of the investigator.

Consequently, I make no claims to infallibility. My conclusions on gamblers have been influenced neither by sympathy nor antipathy for the object of my research. For me, the pathological gambler represents only a pathologic phenomenon which became the object of detached interest during psychiatric-psychoanalytic treatment.

At this point, the ironically minded reader might protest: "Medical treatment for gamblers? Why treat them in the first place? Anyhow, you claim that everybody is a potential gambler, so it would be necessary to treat everybody. Which is nonsense!" This objection rests on a misunderstanding in terminology. Obviously, we must first define that pathologic phenomenon, the gambler. What are his purely descriptive characteristics? There are six of them:

## 1. The Gambler Habitually Takes Chances

Is the movie-goer who used to play "screeno" or "bingo" a gambler? Is the man who risks five dollars betting on the gubernatorial election a gambler? Or the *Times* reader who, in a joking mood, bets that the editorial page in the next edition will be numbered 22 or 28? The answer in each case is "no." The movie-goer does not go to the theater for the specific purpose of playing "screeno." He goes for the film, and even though he may enjoy the game of chance, he is not a gambler in the clinical sense. The man who bets on gubernatorial elections does so every four years; the *Times* reader is not in the mood to wager on such nonsense as the sequence of pages every day in the week. The whole picture would be changed, however, if any of the three were to leap habitually at every chance to make a wager. If, for example, the first man's primary objective is not the feature but the game, and he sees the same boring film again and again just for the sake of playing it, then he may be defined as a gambler. The quantitative factor is indispensable for differentiation. In the same way, we do not classify as an alcoholic the person who takes a cocktail before dinner.

## 2. The Game Precludes All other Interests

The mental energy of the pathologic gambler is almost constantly concentrated on gambling, on computing chances and making prognostications. His fantasies and daydreams center around this one idea; the pathologic concentration overshadows everything else—vocation, love, hobbies.

## 3. The Gambler is Full of Optimism and Never Learns from Defeat

The gambler is apparently the last optimist; he is a creature totally unmoved by experience. His belief in ultimate success cannot be shattered by financial loss, however great. He did not win today? So what? Tomorrow will be lucky. He's lost again? It doesn't prove a thing; someday he's bound to win. There is nothing more tragic than the gambler who has lost his last dollar and is still absolutely convinced that he will "surely" win a fortune, if only he can get hold of the money to tide him through this temporary run of bad luck. Every gambler gives the impression of a man who has signed a contract with Fate, stipulating that persistence must be rewarded. With that imaginary contract in his pocket, he is beyond the reach of all logical objection and argument.

## 4. The Gambler Never Stops when Winning

The result of this pathologic optimism is that the true gambler never stops when he is winning, for he is convinced that he must win more and more. Inevitably, he loses. He does not consider his winnings the result of chance; to him they are a down payment on that contract he has with Fate which guarantees that he will be a permanent winner. This inability to stop while fortune is still smiling is one of the strongest arguments against the earnest assumption, common to all gamblers, that one can get rich through gambling. Of course a man may win a certain amount of money in a game of chance. If he were able to stop at that point, his bank account could profit. But almost without exception, the game is continued until the gambler proves that sensible people are right in calling

him a "sucker." It is this fatal optimism which drives the
gambler to push his luck too far, that ensures the solvency of
gambling houses.

One of my gambling patients visited a fashionable French
resort and paid a social call on the manager of the casino,
to whom he had a letter of introduction. He was asked
whether he had visited the casino. "Of course," my patient replied, "and I have even won a few thousand francs." At this,
the manager seriously advised him to leave town promptly.
"If you don't," he said, "you will continue to gamble and lose
everything. We make money because the gambler cannot stop
when he loses—nor when he wins."

### 5. Despite Initial Caution, the Gambler Eventually Risks Too Much

The gambler is always motivated by feelings of guilt, conscious or unconscious. Consequently, he uses certain mechanisms to appease his conscience. The most typical mechanism
is that of the small stake: "It doesn't matter if I lose that sum; I
can afford it." Gradually, however, the stakes increase, with or
without scruples as to their size. It is here that the pathologic
optimism described above comes into full play. The man who
risks the money needed to feed his family is an all-too-familiar
and tragic figure to need further description. Even closer to
the abyss is the man who defrauds clients or his employer,
using the eternal excuse that he thought he was "bound" to
win. Sooner or later every gambler loses his head, forgets
his good intentions, and risks everything on one card—only
to lose. Some inner compulsion drives the gambler to repeat
these actions which cannot be logically explained (it is plainly
senseless to risk everything at once), and the fact that his
behavior cannot be explained by logic decisively proves the
importance of unconscious motives in gambling.

### 6. "Pleasurable-Painful Tension" (Thrill) Is Experienced During the Game

Pathologic though his behavior is, the gambler feels some
need to appear rational in the eyes of society. He offers, therefore, "rational" explanations for his gambling. The two most

familiar are: "I do it to make money," and "I enjoy the thrill of the game." Gamblers who are not too hypocritical freely admit that they seek the strange tension experienced in the game. An understanding of this mysterious tension is one of the pivotal factors in deciphering the psychology of gambling; a purely descriptive analysis of this thrill component, however, would be almost meaningless. Well known as this sensation is to anyone who gambles, it has not been correctly described in either scientific literature or in belles-lettres. This is not accidental, for it is a psychological state impossible to understand without knowledge of unconscious factors. This tension is a mixture, part pleasurable, part painful; it is comparable to no other known sensation. The formulation itself, "pleasurable-painful tension" (I am quoting an observant patient of mine), shows the *a*logical element involved. It is enigmatic, to begin with, to derive any pleasure from expectancy when the outcome of the awaited event is most uncertain. The normal person does his best to avoid painful uncertainty, but uncertainty is precisely what the gambler seeks. A glib rationalization for this might be that the gambler expects to win and therefore feels elated in advance. Even if this were true, it would still leave unexplained the presence of the painful element in the tension of gambling. To ascribe the painful component to the fear of losing merely closes a vicious circle. The question still remains: Why does the gambler gamble?

The tension of gambling, I repeat, is logically inexplicable. It is erroneous to assume that it arises from the inevitable interim between the placing of a bet and the end of the game. The gambler looks forward to that interval, and to the accompanying tension. This is true whether the gambler realizes it or not, whether his feelings are conscious or unconscious.

The craving for this strange thrill frequently overshadows the desire to win. Even professional cardsharps become victims of this craving from time to time, gamble for gambling's sake, and lose. Casanova is a famous example of the professional gambler who falls victim to this longing for the thrill itself. Striking evidence of the predominance of the thrill component was offered by a patient whom I was treating for pathologic gambling.

He described a game played by two persons with fifteen matches. Each player, in his turn, had the right to take from the central pile one, two, or three matches. The loser was the one who, because it was his turn, had to take the last match. The initiate always won if he began by taking two matches, and was careful, whenever his turn came, to leave an unequal number for his opponent. My patient found this cat-and-mouse play financially lucrative, as even an intelligent but inexperienced opponent could be expected to play ten or fifteen games before catching on to the trick. But he told me that after a while he always became bored. "There was no thrill to it." In other words, once the tension is gone, the pleasure of gambling is destroyed. The element of insecurity, win or lose, is of prime importance, and one of the prerequisites for that strange thrill.

To sum up: From the great mass of merely potential or occasional gamblers we have isolated the *real* gambler. He is marked by the following characteristics, or clinical symptoms:

1. Gambling is a typical, chronic, and repetitive experience in his life.
2. Gambling absorbs all his other interests like a sponge.
3. The gambler is pathologically optimistic about winning and never "learns his lesson" when he loses.
4. The gambler cannot stop when he is winning.
5. No matter how great his initial caution, the true gambler eventually risks more than he can afford.
6. The gambler seeks and enjoys an enigmatic thrill which cannot be logically explained, since it is compounded of as much pain as pleasure.

Thus the title of gambler is reserved for a *specific* group of neurotics, and it is with these types alone that we are here concerned. Simple description has made it clear that the person who indulges only occasionally in games of chance is not a pathologic gambler. Not every "Sunday gambler" is meant.

## THE GAMBLER'S CONSCIOUS
## MOTIVATIONS

The gambler has two stock answers that he uses either individually or in combination for the question, "Why do you gamble?" "I gamble because I want to win money," he will say, or, "I gamble because life is boring, and the game gives me thrills and excitement."

Further probing into the gambler's conscious motivations reveals this line of reasoning: The possibility of earning "real money" by normal work is greatly restricted, if not impossible. On the other hand, there are people who make fortunes quickly through gambling. Why not try that way? The most obvious objection—that the gambler will inevitably lose in the long run—is vigorously denied. Every gambler is glib with examples that allegedly prove it is possible to get rich by gambling. It is interesting that these examples are frequently known to him only through hearsay.

Many of these success stories about gamblers give the impression of "arrested movement." It is as if you were seeing a motion picture in which one specific situation had a powerful attraction for you. You stop at that scene, disregarding all the subsequent action. The moment which is chosen and, as it were, crystallized, is exactly the moment of success. The aftermath, the tragic end of the one-time big shot, his penniless old age, his eventual suicide—all this is ignored. His admirers remember him only as he was at the pinnacle of his success.

In the myth of the eternally lucky gambler only the success is remembered; the failure is forgotten. But this mythical creature provides the gambler's essential alibi. If this hero did not exist, he would certainly have been invented. The tenacity with which this myth of the permanently successful gambler is maintained proves that gamblers need it as an inner excuse. The gambler's guilt, visible only after removal of the screen which this alibi provides, must be traced genetically.

The gambler calls upon three additional arguments—all of them irrational, but to him completely convincing. First, he is subjectively certain that he will win. How can he be so cocksure? He "just knows." Neither his sneer nor his conviction can be refuted. Fanatics are never moved by logical argument, and the gambler is a fanatic in his belief in ultimate success.

Second, the gambler has unbounded faith in his own cleverness. With a supercilious and mysterious smile, the gambler will assure us that he will hit the jackpot. It is tragicomic to observe the deep contempt with which the typical gambler regards other gamblers; in his opinion they are inferior creatures. He is the prototypic individualist. His conviction of his own superiority, however, derives from affective and unconscious reasons, and arguments taken from the arsenals of logic, morality, or even statistics do not impress him in the least.

Third, the gambler claims that life itself is nothing but a gamble. What about the men who accumulate great fortunes in business—don't they all take chances? When pressed, the gambler will concede that luck alone has made very few millionaires, and that more often than not the man who regards business as nothing but a game of chance winds up penniless, or in jail. But there is a stock answer to cover even this concession: "Why shouldn't I be one of the lucky ones?"

The gambler's first two arguments are hardly worth discussing. They are simply results of irrational faith in oneself; they are objectively entirely absurd; they become significant only when the unconscious reasons that prompt them are examined. The third argument—that gambling is a microcosm of the commercial macrocosm—is worth serious consideration. It embodies a common fallacy, the wishful belief that luck alone determines the outcome of a business venture.

The Oriental proverb "Throw a lucky man into the sea and he will come out with a fish in his mouth" is as far from true as Chatfield's epigram, which is its exact opposite: "Good and bad luck is but a synonym, in most instances, for good and bad judgment." The truth, as usual, lies somewhere in between. Without luck, success is impossible. But luck alone is not enough. Only the combination of luck-plus-personal-initiative spells success.

It is obvious that the man who is a failure will lay heavy stress on the element of luck when he is forced to concede a competitor's success. As an anonymous writer put it: "Good luck is the lazy man's estimate of a worker's success." Add personal ingenuity and hard work, and the definition draws nearer to the facts. The identification of gambling and commercial activity is a fallacy which is easily exposed. The identification is based on the fact that both activities, up to a point, are affected by similar conditions. The roulette ball is influenced exclusively by factors beyond the gambler's control—to all intents and purposes, by chance. In business, too, the individual cannot regulate the element of luck or chance. But personal initiative must be completely ruled out of the gambler's fight with the machine, whereas initiative, intelligence, the ability to use imagination in combining external factors—all these are of telling importance to the individual's potential business success, and are very clearly influenced by the individual.

This last statement can be proved. There are people who for *unconscious* reasons counteract their own success. Psychiatrically, such people are called "psychic masochists." Without discussing the reasons for this strange behavior, let us consider a few clinical examples.

One of my patients was a gifted advertising man. "Unfortunately," to quote him, he could not get along with his superiors. By provoking the vice-presidents, and later the president, of his firm, he managed to be dismissed from every job. Interestingly enough, he was very conciliatory at the beginning of every new job. He would begin by being interested only in creating an aura of smartness and success. But after this initial stage, he would start on his routine of merciless provocation, which would continue until the inevitable fiasco. The man was not at all conscious of this procedure, as described. He knew only that he had a "terrific temper," which he tried to control.

There were deep-seated reasons for the man's course of conduct. One got the impression that he was still, inwardly, a parasitic child who considered it a terrible injustice that he had to earn his own living. His wealthy parents should have supported him in grand style—that was his half-conscious aim. Unconsciously, he wanted failure; it would prove that he could be nothing but a parasite. That wish was counteracted by his exaggerated self-esteem; before he could allow himself to fail, therefore, he had to justify his childlike, megalomaniacal opinion of himself. Megalomania accounted for his initial successes; the self-damaging component for his ultimate failures.

The parasitic aim was *not* the result of laziness and the "wish to get"; it was a technique used to railroad his parents into the situation of refusal. He knew that his wealthy and penurious parents wanted him to make a success of his own. By constantly losing his jobs, he constantly returned to a state of dependence upon his parents. Then he could revel in orgies of hatred, and self-pity for his parents' "unjust treatment" of him, as exemplified, for instance, in the small allowance they gave him. He did not in the least realize that he himself had unconsciously provoked the entire situation.

Hadn't he proved that he was gifted? He had. Was he responsible for the fact that in childhood he had been taught "always to tell the truth"? He was not. All he had done was tell his superiors what he thought of them. Thus, by reducing all educational commands to absurdity, he could "with good conscience" talk about his "bad luck in having impossible parents and superiors."

A second example: A gifted student of technical engineering, whose "great future" was assured by his father's connections, labored for years under the inability to take his professional examinations. He procrastinated endlessly, always claiming that he was not yet "thoroughly prepared." His father, himself a professor of technology, accused him of wasting time, and urged him to "pass those stupid examinations and get it over with." All this was to no avail. The son stubbornly refused to take the necessary tests.

The unconscious reasons for this self-imposed failure, first proved and then changed by psychoanalytic treatment, was this: When the boy was three and a half, the father had taught him the alphabet. At that time the father constantly complained that his son was "flighty and not thorough enough." The son's unconscious retaliation came twenty years later, when he turned the tables and beat his father with his own stick, refusing to take his examinations because he was so thorough in his preparation. But this unconscious ironic aggression was only a pretense ("pseudo-aggression"), covering the wish to be rejected and to suffer. A revenge that harms the avenger is neurotic.

The owner of a large bookstore—our third example—ruined himself by "poor judgment" in the following way. Believing that certain books would sell extremely well at Christmas, he not only overstocked, but bought the books outright. Ordinarily, he would have taken the books on consignment (this was the rule in his country), but he was lured by the prospects of a "bargain." His unsound moves were followed by a business depression, and he lost a great deal of money. After repeating the same mistake twice, he went into bankruptcy.

The unconscious reason for his "mistake"? Previously, the man had earned a reputation for sound judgment, proved by the fact that he had built a sizable business "out of nothing." Therefore, nothing but neurotic conflict could explain his sudden "bad judgment." The man was engaged to a girl whom he suspected of being a gold-digger. Instead of getting rid of her—the normal solution—he got rid of his business, unconsciously in order to test his fiancée. The test produced the predictable result: she left him. The entire process was unconscious, as had been his motives for choosing so disappointing a girl in the first place.

We must conclude that the gambling and commercial spheres are not identical, and that the gambler's formulation, "Gambling is only another form of business," is totally erroneous.

More intelligent gamblers stress the irrational motive in gambling: the thrill component. The thrill of that tension was recognized by Dostoevski, who wrote the greatest description of a gambler in literature, *The Gambler*. Dostoevski was himself a pathologic gambler. In one of his letters he confesses: "The main point is the game itself. On my oath, it is not greed for money, despite the fact that I need money badly."

The gambler is neither willing nor able to explain the thrill of gambling. One gambler told me emphatically: "Does the lover care about a psychological analysis of his sweetheart, or the satisfied eater about a chemical analysis of his food?" "You are right," I replied, "but you cannot compare the dangerous and harmful process of gambling with the harmless processes of loving and eating. Don't you believe that the lover and the eater are uninterested in psychology and chemistry only as long as everything goes well? What about a case of jealousy-paranoia or food poisoning?"

The last argument in the gambler's rattling arsenal is this one: "Who cares *how* I make money, so long as I stay out of Sing Sing?" It is easily refuted. Gambling as a profession is too dangerous and insecure to be made the foundation of one's whole existence. The margin of error and defeat is just too great, even if one feigns naïveté, forgets psychiatric facts, disregards the moral disapproval of the community, and accepts the gambler's rationalizations. The ups and downs are too hazardous—merely its insecurity excludes the possibility of making gambling one's profession.

Gambling is not a profession. It is a dangerous neurosis. The gambler doesn't gamble because he consciously decides to gamble; he is propelled by unconscious forces over which he has no control. He is an *objectively* sick person who is *subjectively* unaware that he is sick. But this ignorance does not make him any the healthier.

## WHERE LOGIC ENDS, THE UNCONSCIOUS TAKES OVER

The psychology of consciousness is a tool inadequate for the task of unraveling the complex personality of the gambler. If we remain on the conscious level, we soon reach an impasse of rationalizations and illogical reasoning. To take the gambler's own evaluation of his motives at face value is as naïve as the belief that a drop of water is the same to the naked eye as it is to the eye of a microscope. Just as the microscope reveals the millions of dangerous bacilli that may lurk in a drop of "clean" water, the psychology of the *unconscious* exposes facts hidden in the gambler's psyche.

The best approach to the problem of the gambler's *unconscious* psychology is, first, to examine his illogical, senseless certainty that he will win. A literary example of this may be found in a passage from the diary of a woman who was the victim of her famous husband's gambling. Feodor Dostoevski's wife wrote:

Fedja took eighty gulden, gambled and lost. He took the same sum once more and lost. . . . He fetched the last forty gulden and promised me *unconditionally* that he would bring home my earrings and my ring which he had pawned for 170 francs. He said that *in a tone of complete conviction, as if his winning or not winning depended on him alone.* Of course that conviction did not help him; he lost the last forty gulden too. (August 22, 1867.)

It is virtually impossible to match this lordly self-assurance with an equivalent attitude on the part of an average person leading a "normal" life. A phenomenon like this can be found only among pathological fanatics. Fanaticism is a megalomaniacal condition, and the gambler, in his optimism, is a fanatic too. The structure of this megalomania can best be understood by briefly examining a common phenomenon of the psychology of the child: the "fiction of omnipotence."

As Freud and Sandor Ferenczi have shown, the child lives in a sort of megalomania for a long period; he knows only one yardstick, and that is his own overinflated ego. He conceives of the outside world as something over which he has complete control. This misconception of reality is fostered by his parents, who automatically attempt to fulfill his every wish for food, sleep, affection. This fulfillment of his physical and emotional desires the child regards, not as the result of his mother's love, but as the result of his own omnipotence. Real experience gradually destroys this fiction, an experience which is probably the deepest disappointment of childhood.

A beautiful example of this childhood megalomania is found in Romain Rolland's novel *Jean Christophe*. The author describes Christophe as a child:

> He is a magician, too. . . . He commands the clouds. He wants them to go to the right, but they continued to the left. He scolds them, and repeats his command more urgently. His heart beats more quickly as he watches to see if at least one little cloud obeys him. But they continue to move to the left. He stamps his foot, menaces them with his little stick, and changes his command. Now he wants them to go to the left, and this time the clouds obey. He is happy and proud of his power.

The novelist is describing a transitory phase in the child's development, just as if he were outlining a clinical case. Reality forces the child to acknowledge that he is not an omnipotent magician, but still he must save at least a small part of his cherished fiction. It is as if someone, glancing at his watch at one minute to six, were to command the watch to point to six in exactly one minute, and then—his "command" obeyed—were to feel omnipotent.

To become an adult in the real sense of the word means to relinquish the "pleasure principle" (Freud) for the "reality principle." The child is educated, through love, persuasion, and threats, to realize that there is an objective reality outside the world of his private wishes. But no one accepts this harsh truth without inner protest, and the clinical fact remains that only with great reluctance and difficulty does the child give up his fantasies of omnipotence. In fact, we all have remnants of this fiction in our unconscious, no matter how "grown-up" we are.

Further life experience convinces the child that certain facts are unchangeable. After he has tried it a few times, he learns that it does not pay to run his head into a stone wall; the wall, despite his command that it give way, remains unyielding. And in a form of protective mechanism, he learns to avoid battle when defeat is predictable. He "gets wise," but without enthusiasm. Still buried, deep within him, is the old fiction of omnipotence, and under certain circumstances it can be resuscitated, just as Homer's dead heroes in Hades came alive again when they drank blood.

The power of the "reality principle" lies in the fact that its acceptance by the child, and later the adult, eliminates many defeats. *There is one exceptional situation in life, however, in which the reality principle has no advantage over the pleasure principle:* that is gambling. There blind chance rules, change which in games of "pure" gambling cannot be influenced by logic or intelligence.

An old anecdote told by one of my patients is illustrative. A college student won ten thousand dollars betting on a dark horse at the races. His mathematics teacher was curious to know how he had picked the winner. "Very simple," was the reply. "I dreamed about the figures 2 and 3 and thought that $2 \times 3$ equaled 12, therefore I placed my money on number 12." "But $2 \times 3$ is not 12!" objected the professor. At this, the pupil became indignant. "You want to teach me how much $2 \times 3$ is?" he expostulated. "I won!"

In this particular instance, the student could afford to ignore facts, and give priority to his private, *a*logical system of mathematics. A continued flouting of reality, on the basis of one piece of good luck, would be sure to lead him to disaster.

Gambling unconsciously revives, therefore, the old childish fantasy of grandeur and megalomania. More important, it activates the *latent rebellion* against logic, intelligence, moderation, morality, and renunciation. The "pleasure principle" is never entirely relinquished; traces of it, strong or weak, always remain in the unconscious. From time to time the latent urge to surrender to it becomes a propelling tendency, which leads the individual to scoff ironically at all the rules of life he has learned from education and experience. Heavy inner retaliation is the result. Since the child has learned these rules from his parents and their representatives (teachers, priests, superiors, etc.), his rebellion activates a profound unconscious feeling of guilt.

In clinical terms, this is the psychic situation of the gambler: first, *unconscious aggression;* second, an unconscious tendency toward *self-punishment* because of that aggression. The self-punishing factor, which is always present, is almost never recognized except in psychoanalytic treatment. Thus, the childlike, unconscious, neurotic misunderstanding of the whole gambling process creates a vicious, and endless, circle. Hence the inner necessity to lose.

The act of gambling in itself is a denial of the "reality principle." In this act of denial, the gambler is expressing his neurotic aggression against those who have taught him the "reality principle"—in most cases his parents. In losing, he is simply paying the penalty for this aggression. Long analytic experience teaches us that in neurotics all aggression is paid for by some form of self-punishment. The whole concept of neurosis is based on the knowledge that neurotics unconsciously transfer conflicts, originally experienced with their parents, to innocent persons whom they unconsciously identify with their parents. Since aggression toward the mother and father was forbidden, every aggression toward the substitutes is inwardly forbidden, too. If the aggression is actually performed, it is expiated by severe self-punishment. Here is one of the important differences between normal and pathological aggression. In normal aggression, hostility is directed at the real enemy, not the imaginary one (i.e., the parent). Normal aggression arouses no feeling of inner guilt, because it is used in self-defense; and, since the enemy is not unconsciously identified with a person who figured in childhood experiences, the feeling of righteous indignation has no aftermath of guilt.

It is on these psychoanalytic facts that I base my conviction that the gambler cannot win in the long run. For him, losing is essential to his psychic equilibrium. It is the price he pays for his neurotic aggression, and at the same time, it makes it possible for him to continue gambling.

This unconscious attack on rationality and intelligence (an attack on reality, actually), which is activated—also unconsciously—in gambling, is vicious and not at all harmless. Quite the contrary. Although he never gives his thoughts conscious expression, the gambler is really saying: "You, parents, taught me that every good deed would be rewarded, every bad one punished. But what happens instead? Honest men work hard and earn little. The crook gets money and fame. You preached that there is a moral order of things and that heavy retribution follows if the path of decency is abandoned. What is the reality? The racketeer triumphs, the decent man is pushed around. You instilled in me the foolish notion that only honest work brings success. At the gambling table the opposite is true—people get rich without working at all. You wanted me to believe that logic rules in this world and that justice and reason prevail in the end. All lies. In gambling all your logic and reason and justice are meaningless. None of your rules can explain how the roulette ball rolls, how the dice fall, how stocks climb, or cards are dealt. You claimed that in this best of all possible worlds nothing is left to blind chance. But what happens in gambling houses, on the stock exchange, or at the racetrack shows you up as fools or hypocrites. Blind chance does rule in many places, and I intend to take advantage of it!"

It is in the gambler's *unconscious,* it must be remembered, that this monologue is delivered. Unconscious motivation is a clinically proven fact, but experience has shown that the psychologically uninformed person is extremely skeptical of such clinical facts. However, he is often willing to accept the same facts when they are presented in a nonscientific medium; in a novel, for instance.

For this reason, I should like to compare, from time to time, actual case histories with examples from literature. There are many such "matched pairs" available, in which the main outlines of the fictional and real-life situations are basically the same. The following example will illustrate a typical way in which the gambler uses his pseudoaggressive tendencies:

### CLINICAL CASE

A gambling patient, while playing roulette in a New Jersey casino, was caught by his senior partner. The older man lectured him, pointing out that gambling and business did not mix. My patient's retaliation was to make friends with his partner's son, whom he introduced first to homosexuality, then to gambling. This action constituted a con-

### LITERARY EXAMPLE

In Otto Soyka's *Master in Gambling,* the gambler, Wehlen, is in love with a young girl from a middle-class family. But she believes in stability, morality, and financial security, as represented by her fiancé, Walter. Wehlen's revenge against the girl as to introduce her fiancé into gambling circles. Walter wins at first, then loses every-

scious rejection of bourgeois values. "I couldn't stand the old fool's moral nonsense." The fact that the son of the highly moral father could be seduced to perversion and addiction represented, in my patient's words, "one of the triumphs of my life." What he did not even suspect was that, behind the pseudoaggression, was a hidden desire for self-punishment. The desire was fulfilled: his partner learned the truth and dismissed him under very humiliating circumstances. The patient suffered a nervous breakdown and later came for psychoanalytic treatment.

thing and ends saddled with a debt representing two years' salary. Further to reduce accepted rules of normality to absurdity, Wehlen teaches the girl's brother the "pleasures" of insecurity and danger. He races his car recklessly, and even arranges an automobile accident. The youngster "learns" fast and enjoys it. Then, together with a psychopathic inventor, Wehlen conceives the idea of a device that will cut through steel like paper. This is Wehlen's ironic way of proving the absurdity of the bourgeois faith in the "safety of the safe."

The gambler is quite a rebel. He is the organizer of a private tempest in a teapot. He is invariable in his individualism; his rebellions take place, not within a political party, but in splendid isolation. This *private* rebel fights with neither guns nor ballots; cards, stocks, dice, chips are his weapons and his invisible colors. Out of inner necessity, therefore, he becomes a specialist in reducing bourgeois values to absurdity, because all who hold such values are a source of inner reproach to him. At the same time, his neurosis forces him to follow his pattern of pseudoaggression in an attempt to expose the hollowness and "moral weakness" of the rest of the world.

# The Gambler and His Love [1]

*IAGO GALDSTON, M.D.*[2]

The psychiatrist, unlike the clinician, does not have either ample means or frequent opportunities for testing out his postulations as to the aetiology, the basic pathology, and the therapeutic handling of a given case. Psychiatry has nothing that equals in specific relatedness the tuberculin, the Schick, or the sugar tolerance test. Psychiatry lacks the equivalents of Koch's postulates, so determinate in establishing the authenticity of the causative agents of the infectious diseases. It is therefore rewarding to come upon an instance wherein the patient's own life experience confirms, at a later time, the validity of the formulations, postulated earlier, to account for the dynamics of his psychopathology.

It is such an experience that I wish to detail here. I initially described the patient in a paper published in *Mental Hygiene,* in October, 1951. The title of that paper was "The Psychodynamics of the Triad, Alcoholism, Gambling, and Superstition." The gambler was one of the "triad." Here I will describe him only sketchily, leaving out many details of his anamnestic history. They are not really relevant to the substance of this presentation.

The patient was, as he is today, an habitual and compulsive gambler. He did not in the first instance come for therapy because of his gambling; on the contrary he accepted gambling as a normal and even desirable component of his life pattern. His complaint was of a mild and, as it proved, a transient sense of depersonalization. It was associated with and had been precipitated by, the development of a psychotic

Reprinted by permission of Iago Galdston, M.D. and the American Psychiatric Association from *The American Journal of Psychiatry,* Vol. 117 (1960), 553–555.

reaction in his older brother. The patient had identified with and had introjected his sick brother.

The patient was an almost completely illiterate Jew, 44 years of age, married, and the father of two children. He was successful in business, shrewd, intelligent, and wealthy. He gambled consistently, and had done so since he was 12 years of age. He was in no sense a professional gambler. He gambled, as he phrased it, because he *had* to gamble. It temporarily relieved him of some kind of tension, the nature of which he did not understand and could not describe. I was intrigued by what he termed his "tension," and endeavored to trace its aetiology, as well as to fathom the mechanism by which he gained relief in gambling.

Here I will only present my conclusions as to the aetiology of his tension, without citing the anamnestic data from which they were derived. These data can be found in the earlier paper.

The patient had suffered early and severe deprivations in his affect relations with his parents. He was born in a small village in Poland, and grew up in poverty and squalor. His father was early separated from his mother and lived in a distant village. The patient was apprenticed to a shoemaker at the age of 7. From that age until he married, he had had no home. He was thus deprived of that rounded cycle of contacts and interpersonal reactions with parents and siblings that is so essential to a healthy development through infancy, childhood, adolescence, and youth. In consequence, he was, psychologically, continuously harking back to that childhood period in which he had suffered his arresting deprivations. There he had become compulsively fixated and unable to advance. He thus carried into the age of maturity, and included in his adult personality, the emotional and psychological dynamisms and the relational configurations of his childhood and pre-adolescent periods. His gambling was figuratively the behavior of a child to whom gifts may come by mere solicitation, or by teasing for them, as indeed *is* the case in the child's experience.

In this aetiologic perspective the neurotic gambler can be seen as compulsively acting out a plea to Lady Luck, symbolic of the surrogate figures, mother and father, but mainly mother, for a show of favor, for the affirmative response to the questions: "Do you love me?" "Do you approve of me?" "Do you think I am good, and smart, and strong?"

The neurotic gambler is compulsive in his need to pose these questions and obsessive in his uncertainty. Since he cannot gain a definitive and a for all time reassuring answer, the gambler continues to gamble until he loses. The neurotic gambler seldom, if ever, "quits" when he has made a "killing." He has a compulsion to lose and stays in the game until he loses, in other words until he is without the means to continue gambling. The neurotic gambler's compulsion to lose is understandable, for the more he wins, the more means he has wherewith to gamble, and the more intensive becomes the gambling. Release is to be found only in losing. The questioning can thus be deferred until the next time: until the next game.

Few gamblers come for psychiatric treatment, with gambling as their chief complaint. My patient complained of his sense of depersonalization, not of his gambling. In treatment he reintegrated his personality without much difficulty. After a year of therapy he returned to his accustomed world and its accustomed ways.

Five years later the patient called for an appointment, complaining of what amounted to an acute anxiety. He was again accepted for therapy, and therein we come to The Gambler and His Love.

The gambler, as I reported previously, was married and had two children. He was fond of his wife, as a son might be of his mother. He provided her with all the comforts she desired, but did not share life with her, socially or sexually. She concurring, he arranged to have her vacationing or visiting away from home for the greater part of the year, in Florida, and/or the Catskills. The children were placed in boarding schools. He had never wanted and never thought of legally separating from, or divorcing his wife. He was indeed fond of her—in his own way.

The patient was sexually active, mainly with costly call girls, and casual women. His business required him to travel frequently and widely. His excursions were enlivened with many and bizarre sexual adventures. But these were more in the nature of an exercise than of an orgiastic indulgence. In telling of his sexual ventures he always spoke as if he had been "external to the experience."

But once something extraordinary happened to him—a woman fell in love with him, and she refused to be put off, or to accept the role of a casual partner. The woman was married and the mother of two children. Her devotion to the patient knew no bounds. She pursued him constantly and responded to his every beck and call. She asked nothing of him but his love.

At first he was emotionally unresponsive, aloof, and casual. He relished her sexually but wanted no involvement. In time, however, the woman prevailed, at least to the extent of engaging him emotionally more than any other woman had ever done before. He even suspected that he was beginning to love her. But the more his affections became involved, the more his suspicions grew. Did she really love him? Was it for the love of him that she was sacrificing her husband (who was in fact a shady character with a criminal record), and her two children? Or, was she just a "bum," and after something other than his love. She had "carried on" with him for 18 months, and during that time had not asked him for any money. That puzzled him greatly, and fed his suspicions copiously. He queried her on every score, and though she offered him infinite reassurance and a thousand proofs of her love, he remained unconvinced and suspicious. He was, to quote him, "tortured, nervous, tense."

And this is the way he set about to gain relief! He enlisted the cooperation of his most intimate gambling crony, and with him conspired to put the woman, his love, to a test. The patient was to leave the city for a week, and during this time the friend was to try and "make" the woman. As it was agreed, so was it done! And then came the *Nemesis*. The patient returning, his friend reported that though he had tried his very best, employing his every stratagem and resource, he could get nowhere with the woman. She was, he assured the patient, steadfast in her loyalty, and committed in her love.

But, as I am sure you can anticipate, this did anything but reassure the patient. It only enlarged the range of his suspicions, for now he not only doubted the love of the woman but also the fidelity and truthfulness of his friend.

It was all too much for him, and he came back for help. Under the circumstances therapy could only be supportive with a minimum of uncovering and insight. Yet in the end he managed to regain his singular balance. This is the pattern he followed. He gave up his "love," and simultaneously regained his friend.

The unconscious homosexual component in this constellation is, of course, self-evident. But more interesting and significant is what happened with his compulsion to gamble. He had abandoned gambling during the 18 months of his involvement, and resumed it when "the love" was discarded. He now gambled recklessly and lost a good deal of money. His game of preference was gin rummy. Now he played dice and bet on horses. He resumed his sexual contacts with call girls and casuals. He made an abortive attempt to "get closer" with his wife. Nothing came of it. And yet, he found living more tolerable. He returned to the old and endless pursuit of Lady Luck, who never answers but only smiles the enigmatic smile of the Sphinx.

During therapy he reported an interesting dream. "He was walking somewhere in Chicago. A man and a woman tried to hold him up. They took everything from him. He ran to find the cops. Then ran further and finally gave up."

This slice of life, treated as a psychiatric biopsy, confirms, I believe, this much, that the neurotic gambler always plays to lose, that in his gambling he is obsessively teasing his surrogate figure Lady Luck for a show of favor, yet cannot and will not accept "Yes" for an answer. Such an answer does not square with the deeper facts of his life, nor with the unconscious memories of his irremediable deprivations. And in some ways I am persuaded the gambler is right; for who can make up, and what can cancel out, the egregious loss of the mother's assuring love and the father's supportive sanction. Such a one is doomed to wander through life asking unanswerable questions.

More pointedly, the Gambler and His Love are an unrealistic pair. Only the gambler is real. The gambler has no love. He is incapable of love. Gambling is the gambler's addiction, not his love. For love has the requisite of an antecedent ego maturation—to which the gambler has not attained. He is in these respects severely retarded, a victim of his deprivational experiences.

# Analyzing a Pack of Cards

## CHARLOTTE OLMSTED

As good a place as any to start our analysis is with a very familiar but somewhat complex game tool—the pack of cards. Looked at as a symbolic system, the card pack is compact and ingenious, with a maximum number of variables handled in a neat and economical way. It lends itself extremely well to expressing a wide variety of human conflicts and problems, and to all sorts of interactions between the variables that can symbolize many different styles of human interaction. This is, of course, why it has retained its popularity so long. You are not confined to one sort of game or one style of play, but can vary both to suit your individual needs.

The most prominent divisions in the card pack are the four suits, the two colors, and the face-card, numbered-card divisions. Two other features are the movable ace (which can be either top or bottom and can be used to make the suits circular at will), plus the highly variable joker. Several packs

Reprinted with permission of The Macmillan Company from *Heads I Win Tails You Lose* by Charlotte Olmsted. Copyright © Charlotte Olmsted, 1962, Chapter 4.

can be used in any individual game, or part of the pack can be dropped out for particular purposes. All of these various divisions are interrelated in a way that is both complex and flexible, but which is clear, unambiguous, and easily learned—all highly desirable characteristics in a symbolic system.

Historically the English pack, which is the one with which we are most familiar, arose out of an earlier French pack. Modern French packs use different figures for the court cards, but otherwise the two packs are interchangeable. The Spanish pack and some local German and Italian packs differ in the suit symbols, don't have distinctive suit colors, and don't employ a queen, but are otherwise similarly organized. Linguistic clues point to a probable Persian source for our European pack (as in the case of chess), but forerunners can be traced back to China, where many similar devices are used. The most familiar Chinese example to the Western world is probably mahjong. The mahjong tiles are organized in a very similar way to the card pack, although they differ widely in detail.

Among the ancestors of the card pack is the sun-game series. The clockwise, circular direction of play is retained, and a number of calendrical features—the four-part division into suits, and the fifty-two card series (with a sort of fractional extra card in the form of the joker), which can stand for the weeks in a year. But these very slight traces, while they may help to form a framework for the world of the card pack, have been subordinated to other features.

The four-part division is so fundamental in early thought (and even in modern thought, because of the conservative tendency of linguistic habits) that it can stand for many things, and the most important immediate point of reference in the card pack is social. The four suits historically represent the four estates of medieval social theory, identical in composition to the four castes of intellectual Indian theory. Spades, whose name is taken from the old southern pack, still retained in Spain, come from "spada," "swords," although the symbol used is borrowed from the old German pack and represents a leaf. They represent the fighting man, the nobility. Hearts, whose name and form both come from the German pack and which correspond to cups in the southern pack, stand for the church, religion (Brahmins in Indian theory). In early games from the Renaissance period they ranked above spades but have since been downgraded. Diamonds stand for merchants, and clubs for the peasantry. The name of clubs, like that of spades, was borrowed from the southern pack, while the symbol is a copyist's version of the old German acorn. Acorns were very important in old German peasant economy, as providing food for pigs. Diamonds are interesting; in France they are called "carreaux," from the shape, a word also used to mean paving tile. The same suit is coins in the southern pack, while the old German pack used hawkbells, an extremely old medium of exchange and trade article. The English pack retained the idea of article-of-concentrated-value in the name "diamonds," but the shape is probably ultimately derived from a hasty copying of the bell symbol. When we refer to "diamond-shaped" we are borrowing from the card pack itself, as real diamonds are not customarily of this shape; the older English word for the shape was "lozenge."

These suits have also picked up emotional connotations with the years. Spades-aggression, hostility; hearts-courage, love (both in the churchly meaning of altruism, good will, and in the sense of sexual love); diamonds-ambition, greed; clubs-fear, the state of being exploited. The association of courage and love in the hearts does not quite fit modern notions and may need a little explanation. The basic idea seems to be that these people have the supreme courage to drop their weapons, their defenses, and are thus able to love. It at least avoids the confusion of courage with overt aggression and (by implication) hostility which our age seems particularly prone to make.

The face cards represent the old European family system of father, mother, and eldest son or heir; our pack is very good at playing out family role conflicts and is often so used. It does reflect a particular type of family structure—one where father-son conflicts are seen as more important than mother-daughter conflicts, since there is only one female in the pack, wife to one and mother to the other. The unattached female is not seen as important enough to have a card to herself, although the mother-wife is central to the family structure. You would expect such a society to have a great many Oedipus conflicts—they would probably be based so solidly on family structure as to be all but universal. There would also probably be a strong drive on the part of unmarried females to secure a husband and thus a place in the family structure for themselves, probably not matched by a like desire on the part of the male, who could continue to use his mother for emotional support if he chose. These are, of course, all features that are very prominent in the European area where this pack arose. The Spanish and German packs do not employ a queen, but have king, knight, foot soldiers, or servant instead—they are more useful for playing out social role conflicts than intrafamily conflicts.

The face-card, numbered-card division is often used to symbolize people versus things, or significant people in one's life versus strangers, people in the mass. Ace represents ego, and can be either top or bottom of the pack at will, depending on a variety of factors and corresponding to one's own self-image. Ace of spades (aggression-ego), possibly one's own death, has a very special marking in the English pack. This originated in the custom of printing this one card separately in the government printing office to facilitate collecting taxes, but the particular card chosen may have a certain symbolic significance as representing the ultimate sanction of government.

The joker is the last lingering remnant of the tarot pack. This tarot pack is sometimes considered the oldest form of cards in Europe—there has been some controversy on this, but it is certainly very old. There are the usual four suits, usually employing the symbols of the southern pack, and with four face cards (king, queen, knight, jack), plus a special series of twenty-one cards that are symbolically very interesting, representing as they do late medieval ideas. The number one of this suit is the bateleur or juggler, and he is sometimes duplicated by an extra card. The earliest mention of cards in Europe is from Italy in 1379, and it may have been this tarot deck. It is occasionally still used for fortune telling purposes. The juggler or jester is the only tarot card that retains a somewhat precarious toe hold in the modern deck. His wandering presence lends a certain flexibility and picturesque disorder to the rather rigid pack, and he still finds employment in certain modern games. Since he was originally number one, or ace, in the tarot suit, he usually also represents ego, and a particularly free and independent ego at that, not attached to the social order at all.

The English and French packs employ color in addition to symbolism. Red and black are used in many games, especially in the European area. In Europe in general, especially western Europe, they both carry slightly hostile and derogatory connotations—devils come in both colors. White is too good a color—the color of angels—to be much used in games, since if the two colors were black and white, few people would voluntarily choose black. The one exception is chess, and in chess white does have the advantage—it always plays first. This white and black (or occasionally white and red) coloration of the chessmen is found both in Europe and in India —both areas where there tend to be rather elaborate social distinctions based on skin color. Chess sets from the farther Orient seldom use these distinctions—either they use red and green with the Asian connotation of red-good, green-evil, or they employ distinctions of shape and direction-in-which-pointed, like "shogi," the Japanese form of chess, and not color distinctions at all.

Red and black as used in Europe usually represent revolution, change versus conservatism, *status quo*. It is probably significant of the Renaissance origin of our modern pack that the nobility and the peasantry are seen as conservative, while the church and the merchants are seen as the party of change. This reflects the Reformation and the Counterreformation. It is appropriate in emotional terms, also, with altruism, courage, and ambition seen as forces working toward change, while aggression, greed, and fear try to maintain the *status quo*.

Incidentally, since Russia overlaps both the European and the Asian area, it can be seen why she uses red so extensively as a symbol—it can stand for revolution and change, and also carry overtones of the Asian good versus evil.

There are three one-eyed face cards, probably representing the most single-minded of the people; these are the jack of spades (the young aggressive or hostile male) and the jack of hearts (the young, either altruistic or amorous male)—both representing different aspects of the conventional mythic hero of the West. The other single-minded character is the king of diamonds—the mature businessman. All the queens hold flowers—old symbols of female sexuality—and the queen of spades (the aggressive or hostile female) has a scepter of rule as well. The jack of spades holds a rather twiddly object in his hand that has completely lost its meaning—it looks more like a mathematical symbol of infinity than anything else —but it was originally a sword hilt.

The jack of hearts has suffered a sad fate. Originally he held a splendid torch as tall as himself, the torch of Hymen, a phallic symbol, neatly symbolizing the source of his drive— either directly for an amorous male or sublimated for an idealistic one. Generations of copyists have reduced this once proud symbol to the wilted leaf he now holds—no wonder he looks depressed! Three of the kings carry swords; spades and clubs directly, ready to be used as weapons. Both nobles and peasants may use these, and in emotional terms both aggression and fear may use weapons. Or if one prefers to take the sword as a phallic symbol (remember that games are over-determined), the nobility and the peasantry, both country dwellers, are apt to have larger families than either church or merchant, seen as town dwellers. The king of hearts has a sword, but he has buried it in his own head. He has suppressed his aggression, or if you prefer to see it as a phallic symbol, he has suppressed his own sexuality, either by becoming a celibate priest, or as the kindly, benevolent head of a family who must use his libidinous impulses to be especially nice to the daughters in the family while holding tight to his incest tabus.

The ambitious and single-minded king of diamonds and the jack of hearts not only do not carry weapons, they are driven by a weapon back of them. Apparently the love that drives the young, amorous male and the ambition that drives the mature businessman may not be wholly his own, but forced on him from outside; these are seen as in some sense the most driven members of the society. The battle-axes back of them may be among the forces that have helped to castrate them—I wonder if the queen of spades and her scepter had a hand in this? It may not have been conscious, but it makes a fairly sharp social commentary all the same.

Although very few people are consciously aware of the meanings of the card pack, it has retained sufficient unconscious force so that practically all games use the pack in very similar ways to play out various interaction patterns. It does this so efficiently that I think we might well begin to make use of this tool consciously for working out the implications and probable results of a variety of human systems of organizing relationships. It hasn't graduated to any practical use as yet, but perhaps it is almost ready.

Using this symbolic vocabulary, one can analyze the meaning of practically any card game; it is amazing how closely individual games retain them, even if their inventors and players are not consciously aware of them at all.

Modern or contract bridge is based on the older auction bridge, which came in at the very end of the nineteenth century and was in turn based on whist, a very popular English game since at least the early eighteenth century. It is a game that appeals to highly conventional people who wish to enhance or increase their social status; sociological studies show it to have very little appeal to lower-class players. In it the cards are all dealt at the beginning of the game and there are exactly four players; it is a game that appeals to people with a rather fixed and static view of the social order, who seem to have tendencies toward constructing a closed circle in any social situation, with a fixed number of roles. Unless one of these roles happens to be vacant and a newcomer can demonstrate that he or she is ready, willing, and able to fill this role in a manner that has become conventionally acceptable, the bridge player is not receptive to newcomers. Bridge involves a certain amount of cooperation between the players, but unlike whist, where all four players continue to play throughout the game, only the opposition, the people in least favored position, so play in auction or contract. Cooperation is thus seen as most useful in a destructive way, in endeavoring to obstruct a player's actions, and not used in a constructive way, to get the most out of a good hand. Two people may work together to pull down a third, but if one has good cards one is strictly on one's own as a player. However, all four still work through the bidding situation, when values are being established. Social interaction is thus seen as necessary to establish values, but otherwise an external enemy, or scapegoat, is necessary in order to secure cooperation in this society.

The four suits are ranked. The nobility and/or aggression, hostility to outsiders is ranked highest; next comes the church and/or courage or love. The other two suits are not as highly ranked, with merchants and/or ambition and acquisitiveness seen as better than the peasantry, and/or fear. The ace is always tops—this is a game for egotists, with a rather high opinion of themselves. Tens are ranked with the court cards; we would expect a certain amount of personalizing of possessions, making a house, a car, or a fortune in money almost equally emotionally important as a member of the family.

Conservatism (the black suits) rank both top and bottom of the scale, with change in the middle; the conservatism of the noble is highly desirable, probably much admired, but the peasant who refuses to change his ways is not ranked highly. This is consistent with the upward mobility of bridge players. They themselves feel capable of change, but are on the move from a low status seen as fixed to an equally fixed high status. First they become rich (diamonds), next altruistic (hearts), and may finally work their way up to the hostile, exclusive, upper circle (spades).

The way in which trumps are determined and used is interesting. In the ancestral whist, trumps are determined by turning a card, by chance; the matter of which characteristic is most valued in a particular social circle is seen as fixed, not to be altered, a variable not under the control of a player. It is a society of hereditary ranking, where one's value system was determined by accident of birth. Later, auction made it possible to bid up the value of whatever one had the most of —whether this was old family birth and aggression (hostility to outsiders), an enthusiastic membership in the proper church or charitable organization, just plain wealth and ambition, or even a willingness to be exploited by others, if nobody else had too much of any of the other qualities. Or all can be valued equally if one has the necessary cards, in no-trump.

In contract, this is also true, but one must determine beforehand exactly how far one is able to go. It would seem to demand a much earlier setting of goals than auction, and considering the period when it first became popular (around 1930), probably represents the sort of society where one's education and early business and social connections pretty well determine one's status. It is still desirable to set these as high as possible—high status is still valued—but one is penalized for setting one's sights too high and failing to make good on these early expectations more than if one had not been so overly ambitious. It is better not to try than to try and fail. Conversely, overfulfillment of one's goals does not help very much; one must assess one's abilities very accurately at an early age.

The attitude toward communication is interesting in bridge. Conventional signaling through the bids is perfectly all right, and elaborate code signals have been worked out, but other communication between partners is very much frowned upon, and considered cheating. Only those types of communication which are in theory equally open to all members of the game are allowed. Behavioral characteristics that have become conventional—that is, fixed, static, and therefore able to be learned—are much easier for an upwardly mobile group to handle, and they will tend to value these more highly than more spontaneous behavior. Novelties are tolerated—there are many bidding systems, just as fashion determines many conventions—but these must be set out carefully and explicitly beforehand, and are usually left to the expert and not to the individual player. Originality is not desired or expected by a bridge player, although adherence to the latest fashion handed down from above may be.

There are not many sexual connotations in bridge. The family—the court cards—are highly valued, but in social terms. The two-person teams may be, and often are, husband-and-wife teams, but bridge symbolizes marriage-as-a-working-social-group rather than marriage-as-a-sexual-outlet. One would not expect sexual frustrations to be particularly high among bridge players as a group, since they seem to have few conflicts in the area that need expression in their game. Either they have fairly satisfactory sexual outlets, or they have successfully devalued sexuality altogether. The two-person teams can equally well be man-sister or man-secretary, or even mother-daughter, father-son, or other pairs. The woman may perform specialized functions in view of her sex, as hostess and the like, but these are social rather than directly sexual. A husband or wife is necessary to this group for social reasons rather than for personal sexual satisfaction. A conventionally sexually desirable partner might be valued, but more in the service of status, impressing one's friends, than for personal pleasure; spades (aggression, putting oneself forward) outrank hearts. There are no wild cards or especially valued cards in bridge; a certain rigid, conventional ordering is preferred.

In contrast, poker is mostly a man's game, and represents a peer group. Women can and do play it, too, but women who aspire to be the equals and companions of men and to be treated "just like a man." There is no fixed number of players, and only some of the cards are dealt out—people can enter or leave the game at any time, and it is much more fluid in this respect than bridge. It represents a group of strangers trying out one another's reaction patterns and is often so used. Nonverbal communication is watched for, but if it is involuntary and therefore honest, it works to a player's disadvantage; it is advisable to cultivate a "poker face." Any cooperation between players is one of the worst possible sins, and it is always strictly competitive without the socially expected teamwork of bridge.

Poker is decidedly more flexible and open to innovations than bridge. There are many variations, differing almost as much among themselves as whist does from bridge, but these are not considered separate games but only variants of poker.

Although sequences rank high, and particularly "royal flushes" —a complete family—three and four or even two of a kind rank high, too. The family is valued (sequences, since they include the family structure of KQJ, usually represent the family in cards), but peer groups are almost as highly valued. Ace ranks high—this is another game for egotists. The wild cards are interesting in poker. Deuces often are used as wild cards, and other common ones are "one-eyed jacks." Many American card games rank the jack rather high; there are many games with jack in the title and none with king in most American game collections. This indicates the high valuing of the young, unattached male in our society. The one-eyed jacks (spades-aggression and hearts-love) are, as we have seen, our old friend the Western mythic hero. Ranking deuces high in this way probably indicates a certain self-identification with a low, disregarded status, ranked high for this one special game. The poker player is not quite as secure in his self-esteem as the bridge player—he is less self-satisfied. Jokers are also sometimes used in poker, always ranking as wild cards. These wild cards are more adaptable than ordinary cards, since they can be used to replace any card of the deck at will. A game that uses wild cards usually values a certain flexibility, a willingness to accept a variety of roles according to circumstances, in contrast to the rather rigid definition of roles in such a game as bridge. A poker player seems to have more imagination, more room for fantasy than the bridge player; he is also probably less realistic.

The suits are not ranked in poker; it is more democratic than bridge, and has more regard for personal characteristics and less for social status. This is probably partly because in the rather fluid society of the poker game, where strangers are readily accepted, it is impossible to assess social class other than by personal characteristics. The possibility of misrepresentation is well understood, however, and is fine if you can get away with it. A successful bluff is just as legitimate as any other form of winning in poker.

There are quite a few sexual connotations in poker. Mr. Fresco of the Department of Psychology of San Francisco State College has done some very interesting work in the field of gambling, correlating game behavior with other characteristics. He sees the motion of the hands in dealing, and much poker terminology—"stud" poker, "hit me" for deal me another card (hitting oneself is also used as a synonym for masturbation) and "I sure got screwed that time" as masturbation equivalents. With the male peer-group structure of poker, it seems to be an exhibitionist but diffused sexuality that is expressed—not directed *toward* anyone in the group. This form of expression of sexuality would seem an ideal outlet for and defense against homosexuality in an all-male group; poker thus is very popular in such a situation as an army camp or lumber camp, since it allows for the expression of sexuality (and also aggression) in a highly symbolic and impersonal form that will offer the least threat to the individual or to group cohesiveness. Sexuality openly expressed as between individuals in an all-male group must by definition be homosexual, and the strong cultural barriers against this lead to building up all sorts of elaborate defenses. Gambling and game behavior are a socially well accepted activity that enables the individual simultaneously to express and deny the emotion, so it is not surprising that this outlet is often used in such situations.

As to the expression of aggression, all gambling forms a way to express aggression and competition relatively safely— the loser tends to blame his own luck or bad cards instead of feeling directly hostile toward the winner, so that this form of competition is comparatively free from threats of reprisal and thus tends to appeal to timid people, afraid of the results of expressing aggression more directly. Sometimes, however, the attempt to impersonalize the hostility is not altogether successful; direct expression of aggression against the other players not uncommonly arises out of the gambling situation.

Many compulsive gamblers express sexuality through poker in an almost overt way—this interpretation seldom seems alien to them, although it is apt to disturb the more casual player. It may be that motivations vary—or it may be that the compulsive player's conflicts are closer to the surface and less deeply buried. The compulsive player's thrill generally comes

from losing rather than winning, which has many implications for the gambler's view of sexuality, and will be explored
in more detail later.

Twenty-one or blackjack is a game much used in the gambling houses of Nevada. It seems to symbolize mostly dominance-dependency conflicts, and the attainment of full adult
status without assuming adult responsibilities. All the face
cards are ranked alike as ten—ace is either one or eleven,
top or bottom, according to which is most desirable at the
moment. Twenty-one, the traditional age of attaining adult
status, is aimed for. But sequences are not valued at all in
twenty-one—family ties are not desired or required, simply
independent adulthood with no ties. Blackjack, the other name
of this game indicates this also—the single, unattached male,
doubtful whether to be aggressive or give way to fear, is
also the ace, not certain whether to be top or bottom of the
pack.

Unlike most gambling-house games, such as craps, roulette,
or slot machines, the representative of the house, the dealer,
also deals himself a hand in direct competition with that of
the customer. The dealer, backed by the house, represents
the family figure, backed by the society or the family structure, against whom the player is in rebellion and with whom
he has a direct, personal conflict. Twenty-one is played for,
but it is even more dangerous to go over this figure than to
fall short of it. Independence, adult status, is aimed for, but
no responsibilities.

Although the player is thus in rebellion against his family,
he is basically rather conservative (black jack, not red jack).
He does not contemplate changing the social order in the
slightest, only his own role in it. He does not aspire to become a king, either—he wants the privilege of adult status,
but wants to stop right there and remain a jack all his life.

There does not seem to be much direct expression of sexuality in twenty-one, but of course dominance-dependency conflicts are by no means confined to father-son duels and,
indeed, cross sex and age lines rather freely in our society.
Although the author has done no work on this problem, it
might be interesting to find out if people with a high degree

of intersex dominance-dependency conflicts seek out dealers of the opposite sex in playing twenty-one. This may well be the case.

Aside from the dominance-dependency conflicts that may form an important part of sexual role conflicts, only those players with an exceptionally high degree of equation between monetary loss and sexual satisfaction would seem to be able to express much sexuality through twenty-one. It does not lend itself to this purpose nearly as well as many other games.

Other popular games are the rummy group. The forerunners and many of the modifications of this game have come out of Latin America; it was originally called "rum poker"—queer poker—and first became known in the United States at about the time of the Mexican War. It is one of the few games where you can directly exploit your opponent's gains to your own advantage; if he has sequences or several of a kind in front of him, you can add to this grouping on your own in order to add to your score. These fifth-column aspects of rummy are appropriate both to the Latin American countries, which exploited many factors already existing in the Indian societies which the Spaniards came to dominate, and to American methods of territorial expansion during the nineteenth century. California, Texas, and Hawaii were all gained by fifth-column tactics—a group of American nationals became powerful enough in the country to foment a revolution, ostensibly internal, and subsequently ask to become attached to the United States. Similar tactics are sometimes used in modern times as between corporations, which may explain the great revival of popularity of rummy (particularly in Hollywood and among corporation executives) in the 1930's. It may be no more than a coincidence, also, although an interesting one, that this revival of rummy in the United States also coincided with a period of increasing American influence and marked local fears of this influence in two areas that had seen former American territorial expansion—namely, Latin America (particularly Mexico and Cuba) and the Pacific islands (Japan).

Sequences are fairly important in the rummy group—the

family structure is fairly highly valued—but peer groups are becoming increasingly important, especially in the newer variations such as canasta. Modern variants have a tendency to use an increasingly large number of packs; this probably represents the individual's feeling of being swallowed in an increasingly large number of duplicates in an industrial society. Deuces are wild in some versions—the lowliest individual can have immense strategic importance in this type of organization. So can the joker, the erratic individualist.

One modern form that is much played in the card rooms of California is "panguinguie." This uses between five and eight packs—the individual feels himself really submerged in an overpowering number of duplicates. It also drops out the eights, nines, and tens. This is common in many Latin American games; United States games tend, like pinochle, to drop out the low-ranking cards instead when cutting down the pack. The Latin system probably represents a self-identification with the poor—wealth is no longer expected or perhaps even hoped for, since it may be feared as too dangerous a distinction. Ace ranks low—again the individual has settled for a relatively humble position. Sequences (called stringers or ropes) are valued, but sets of cards all-of-a-kind are also valued. They must be of different suits except in the case of aces or kings (called "non-commoquers"). This represents a certain identification with the male head of the family, unlike the common American identification with the jack. The king of spades is especially highly valued, and spades in general rank high. This represents a valuing of the family with an aggressive male at the head, poor, and accepting a rather low status. The game arose among the Mexicans in this area, but has spread to many other lower-class non-Mexican groups, whose situation and values may be similar. Threes, fives, and sevens are also especially valued. Three, five and seven have special significance in a number of games throughout the world, in Africa and Asia and elsewhere. There is probably no direct connection whatever; since odd numbers are much more stable in terms of social structure, as there is always a clear majority that can coerce the outnumbered minority, they have probably acquired "magic" (that is, emotional) significance independently.

Pinochle has been mentioned. This was once much more popular than it is now, but is still often played in the family setting. Nobody seems to know exactly where the name came from (it may be dialectic German) but the game itself is very similar to the old French bezique, with many of the same features. It is a model of middle- and lower-middle-class life of a rather old-fashioned sort. There are trumps, used in a way similar to bridge or whist trumps. In the earlier form, these are determined like whist trumps, by turning a card— one's place and consequent value system is determined by chance of birth, and one must accept this and not try to alter it in any way; there is also a more modern form which allows for auction, also like bridge—a more flexible attitude toward values, with some manipulation allowed.

All cards below nine are dropped, but the other cards are duplicated, and thus emphasized. Family relations are seen as much more important than all but the top possessions. But the top possessions—as much money as possible—are ranked very high; this is a society that values wealth and becoming rich. In taking tricks, the cards are valued (in order), A, 10, K, Q, J, and ace and ten far outvalue the other cards when taken as tricks. But in the melds which are made on the table after taking a trick, only one allowed at a time (the cards used for this can subsequently be played as tricks), the values are different. A, K, Q, and J are valued in that order, and in addition there are special values on, first of all, a "royal marriage" (K, Q of trumps), then other marriages. A pinochle —queen of spades and jack of diamonds—the aggressive female and the male either actually a son or a husband-treated-as-a-son pushed into wealth—ran with a royal marriage. This game seems to symbolize two different types of interaction and value systems—within the family and outside the family. The melds then represent family values, the tricks values for dealing with outsiders. Money is supremely important—next only to ace, ego, one's own self-esteem—in dealing with outsiders, with family backing running a bad second. Money is not so important inside the family, although since only one meld can be made at a time, and must immediately follow a scoring trick, it is seen as vital to go out and win outside the family to carry much weight in the family situation. The lowest trump is valued, but not very highly—it probably represents the child in the family.

This is a game for a society of wage-earners; their only interest outside the family is to get enough money to push their weight around inside the family. The wage earner has prestige only as long as he is bringing money in. In order to have a family, he also has to have a wife. She is aggressive and pushes him rather hard inside the family; his ego is in much better shape when dealing with outsiders (ace ranks relatively much higher in taking tricks than in the melds, where it is pretty well ignored). The wife treats him like a mother when she is being aggressive, and he feels like a son being pushed into being rich.

The similarity of this pattern to the life-style of many Americans, especially of an earlier generation, is apparent and explains the wide popularity of this game.

Other card games may be analyzed in similar terms, but these seem to be among the most popular, and are perhaps enough to demonstrate the method.

# Inspirational Group Therapy: A Study of Gamblers Anonymous

*ALVIN SCODEL, PH.D.*[1]

It is the purpose of this paper to discuss the writer's involvement, for an eight-month period, with an inspirational therapy group.[2] The writer, an academic psychologist with clinical training, was essentially a participant-observer, a term as good as any since it implies a kind of professional reputa-

Reprinted with permission of Mrs. Alvin Scodel and the *American Journal of Psychotherapy* from the issue of Vol. 18 (January, 1964), 115–125.

bility while it hints at the ambiguity that characterized his position in the group. After the group has been described, some speculations will be offered on the position of this and similar groups in a larger sociologic context and, finally, the dynamics of the group will be explored.

The name of the group is "Gamblers Anonymous." Its model, as one might suspect, is Alcoholics Anonymous, and the group comes complete with an official credo in pamphlet form that outlines the problems created for oneself and others by compulsive gambling, together with a suggested 12-step recovery program. The format for the meetings of the San Francisco chapter is simple and unvarying. The secretary, whose office is elective, designates a member at the end of each meeting to serve as chairman for the next meeting. The chairman reads the little pamphlet, or preamble, as it is known officially, and at the conclusion of this reading, which takes about 10 minutes, generally comments on the profundity to be found in the preamble. It is good form to comment further that every additional reading of the preamble yields new and deeper meanings. The chairman then calls on each member of the group to give a "weather report." At the conclusion of the weather reports there is a brief prayer to close this portion of the meeting and a bull session follows during which refreshments are served and members talk more informally. One unusual feature of this group is that wives are encouraged to attend, and at least six members of the group are invariably accompanied by their wives who sit passively in the back throughout the weather reports, but interact occasionally with group members during the bull session.

Membership in the group numbers about 25, with approximately 11 or 12 hard core members. Exclusive of wives there are usually about 15 local members present and one or two guests from other chapters in the San Francisco Bay Area. Telephone contacts among members are frequent and there is considerable between-meeting fraternization in the form of parties at the homes of one or the other of the members.

The age range of members is, roughly, between thirty and sixty. The occupations of some are unknown to the writer, but of those that are known there are two skilled laborers, a

cab driver, a song plugger, a newspaper reporter, a sales promoter, four men who have their own businesses or are employed in business firms, and one man who describes himself
simply as a con artist. Two men have served time in jail for
bad checks. About half the group are Jews, and there is one
Negro. Some of the members have restricted their gambling
to either horse-playing, card playing or crap shooting while
others have engaged in all of these.

The weather reports reflect modes of expression that are
highly urbanized and idiomatic, and they manage to be simultaneously cynical and platitudinous. Several members employ
a "Guys and Dolls argot," occasionally mitigated to meet the
demand of respectability imposed by the presence of women.
Levity is sanctioned, even encouraged, if it has a wry, mock-
ing quality designed to give the impression that underneath
it all the person is talking about deadly serious business. Self-
flagellation is also common, and members are invited and,
if necessary, not too subtly coerced by the attitudes of other
members to admit that they have serious emotional problems.

It is a cliché of the group that one is not only a compulsive
gambler but also a compulsive loser; however, the reasons for
wanting to lose are never explored, at least publicly. What
frequently happens is that a person will talk at length about
the severity of his neurosis without verbalizing much content,
or, to put it another way, he is much more guarded than the
quality of his performance would indicate. Since religion of a
generally accommodating and vaguely specified variety is part
of the group's official ideology, weather reports will also refer
to the spiritual nature of the program and frequent mention
is made of a newly acquired religiosity which is incorporated
into the person's pronouncement of a reformation of character.

The anecdotes in the weather reports are often variations on
the gambler's perennial prayer, "I hope I break even today,
I sure need the money." Jokes are frequently old-time vaudeville one-liners, for example, "I bet on a horse at 20 to 1 and
it came in at 10 after 6." Jokes may also express the theme of
the renunciation of hedonism and the (avowed) internalization
of new, austere values. ("It used to be wine, women and song,
now its Metrecal, the same old gal, and Sing Along With

Mitch.") Possibly the flavor of a weather report can best be conveyed by giving one which is a composite.

I'm Jack R., compulsive gambler. I'm a compulsive loser too, but I don't lose no more because I don't gamble no more. I want to tell you that six months ago when I first walked through that door, I had reached the depths of degradation. To give you an example how low I was, my wife was in the hospital having a baby, and I was holed up in some stinkin', petty larceny joint over in Emeryville playing lowball. I was in hock up to my ears, I had lost all my self-respect, I couldn't look anybody in the face, I was the kind of guy that if you had a sawbuck to your name, I'd figure out a way of conning you out of $9.98. I was always trying for the big score, and later I was trying just to get even and the harder I tried, the more I kept getting in deeper and deeper. And what the hell was this big score anyway? I made it a couple of times so what did I do with it? I blew it, I had to blow it, it wasn't real money, it was Mexican money, strictly counterfeit. My wife never even got a dress or a pair of shoes out of it. I mean, I was in bad shape. I was writing lousy checks, thank God I was able to cover them in time, but for the Grace of God, I'd be in durance vile right now. But you know the routine as well as I do, we're all the same, we've all gone the same route.

But things are different now since I've joined G.A. I'm not out of hock yet, but I can see that silver lining up there in all those clouds. I don't know what it is, maybe it's just coming to these meetings, maybe it's some higher power, but I'm getting serenity, some peace of mind now. Like Harry G says, "Progress is Our Most Important Product," and I'm progressing all the time. Just lately, after an absence of many, many years, my wife and I rejoined the church of our faith. When I joined G.A., I didn't even come in on my own, I had to square a beef with my wife, I admit it, but I decided she was right. I looked in the mirror one morning and I said to myself, "Schmuck, what are you doing with your life?" I know I'm still a compulsive gambler, if I start staying away from here, I'll be right back where I started from. But I take it one day at a time, I haven't gambled in the last 24 hours and tomorrow's another day. That's my weather report.

And so it goes; all traces of poignancy are quickly obscured by the sentimental and the farcical.

In the bull sessions, conversations are sometimes confined to gambling, sometimes not. References to sexual behavior, unofficially tabooed in the weather reports, crop up periodically when the wives are out of earshot. Here is one illustrative brief exchange. A man said to the writer, "Are you bothered much by the two-headed devil?" "The two-headed devil? I don't know what it is." "Well, these guys don't talk about it in the weather reports, but you know it as well as I do, if you're not gambling, you're out chasing broads. It's one or the other." (Subsequent confidences by other members revealed that instances of infidelity had in fact been frequent.) In the course of drifting from one small group of two or three to another during the bull session, a random sampling of comments might be, "Bob's given up on psychiatry. Those guys are only out to make a buck like everybody else," or, "Oh, I conned him good, I conned him real sweet, but I'm not proud of it. Do you follow me?" or, "This guy walks into this joint and 45 minutes later he's taken a swim for six and a half bills."

Values and attitudes of this sort are as much of sociologic as psychologic interest. What is at stake here is the relevance of theories of alienation to people like the members of Gamblers Anonymous. The emergence of alienated man (or mass man or marginal man) is often viewed as a product of the change from *Gemeinschaft* to *Gesellschaft*, that is, the transition from small, organic communities to the impersonal, mechanized urbanization of contemporary life, and concurrent with this change, supposedly, has been an increasing tendency toward alienation.[3] The concept of alienation, once the property of Marxists, is not without its ambiguities, but if it is given the meaning of a feeling of estrangement from oneself and the world, it has now appeared in the field of psychopathology in the form of an "identity problem." To lack an identity is to be cut off from a sense of historical continuity in one's life and any awareness of one's place in the social scheme of things. The quest for identity—to use Wheelis's phrase—must necessarily involve, then, attempts to reject one's anomie or feelings of marginality.

For the most part psychoanalysts of whatever persuasion (excluding some notable exceptions like Fromm and Lindner and Reich) have not been given to prescriptive social and political messages, but social critics have long warned against the totalitarian implications of widespread alienation. Frustrated and isolated, the alienated man is easy prey for the charismatic leader who promises a state of grace or, in the language of today, a sense of identity. People whose inner emptiness and lack of relatedness have forced them into a position outside of society can find sanctuary only in the spurious utterances of false prophets. One important qualification of the theory is that the raw material of mass movements is not to be found in the totally disenfranchised who have never entered the social mobility sweepstakes, but is recruited from those whose expectations have been aroused and unfulfilled. The alienated man is quite literally a loser.

When the absence of identity blends with open defiance of societal conventions to form the psychopathic syndrome, the potential for political exploitation has been noted by more than one writer. Here is a statement by Lindner:[4]

> This is the menace of psychopathy: the psychopath is not only a criminal: he is the embryonic Storm Trooper; he is the disinherited, betrayed antagonist whose aggressions can be mobilized on the instant at which the properly-aimed and frustration-evoking formula is communicated by that Leader under whose tinseled aegis license becomes law, secret and primitive desires become virtuous ambitions readily attained, and compulsive behavior formerly deemed punishable becomes the order of the day.

Now a close empirical look at the fate of this type of monolithic generalization suggests an inaccuracy in prediction and one wonders about its applicability to the American scene. Bell, for example, asserts that the important fact of Americans as joiners is being overlooked. The groups that people join may be full of absurd rituals, but the satisfactions obtained from them are genuine nevertheless. Yet, the kinds of groups that according to Bell would represent a bulwark against totalitarian ideology are ordinarily associated with middle class status. These group memberships are generally a sign of successful social mobility rather than the reverse; certainly Rotarians are not among the disinherited.

Of course, there are explanations of the current "radical right," particularly those of Lipset and Hofstadter,[5] which stress the status anxiety of some middle-class groups, afraid of either losing their position or, in the case of upwardly mobile ethnic minorities, insecure about their claims to Americanism.

The concern here, however, is with those people who have always been distinctly marginal (and for that reason have been viewed as prospective adherents of extremist movements) but are still apolitical. Within Gamblers Anonymous the writer has some concrete evidence concerning the members' lack of political interest. In a period when Dr. Fred Schwarz and his narcissistically projected preoccupation with good and bad apostate Jews, specifically Christ and Marx, inundated the San Francisco Bay Area with the Christian Anti-Communist Crusade, the writer tried diligently to elicit the attitudes of Gamblers Anonymous toward this campaign. At the time, the Schwarz campaign was given reams of publicity in the local press and had preempted conversation, both pro and con, in many circles. Yet here was a group of 15 articulate people who could not have cared less. True, the ethnic membership of the group is decidedly atypical, but adverse attitudes were as absent as favorable ones, and the same indifference prevailed among the non-Jewish members. The hypothesis presented in this paper is that the alienated, the losers, the mass men are becoming immune to blandishments based on irrational and thaumaturgic appeals because they are learning to utilize each other to achieve identity. The losers need only each other to recoup their losses.

It is hardly news that Americans join groups. The American tendency to form associations was described by de Tocqueville[6] in *Democracy in America* about 125 years ago, but the present hypothesis transcends indigenous social virtuosity. What seems new is the exploitation of symptoms or any kind of major defeat in an effort to redress the social imbalance by establishing united fronts. Anonymity implies renunciation, but it has now become a guise for all kinds of narcissistic rewards and, possibly, this trend—if it is a trend—can be regarded as part of the natural history of a society in which failure is reprehensible and isolation intolerable. In the San Francisco Bay Area there currently exist Recovery, Inc., Alcoholics Anonymous, Gamblers Anonymous, Business Failures Anonymous, Suicides Anonymous—the list proliferates endlessly. By way of hyperbole, a drinking gambler who has lost his business and tried to kill himself, can easily become one of the most popular men in the city. Parenthetically, these groups should be distinguished from the customary kind of group therapy in which, hopefully, the group is not a substitute for life and, ideally, the group fashions insights rather than buddies.

The strategy in groups like Gamblers Anonymous is to acclaim kinship through symptom-formation ("We've all gone the same route") and in the process of striving for a radical democracy seeks to obliterate subcultural differences. If symptoms initiate contact and affirm brotherhood, it is necessary to attempt at the same time a rejection of external values which are based in such large part on the narcissism of small differences. It is in this sense that such groups are explicitly and avowedly apolitical because any consideration of large-scale social conflicts revives a whole range of status differentiations which it is the purpose of the group to deny. To achieve fraternity and a derivative identity simply and exclusively because one is a compulsive gambler is an accomplishment that cannot be risked by attributing equivalent importance to oneself as a Protestant or Democrat or workingman. Besides, these other aspects of identity have resulted only in isolation, and it is tantalizing to prophesy that future members of these therapy groups will conjure up symptoms or at least exaggerate them in order to obtain admission.

It should be stressed that the attempted radical democracy of groups like GA is not without its strains. There is certainly more ambivalence toward the values of the external world than the members care to verbalize, and these values keep intruding despite the members' good intentions. Officially, the habitual two-dollar bettor is just as sick and, therefore, as deserving of group approval as the big plunger, but there is little doubt that added status is conferred on the man who has lost large sums. Thus, there is the man who claims not to have gambled in two years, but in eight months' time the losses he mentioned in his various weather reports climbed almost imperceptibly from $65,000 to $85,000. Another man is adept at mentioning his cousin who is supposedly a very distinguished specialist in New York City, a reminder of an earlier, more innocent period when a benevolent Providence

had so arranged the affairs of this country that almost every
Jewish physician was a "top man in his field." Still others
manifest a touching naiveté with respect to social processes
in spite of, or possibly because of, their self-proclaimed ability
to con anybody out of anything. The man who declaims in
stentorian tones, "Progress is our Most Important Product,"
wants to provide the most respectable kind of inspiration, and
he would surely use the slogan more hesitantly if he apprehended fully that it belongs to a corporation whose top officials have been in trouble with the government for price-fixing
practices.

At the level of individual dynamics, the paucity of historical
information about Gamblers Anonymous members precludes
any attempt to recreate the quintessential gambler—probably
a fruitless task, in any case—but any discussion of dynamics
still necessitates a resumé of some of the more frequently cited
psychoanalytic accounts of gambling. Freud's views on gambling addiction were presented as a kind of postscript to the
paper on "Dostoevsky and Parricide."[7] The article is admit-
tedly disjointed and Freud explains in a letter to Theodore
Reik that it was written reluctantly at the behest of a friend.
In any event Dostoevsky is presented as a person with a particularly intense masochistic character structure whose need
for penance derived from death-wishes toward a very severe
father. (Freud also has a very pungent comment for Dostoevsky's final capitulation to the Czar and the Church! ". . . a
position which smaller minds have reached with lesser effort.")
One of the more interesting aspects of Dostoevsky's gambling
was that he apparently never wrote more or better than when
he had lost all his money, that is, when his guilt had been
assuaged by self-inflicted punishment.

Freud illustrates the addiction to gambling as a masturba-
tory equivalent by an analysis of Stefan Zweig's short story,
"Twenty-Four Hours in a Woman's Life." Much is made of
the feverish activity of the hands while gambling and Freud
asserts that the gambler-hero is saying, "If my mother only
knew what dangers masturbation involves me in, she would
certainly save me from them by allowing me to lavish all of
my own tenderness on her own body." The article concludes

with a statement that the relation between the effort to suppress masturbation and the fear of the father is well known. There is no mention of Dostoevsky's partially autobiographical short novel, *The Gambler,* in which the "two-headed devil" is prominently featured. The story in brief concerns a young man with a strong masochistic attachment to the daughter of the household he serves as a tutor. The hero importunes the girl constantly to command him to kill himself so that there can be no doubt of his devotion to her. He is seized with a premonition of good luck and goes off to the Casino where he amasses a sizable sum of money. He presents the money to the girl who rejects him and the money with the accusation that he is trying to buy her. Later, he takes up the life of an inveterate gambler and does not think once of the woman with whom he had been in love until, by chance, he runs into an old friend who informs him of the girl's recent serious illness. He shows perfunctory interest, gets some money from his friend, and goes off to resume his gambling.

This theme of masochism in gambling recurs in the interpretations of Greenson[8] and Bergler.[9] Greenson states that neurotic gambling has two crucial components: (1) The neurotic gambler feels lucky and hopes each time he will be rewarded, despite all intellectualization to the contrary, and (2) The neurotic gambler is impelled to test out luck or fate. Consciously or unconsciously, he believes in his right to ask fate for special privileges, and he mistakes his strong yearnings for a lost omnipotence for the feeling that he is, in fact, omnipotent. Greenson, in his summary of neurotic gambling, says, "Luck and Fate are derived from mother and/or father images and gambling offers an opportunity for the revival of unconscious Oedipal phantasies. In addition, gambling offers satisfaction possibilities for latent and unconscious homosexual, anal-sadistic, oral-receptive drives, and gratification of unconscious needs for punishments." Certainly, one can enter a demurrer to Greenson's summary by asking "What else is there?"

Several considerations can be raised to confuse even further the question of gamblers' dynamics. First, there is an enormous difference in the public character of different kinds of gambling. Winning and losing in games like poker and craps are, in a genuine sense, part of a public performance. The social situation provides a basis for the exploitation of exhibitionistic trends as well as reactions against them so that, for example, one can often observe people assuming an attitude of profound indifference while winning and a determined demeanor of stoicism when luck is against them. By contrast, the horse-player, whether he bets on the phone with the neighborhood bookie or goes to the track to place his money, usually wins or loses in isolation. Playing the horses is essentially a one-person decision-making situation whereas almost nobody would think of entering a crap game unless other players were already present. That, of course, is why casinos employ "shills."

Another point is that it is far from clear that the neurotic gambler invariably, or even usually, transforms his wish for omnipotence into a feeling of omnipotence. As often as not, the need to lose is accompanied by the belief that one will lose. There are all kinds of neurotic gamblers who attempt to impose a limit on how much they will lose before they gamble. It may be that this behavior is an attempt to buy off fate in some magical, obsessional manner, that is, "If I pretend that I am going to lose, fate will be placated and will be kind to me and I will win," but this pretence suggests much more of an ambivalent attitude toward fate than is supplied by Greenson's formulations. Similarly, one sometimes hears of gamblers who willingly go into a rigged game with the knowledge that the game is fixed and they must lose. This voluntary submission to fate is easily transformed into the wish that such humility should be rewarded, but the request for magical intervention is certainly not the same as the belief that one can influence the game unaided.

A third point refers to the uncritical acceptance of the belief that all neurotic or compulsive gamblers have to lose. There are people who "love action"—to use a frequently employed colloquialism—so long as the percentage is in their favor. This issue is resolved quite simply by members of Gamblers Anonymous who would argue that these people are businessmen rather than gamblers. The need to lose defines the behavior as neurotic, and, on this issue, they are probably more dynamic (always an honorific term) than the writer. Still, there are people, properly called neurotic gamblers, who have made a very good thing of gambling. They will play dice every night if they can "book" the game or play blackjack interminably if they can keep the deal, and so forth. This behavior can be said to represent much more of a true feeling of omnipotence since it is associated with a patronizing hostility best expressed by the attitude, "Everybody's a sucker but me." One is reminded of the character played by George C. Scott in the movie, "The Hustler."

To return to Gamblers Anonymous, there is no way of knowing whether they are fairly representative of gamblers or have to be considered *sui generis*. One distinct impression is that they are very dependent on their wives who serve as a provisionally nurturant Greek chorus during the meetings and smile benignly when promises of reformation and restitution are made. The writer's hypothesis is that both the gambling and the unverbalized infidelities represent abortive attempts at emancipation which must fail because independence from their wives cannot be sustained. If there is a certain interchangeability between gambling and sexual exploits, as suggested, for example, by the phallic language of gambling in such phrases as "the big score," the consequent fear of loss of support, if the person is successful either in gambling or extramarital adventures, is of crucial importance. Conversely, the wives manifest a patent need to manipulate and control, and it is quite possible that these women have unconsciously wanted their husbands to lose in order to insure continued domination of them. One of the reasons, then, why the wives have such a vested interest in their husbands' abstention from gambling is their fear that the husbands will, in fact, make a big score. The group culture is decidedly emphatic in its continual protestation of the need to lose, but very few people need to lose that intensely, consistently, and compulsively. The repetitive, public declaration of that need is partly an act of confession which sets the stage for the help that the group can provide, but, in addition, it is a ceremonial device intended to express resignation and surrender in the battle between the sexes. In brief, there is a need to lose other than the one they are talking about.

Certainly the adoption of a humanistic position makes it easy to inveigh against the sentimentality, the facile cynicism, and the lack of any serious attempt to achieve a deepened self-awareness in this particular group, but judgmental and therapeutic stances need not necessarily coincide. There is still the criterion of the group's effectiveness in producing a diminution of distress. On this issue the writer has very little direct evidence except for the frequent statements in the weather reports that described a newly acquired tranquillity. The cab driver, the group member with whom the writer was the most friendly, spoke often in casual conversations of a sense of purpose in life which the group had given him. He believed that he had undergone a moral transformation which now made it possible for him to meet people without thinking in terms of exploiting them. Most of the restlessness and instability of his earlier life was ascribed to a "dog eat dog" view which he still believed to be the dominant value in the lives of most people, but had now been renounced by him in favor of a more trusting, less exploitative approach to the world. He had no explanation for the way in which this change had been effected, but there was little doubt that the group had dispelled, at least temporarily, those aspects of his inferiority feelings which were associated with social status. One evening he said to the writer, "I can't talk to doctors and lawyers and they don't want to talk to me and I sure as hell get tired of talkin' to cab drivers. All they talk about is three things: driving a hack, the number of whores in town, and ways to turn a fast buck. I need more than that and so I found these guys. These guys I can talk to."

## SUMMARY

This paper is an account of eight months' experience as a participant-observer in the San Francisco branch of Gamblers Anonymous. The organization is modeled after AA and its ostensible purpose is to help compulsive gamblers abstain from gambling. Group sessions consist of testimonials or "weather reports," followed by informal bull-sessions. Members fraternize a good deal between meetings and are also available for 12-step calls should one of the group feel an urgent need to gamble.

The group is considered, first, from the point of view of current theories of alienation and their implications for political behavior. On the assumption that groups like Gamblers Anonymous are rapidly increasing in number, the hypothesis is offered that the alienated are learning to utilize each other to achieve identity and, as a consequence, are becoming more immune to the appeals of political mass movements.

At the level of psychologic dynamics any attempt to clarify the motivation behind compulsive gambling is complicated by many considerations. First, there is an enormous difference in the public character of different kinds of gambling; second, it is not clear that the neurotic gambler invariably, or even usually, transforms his wish for omnipotence into a feeling of omnipotence; third, it may not be true that all neurotic or compulsive gamblers have to lose.

For the members of Gamblers Anonymous studied here, it is inferred that one of the motivations underlying group participation is the symbiotic relationship between these men and their wives. The gambling represents an abortive attempt at emancipation which must fail because independence from the wives cannot be sustained, and it is further hypothesized that, unconsciously, the wives would rather have their husbands lose than win so that the wives' continued dominance is assured.

# PART IV

# Gambling, Crime, and Public Policy

I N VARIOUS PLACES and times, gambling itself has been defined as criminal. In addition, both legal and illegal gambling seem often to generate other problems, to corrupt—to introduce procedures and rewards into events so as to alter previously understood rules.

The article by Robert Kennedy, written when he was U.S. Attorney General, summarizes an official administrative position—a view also discussed in a number of articles in the next section of this book. Underwood's article on the one-year suspension of a great professional football player is of interest here because it examines some of the conditions under which corruption is relatively likely to occur. (The reader is urged to compare Underwood's article with any of several recent studies of academic cheating.)

Too few students, in the editor's judgment, have ever read the verbatim transcriptions of congressional committee hearings which are held ostensibly to consider potential legislation. These official transcriptions are often fascinating documents; something of the drama, the personalities of the congressmen and witnesses, and in the case presented here, the humor of the situation is caught in the published record. In 1961, the McClellan Committee of the Senate (Permanent Subcommittee on Investigations of the Committee on Government Operations) undertook an investigation of the relationship between gambling and criminal organization—as had the Kefauver Committee ten years earlier. Most of the witnesses were called to testify to some aspect of communications (especially wire services for off-track horse gambling) and tax matters, but in the section reproduced here, the committee learned of still another ethically marginal practice from the world of gambling.

Starkey, a member of the faculty of the Saint Paul School of Theology (Methodist), Kansas City, has written a book entitled *Money, Mania, and Morals: The Churches and Gambling* (Nashville, Abingdon Press, 1964). The selection included here, a separate article in a Protestant journal, summarizes his position.

# The Baleful Influence of Gambling

*ROBERT F. KENNEDY*

No one knows exactly how much money is involved in gambling in the United States. What we do know is that the American people are spending more on gambling than on medical care or education; that, in so doing, they are putting up the money for corruption of public officials and the vicious activities of the dope peddlers, loan sharks, bootleggers, white-slave traders, and slick confidence men.

Investigation this past year by the FBI, Internal Revenue Service, the Narcotics Bureau, the Post Office Department, and all other federal investigative units has disclosed without any shadow of a doubt that corruption and racketeering, financed largely by gambling, are weakening the vitality and strength of this nation.

But, as I sit down today to write this article, a business executive with an industrial firm on the Eastern seaboard is telephoning a bookmaker to place a fifty-dollar bet on a horse race; a factory worker in a Midwestern town is standing at a lunch counter filling out a basketball parlay card on which he will wager two dollars; a housewife in a West Coast suburb is handing a dime to a policy writer who operates a newsstand as a front near the supermarket where she shops.

These people, and millions like them who follow similar routines every day, see nothing wrong in what they are doing. Many of them can afford the luxury of this type of gambling. They look upon it simply as taking a chance.

But they are taking a chance which the nation and its economy cannot afford. They are pouring dimes and dollars day by day into a vast stream of cash which finances most illegal underworld activities. The housewife, the factory worker, and the businessman will tell you that they are against such things as narcotics, bootlegging, prostitution, gang murders, the corruption of public officials and police, and the bribery of college athletes. And yet this is where their money goes.

Last May I appeared before a subcommittee of the House Committee on the Judiciary and testified in support of anti-crime legislation then pending before the Congress. Relying on rock-bottom estimates of the Department of Justice, I estimated—probably conservatively—that illegal gambling in the United States does a gross volume of $7 billion annually. That is more than the American people spend each year on bread.

Mortimer Caplin, the Commissioner of Internal Revenue, told Senator John L. McClellan's antiracketeering committee that a total of $25 billion a year is wagered in the United States, but he did not provide a breakdown on how much was legal and how much went into illegal channels. Twenty-five billion dollars is almost as much as we spent on education in this country last year.

Last August, John Scarne, who has made a study of gambling for many years, testified before the McClellan committee that the annual gross figure on illegal gambling involves about $50 billion. He testified that the bulk of this money was bet on horse racing through bookies. Fifty billion dollars is eight billion more than Congress appropriated last year for national defense. Our estimate of $7 billion may be low. Mr. Scarne's estimate of $50 billion may be too high, but it could be right. The truth is that nobody really knows. Senator McClellan pointed out that if the figure of $50 billion is accurate, the government is being cheated out of some $5 billion a year in taxes owed by the gambling community.

Is this really the way American citizens want it to be?

The great discrepancy in the guesses as to how much is wagered each year is understandable, because once the housewife, the factory worker, or the business executive gives money to a local bookie or policy writer, it disappears into the pocket of the underworld figure, who is in business to cheat the government—and his customer, if he can. And while many persons may regard the bookie on the other end of the telephone and the neighborhood numbers writer as the gambling racketeers, actually they are usually the small-time front men who stand to make a profit with every person who bets with them.

The bookies make a profit from the bettors because they have an edge on every bet. They pay track odds, but usually not in excess of twenty to one. The odds at the track are calculated after deducting the 15 to 18 percent of the total betting pool which goes to pay taxes and other expenses. The bookmaker pockets that amount.

But he is not a man of unlimited resources. He must balance his books so that he will lose no more on the winner than has been bet on the other horses in a race, after his percentage has been deducted. He cannot control the choices of his customers, and very often he will find that one horse is the favorite choice of his clientele. His "action," as he calls it, may not reflect the action of the track. Therefore, he must reinsure himself on the race in much the same way that a casualty insurance company reinsures a risk that is too great for it to assume alone. To do this, the bookmaker uses the "layoff" man, who, for a commission, accepts the excess wager.

The local layoff bettor also will have limited funds, and his layoff bets may be out of balance. When this occurs, he calls the large layoff bettors, who, because of their funds, can spread the larger risk. These persons are gamblers who comprise a nationwide syndicate or combine. They are in close touch with each other all the time, and they distribute the bets among themselves so that an overall balance is reached on any horse race.

With a balanced book at any level—handbook, layoff, or syndicate—the edge is divided, and no one loses except the men and women who placed the bets. As an indication of the volume of business I am talking about, one of the largest operations in the combine does a layoff business of $18 million a year. His net profit is $720,000 a year. This is a 4 percent return on volume, with relatively no risk, as a result of the balancing of his books on each event.

The term "gamblers" is a misnomer for these persons. They accept money that the small gamblers wager, but they do not gamble at all. This is further illustrated, graphically, by what we know as the numbers racket.

A man purchases a ticket with three numbers on it, paying a dollar for the ticket. Since there are 999 such numbers, he should reasonably expect the odds to be 998 to 1. The numbers bank usually pays 600 to 1 on such a wager—or less—so you can see that the only gambler in this situation is the man who makes the bet. The operator pockets forty cents of every dollar bet—that is, if the game is run honestly. That, however, is too much to expect from this group. If the play is too high on any one number, they manage through devious means to ensure that a number on which the play has been small will be the winner.

While we do have great problems in estimating the total amount gambled illegally, we can get some idea from significant records made available by the Internal Revenue Service through raids.

For example, the records of an Indiana bookmaker indicate that for a three-day period he received a total of $1,156,000 in wagers. A check of the gross receipts of a large department store in the same city indicated its gross for the same three days as $31,863. A Chicago bookie's records showed he took in $6,400,000 in total wagers for one year, while a chain grocery store in Chicago showed total gross receipts of only $293,000. While, actually, these comparisons may be unfair, in that the bookmakers probably are doing considerable lay-off betting from smaller bookies in other cities and other states, these two instances are not unusual, as the following Internal Revenue figures indicate: A Los Angeles bookmaker, Jack Rosen, took in $4,511,000 in one year. A Miami bookie received $1,594,000; a Virginia bookie, $1,221,000 for an eight-month period; and a Tennessee bookmaker, $1,689,000 for five months. A Pennsylvania policy operator collected $587,000 in seven months.

But, invariably, when federal agents try to raid bookmakers and policy operators, the first efforts of the law violators are aimed at destroying all of their books and records. Only a short while ago raiders in Detroit used a ladder to go through a second-story window in a raid in which they found people in the house burning information sheets in a potbellied stove which had a padlock on it. IRS agents in Atlanta recently raided a policy operator who also operates a supermarket. They found records of baseball bets in his cash register. While agents were examining these slips, the operator of the establishment suddenly touched his cigarette to the betting slips, and they exploded in a ball of fire. This bolt-flash paper is now widely used by racketeers so that they can do away with their records in a matter of seconds. A New Orleans bookie who was recently raided raced into his bathroom and dumped his papers into a toilet. Agents were right on his heels and salvaged the soaking documents, which indicated $6500 in bets had been placed with this operator during part of the day.

In January, Internal Revenue agents raided a large-scale bookmaking operation in Florida. The raid was unique because some of the Revenue agents brought fire extinguishers and were able to douse a fire set to flash paper by operators in an attempt to destroy records. However, I was more interested in the agents' report that the bookmaking operation appeared to handle about $250,000 in bets daily.

These cases demonstrate that fantastic sums of money are being handed over to the gamblers by millions of Americans who, like the housewife, the factory worker, and the business executive, think they are simply taking a chance. They are not taking a fair chance. The odds are loaded against them.

Their dimes, quarters, and dollars do not stay in the pockets of the big-time gamblers and racketeers. Just as legitimate businessmen invest their profits in other businesses, so do the capitalists of crime use their gambling profits to invest in other criminal businesses. High on the list is narcotics.

The horrors of the narcotics traffic need no elaboration. The contribution of gambling to narcotic smuggling, however, deserves wide attention. The profits from narcotics smuggling can be enormous, but it takes large amounts of money to finance a narcotics ring, and almost invariably gambling revenues provide the initial investment. Indeed, the use of such revenues to finance narcotics operations is so common as to be virtually inevitable.

During the 1920s and 1930s, such kingpin gamblers as Arnold Rothstein and Waxey Gordon invested huge amounts in the narcotics-smuggling business. An enormous international narcotics conspiracy in the 1950s was financed with the gambling profits and underworld credit of Harry Stromberg. He and seventeen others were convicted for their participation in this five-year heroin-importing operation.

The activities of Vito Genovese, a top racketeer, closely document the kinship between gambling profits and narcotics traffic. The Federal Bureau of Narcotics has described Genovese as having been the motivating force behind an international heroin-smuggling combine, and at the same time the controlling force behind gambling interests in several large cities. At one point, Genovese and several associates attempted to take over the numbers racket in the Spanish-speaking areas of East Bronx, New York. Their plan was to use the gambling profits from the numbers operation to finance heroin shipments into this country. The gang was arrested before it could carry out the entire plan. Genovese is serving a fifteen-year prison sentence for narcotics conspiracy, and his associates also received substantial sentences.

Strong-arm methods, including murder, are common in the illicit narcotics traffic. After a major international narcotics ring was broken up last year, two of the twenty-four defendants were murdered before completion of the trial. One was shot down in the Bronx; the burned body of the other was found near Rochester, New York. The business executive, factory worker, and housewife never encounter the seamy side, but this is what their bets are financing. Again I ask, Is this really the way the American people want it to be?

This Administration is making a major effort to bring organized crime and racketeering under control. Congress, in the last session, with strong support from Democrats and Republicans, authorized the Justice Department for the first time to deal with gambling activities. Our theory is that if we can reduce the gamblers' income, we will take a first major step toward cutting off the funds which now are being used to bribe public officials and finance the narcotics trade and other underworld activities.

In the past, only three effective laws have permitted the federal government to move against gambling. They are the wagering-stamp and excise-tax statutes, which basically were aimed at collecting revenue for the federal government, not at controlling criminal operations in this country, and a law prohibiting the interstate shipment of slot machines.

One of our new laws makes it a federal crime for any person to move in interstate travel to promote or participate in a racketeering enterprise. Some of the nation's most notorious racketeers have been insulated from prosecution by living in one section of the country and having illegal gambling interests in another.

In one case, many of the racketeers who backed one of the nation's big number banks lived in a resort area far from the scene of their illegal operation. Every month a courier with a bag of money was dispatched from the racket enterprise. One month's payment alone was in excess of $250,000. The kingpins of this operation reaped huge profits and remained beyond the reach of the law because they had committed no crimes in the state in which they lived. We plan to move against such activities. The messenger who carries the funds across state lines and those who conspire with him are subject to the new law; and we hope, therefore, that we will be able to dry up this interstate flow of cash, which turns ten-cent bets in one city into massive profits in the hands of big-time hoodlums.

Two other new laws make it a felony to transmit bets and wagers between states by wire or telephone or to transport wagering paraphernalia to another state. Wagering paraphernalia, as defined by Congress, includes tickets, slips, or paper used in bookmaking, sports pools, or the numbers racket.

The new laws, which the President signed on September 13, had an immediate effect on the gambling community. The nation's leading race wire services, including Athletic Publications of Minneapolis, Minnesota—the so-called Minneapolis line, which furnished point spread and other sports handicap information—and the Nola News of New Orleans closed down. Federal field offices and local law-enforcement officials in every section of the nation report that the hoodlums who control gambling have curtailed or shut down their activities. Some are even making plans to dispose of their homes and move to other countries that will permit them to operate in the manner to which they have been accustomed.

But many of the gamblers, while making themselves less vulnerable to federal prosecution, are standing by with a wait-and-see attitude. We know they are worried, and from the evidence already in hand, the FBI has estimated that this year alone we may have as many as ten thousand cases for investigation under the new laws. In the first four months that the laws were in effect, more than three thousand cases were brought under investigation.

The two other new laws extended the FBI's authority under the Fugitive Felon Act and prohibited the interstate shipment of weapons to or from persons accused of certain crimes. The Justice Department sought three other bills in the last session which are extremely important. They were enacted by the Senate and are now before the House. One would protect persons cooperating with the FBI from threats or coercion. Another would permit the government to give immunity to certain witnesses in labor-management racketeering cases, and a third would strengthen the 1951 law which prohibits interstate shipment of slot machines. The proposed measure would cover other types of gambling devices, including pinball machines.

The laws themselves, of course, while enabling the federal government to do a better job, will not make the final difference. That must come from the extra effort now being made by all the federal law-enforcement agencies and many local police officials, and from the support which this effort gets from the American people themselves.

The dishonesty of the gambling operations, the degradation of the narcotics and white-slave traffic are bad enough, but what really concerns me is the great wealth of the racketeers and the power that goes with it—the power to corrupt police and public officials, and in some instances, gain political control of an area.

The fundamental strength of our democracy, which is based on respect for the law, is at stake. Individual citizens, by working to elect honest public officials and raise policemen's pay, can make a major difference in this matter. But in the last analysis it depends on the business executive, the factory worker, and the housewife who have been financing big-time crime with their two-dollar bets and their ten-cent wagers. If they would stop patronizing the illegal bookie, the numbers runner, and the sports-pool operator, they could take the profit out of gambling and bring organized crime down to size quicker than all the combined efforts of the federal and local law-enforcement agencies.

# The True Crisis

### JOHN UNDERWOOD

I think all of us in college athletics have gone far astray—in recruiting, in letting people leech on to us who are known to be of bad character. I think we are gutless not to clean up our own business. You cannot use my name, because I am as gutless as the rest.—Anonymous Coach, Southeastern Conference.

In the first four months of 1963 these incidents made important news in sport: Paul Hornung . . . of Green Bay, one of the best football players in the world, and Alex Karras of Detroit were suspended from the National Football League for betting on games. Six other Detroit players were fined for the same offense. Alabama Coach Bear Bryant and Georgia Athletic Director Wally Butts were accused of conspiring to affect the outcome of last fall's Alabama-Georgia football

From *Sports Illustrated*, May 20, 1963. Reprinted by permission of Time Inc.

game. The University of Indiana and Purdue competed for a talented high school basketball player by offering scholarships to his girl friend. Jack Molinas, a former professional basketball player, was handed a 10-to-15-year sentence for fixing college basketball games from 1957 to 1961. Biggie Munn, athletic director at Michigan State, was found, embarrassingly, to be a stockholder in a management firm owned by a Chicago gangster, Frank (Big Frank) Buccieri. (Munn promptly said he got out as soon as he discovered who "that furniture man" really was.)

The doleful box score of the past few months, together with the basketball scandals of recent years and a Senate investigation that is soon to take place, have cast a nervous shadow over sport. Confused by the dispiriting succession of events, people are disturbed, and they are talking: the subject, articulated in various ways, is, simply, morality. Some Americans who were not so already have become cynical about sports, some fearful, some doubtful, some merely curious. To read all the signs, there is a crisis in U.S. sports. But is there?

In an important sense, unless it is a sin to enjoy oneself, there is no crisis. Pure sport ("that which diverts and makes mirth; pastime; diversion"), the sport of the participant, is healthier than ever in this pastiming nation of bowlers, boaters, golfers, skiers, snowshoe hikers, softball players and fishermen. Some 33.5 million Americans participate. So the concern is not with what people do, but with what they watch others do, the professionals and the heavily promoted college and amateur players of commercial sports. It is toward these performers that would-be moralists point a finger and say, "Yes, there is a crisis." Are they right?

On the surface, they are not. Sensational news to the contrary, there is less outright dishonesty today than there was in the "good old" days which, a dispassionate review would show, were not only not good but often sensationally crooked. In 1877, long before the Black Sox scandal of 1920, Louisville, then a major league club, expelled four players for throwing games. Owner John Morrissey in the same era used his Troy (N.Y.) Haymakers (forerunners of the New York Giants) like "loaded dice and marked cards." Seven members of the Uni-

versity of Michigan's 1893 football team were not even students at the university, and when Yale lured James Hogan,
who later became an All-American tackle, to New Haven in
1902 it was by dint of free tuition, a suite in Vanderbilt Hall,
a 10-day trip to Cuba and a monopoly on the sale of score-
cards. Some of the old recruiters could make the present
breed, with their payments under the table, seem like so many
penny-ante poker players.

Today baseball, football and horse racing, the three biggest
commercial sports, are more efficiently policed than they ever
were in their not-so-innocent youths. Baseball in particular
has been careful. In 1943 Commissioner Kenesaw Mountain
Landis banished the Philadelphia Phillies' millionaire owner,
William D. Cox, from baseball for life for betting on his own
team. Commissioner Happy Chandler suspended Leo Duro-
cher in 1947 for "the accumulation of incidents detrimental to
baseball" (he was friendly with a gambler). Similarly, the National Football League suspended Frank Filchock and Merle
Hapes of the New York Giants for failing to report an attempted bribe. The league, emulating racing's Thoroughbred
Racing Protective Bureau, which has been relentless in keeping known gangsters away from tracks since its founding in
1946, has a staff of 17 detectives on call to check out all
rumors concerning players and owners.

There is a good economic reason for such close surveillance.
Franchises have become so expensive—and generally so profitable—that an owner would be committing financial suicide not
to guard his investment. Too, the probing eye of catechistic
news media has severely narrowed a man's chances of making
a dishonest dollar. The glare of prolonged inquiry has made
even boxing a cleaner sport, although one in dire need of further repair.

Yet beneath the surface of seeming morality there lurks a
true crisis. It is far less spectacular than a Black Sox scandal
or the case of a prizefighter deliberately taking a dive (as
Jake LaMotta admitted doing in a bout with Blackjack Billy
Fox 15 years ago). It is, instead, a subtle erosion of the quality of sport. This erosion affects the individual sports; it affects
the people in them, the players, the coaches and managers,

and the owners. E. Norman Gardiner, writing in *Athletics of the Ancient World*, said, "The very popularity of athletics was their undoing." This is not Greece, but the men who control sport in the U.S. today are courting the Greeks' same risk of failure to cope with success. For it is an excess of success that produces unfortunate cases such as Paul Hornung's.

Paul Hornung is a fun-loving fellow who stands to lose $50,000 in the next year for being untidy in choosing his fun. Hornung gambled on football games, including some in which he played as a star halfback for the Packers. The consequence was that Commissioner Pete Rozelle of the NFL suspended Hornung for a year—which, besides loss of salary, sharply reduced Hornung's chances to endorse products in advertisements, which provided him with upward of $15,000 a year in pocket money. When the decision went out, and Hornung went out to see what people thought, it might as well have been spring. Cab drivers and sportswriters and fellow athletes and ladies in elevators hailed him and told him how Pete Rozelle ought to be strung up by his strait laces. (Others were just as convinced that Rozelle was justified, but Hornung did not hear much of that.) At a banquet in Worcester, Mass., he was given a hero's ovation. "Everywhere I went the people were behind me," said Hornung, understandably relieved. The crime obviously had not fit the punishment. Why, pshaw—there was hardly any crime at all.

But of course there was. Hornung himself is not a criminal; his football play is unassailable, and he has not thrown a game, taken a bribe or sold his soul to Frankie Carbo. He is a generous young man, good to his mother in Louisville and, as a practicing Catholic, he meticulously orders clam chowder on Fridays. No, indeed. Hornung's mistake was not a criminal act, it was an irresponsible one. Naively, and perhaps unwittingly, he destroyed a portion of faith in the integrity of the game that pays his way. One day he was merely the pal of Gambler-Businessman Barney Shapiro. The next day, "scarcely before I realized it," he says, Shapiro was his betting agent and confidant. He had no idea of the consequences of his actions when he placed his first $100 bet. Anybody old enough to chew bubble gum can fathom what suspicions this association aroused.

Encouragingly, Paul Hornung was quick to realize his error. Unlike the recalcitrant Alex Karras, who thought himself railroaded, Hornung has been contrite and has tried to say all the right things. He says if he had it to do over again he would still "tell all" to Commissioner Rozelle. "Hell, yes, I would. I broke the rule. I'm guilty. And what anybody else might have been doing wrong is no matter to me." Hornung admits he is not sure of all the implications of the rule he violated, and he does not consider his action "immoral," but he knows for sure his conduct "wasn't kosher."

Still to be determined is what sorcery could make a Paul Hornung risk his handsome neck and handsome way of living by assaulting, as he did, a rule he can read on every locker room wall in the National Football League. The answer is not too hard to find. In a sense, Paul Hornung was indoctrinated to excess at age 17 with the coming of the first high-pressure college recruiter ("I wasn't offered a car or anything big like that," he recalls, "but in some cases I was promised extra money"). So sought after was he that Paul (Bear) Bryant, now at Alabama but then coach at the University of Kentucky, brought the governor of Kentucky to the modest Hornung apartment in Louisville to help charm Hornung into accepting a scholarship in 1953. Bryant has since said he would have stayed at Kentucky three more years had he landed Hornung. He did not get Hornung, however, principally because of Hornung's mother, whose abiding dream was for her son to go to Notre Dame. Hornung was asleep in another room when the governor came to call, and Mrs. Hornung did not bother to wake him up.

As a Notre Dame man, Hornung found that he could rationalize the firing of his former coach, Terry Brennan, for being "too young," even though Brennan had been hired five years earlier when he was five years younger. Hornung called it part of the game. Used to special treatment as a pro star, it seemed natural to Hornung that the U.S. Army obligingly gave him weekends off so that he might continue his career with the Packers. He had found he could scarcely get out of the way of people wanting to do him favors and give him money. It was by this time quite easy to take lightly "a simple little wager" of $100 or $200. The money didn't mean much to him, why should the rule? After all, he said, "I'm just another one of the vehicles in this business."

The point about Paul Hornung, of course, is that he is not unique among American athletes. Commercial sport is a business. The people who run it—whether they be college presidents or owners of big league ball clubs—want to be successful. They are successful if they win, and they win when they have the best players. But this drive to excel puts terrifying, almost unreasonable. pressure on good athletes such as Hornung. Small wonder that the values of such gifted athletes become relative and that rules become playthings to be toyed with. The young men often develop what ex-West Point Coach Earl Blaik calls a what-the-hell attitude.

They also take their confusion into adult life. Wes Santee, the former star miler, who now sells insurance in Lawrence, Kans., was banned from amateur running for life for accepting $1,500 in "extra" expense money. He reserves the right to be especially critical of promoters who run amateur meets, and he blames them for his downfall. "If a track meet promoter or official tells a boy, 'The present rule on expenses is antiquated. Here's two or three times what you are legitimately supposed to get,' why expect the kid to be simon-pure? I remember when I first began running well. This promoter called to ask if I'd compete in his meet. 'How much expenses do you want?" he said. I didn't know what to say. I was a greenhorn. He said, 'Would $800 be enough?' My eyes almost popped out. I was green as a young runner, then, but I became a pro real quick."

## A QUESTION OF RIGHT

"Did I do wrong to accept these fees? I still don't know. I do know they never stop. After I had got the temporary court order to permit me to keep running, I went to Boston for a meet. I was in trouble. You would think everyone would have been extremely careful. But after the meet one of the officials handed me a program, saying, 'Here's a souvenir for you.' When I opened it there was a $50 bill stuck inside."

This, as anybody who has followed sport even indifferently knows, is minor league stuff compared with what goes on at some colleges where local, state and alumni pride often are motivating factors as powerful as profit in building winning teams. Since 1952, when the National Collegiate Athletic Association took on police powers, it has had enough evidence of recruiting violations to have taken action against schools in 86 cases. Some did not learn their lesson and had to be punished a second time. Auburn lived in the NCAA doghouse for six years. Indiana has been in for three.

Head coaches, either ambitious for better jobs or fretful that the ax will soon fell them, continue to cut recruiting corners despite the threat of penalty. And many feel it would be a mistake to become sentimental about their players. The stringent policies of Coach Charlie Bradshaw resulted in 53 University of Kentucky players abandoning the team by last September. One assistant at another southern school quit his job recently when he became sickened by the ruthless measures his superior was using to get scholarships *back* from boys who had not succeeded on the football field. What happens to allegiance to the sport and the school then? In prosecuting the college basketball scandals of 1961 an assistant New York district attorney, Peter D. Andreoli, said that one pertinent thread ran through all the players' testimony: none of them had any loyalty to his school.

A. Whitney Griswold, the late president of Yale, so disliked athletic scholarships that he termed them the "greatest swindle ever perpetrated on American youth." In his book, *Campus U.S.A.*, David Boroff said that college football players had become so "seriously devalued in recent years [that] they are Saturday's children, neglected the rest of the week. No longer heroes, they are just hulking mercenaries to many students." Sociologist Reuel Denney of the University of Hawaii, a collaborator with David Riesman on *The Lonely Crowd*, says that in the commercialized sports environment the athlete "is first turned into a robot, and then sometimes the robot becomes a burglar. I think the first stage, when the human being is turned into a robot, is worse."

These views are extreme. Sport remains a major assimilating force on the college campus, and there are as many legitimate reasons for letting the superior athlete play his way through an education as for supporting a brilliant violinist. It would be a mistake to kill the athlete's chances of going to college. Better curb the excesses of his elders.

But if some college authorities persist in sidestepping rules, then, alas, the athletes, their parents and friends will have to set a higher tone. For it is important that the man on the field be ethically straight and that his play be right and not merely entertaining. Sport will retain its character, its unique quality as sport, only so long as the player and the fan and the kid who stands three hours in the rain to get Willie Mays's name on a crumpled program believe in its sacrosanctity.

William Saroyan said that baseball is "caring." The obligation of the athlete is clear: he must care. There is an almost spiritual quality to sport. Man and boy identify with the sports hero; the hero must therefore be the quintessence of his sport. "I suspect," says Sociologist Max Kaplan, "that the fan rather enjoys scandal—but only so long as it does not touch or destroy his heroes. That is to say, himself."

It would be absurd to expect unqualifiedly good deportment from an athlete. His world is often a roiling place, and rebellion is never far below the surface. Roger Maris was an impossible character the year he hit 61 home runs. Bo Belinsky likes nightclubs and Tommy Bolt hurls golf clubs. Big Daddy Lipscomb, the Pittsburgh Steelers' giant All-Pro tackle, died in tawdry circumstances last week, possibly of a combination of dope and liquor.

But it is not too much to expect the athlete-celebrity to at least try for good conduct, since where he goes, what he does and who he does it with take on a measure of importance that reflects on his sport. Paul Hornung found out too late that "you just can't *be* like other people."

If college and amateur leaders have contributed to the moral crisis of sport in their own spheres, so have the professionals. These prosperous days the major sports deal in very large amounts. Walter O'Malley's new ball park in Los Angeles is a $22 million showcase. Racetracks in this country handle $2.5 billion a year, and pro football is a $20 million operation. Naturally, the athlete becomes a principal beneficiary. Big league baseball teams cascade hundreds of thousands of dollars in bonuses on big-eyed, little-tried talent (recent examples: $175,000 for Bob Bailey of Pittsburgh, $130,-000 to $150,000 for Bob Garibaldi of San Francisco).

This is not exceptionable. Commercial sport is a business, a part of the free-enterprise system, and the people who run it quite rightly should take as much money out of it as they can. But eventually it will be to their advantage to remember that sport is not a fast-buck business, a get-away-quick racket. There must be a degree of dedication to the game, for hard-nosed business reasons as well as idealistic ones. The purpose of sport is to offer recreation, to lift men out of their humdrum experience and offer them an exultation they cannot find in other puruits. When profits become the only objective, sport dies. The name is retained, but it is a mockery. In death, it kills more important things than itself.

Baseball has not had a scandal in years. Salaries are way up. There is a sound pension plan, and the players have representation. But the players also have a game reduced in significance by continuous capital-gains maneuvers. Franchises are moved from city to city like show troupes. Many owners are wheelers and dealers. Arnold Johnson of Kansas City was involved in so many deals with the New York Yankees—including the sale of Yankee Stadium—that his reckless player-peddling became a national joke. Adulterating the game, management moves the fences in and out to suit the power of their teams. Up goes the number of league games and night games—a staggering 849 in 1963 as compared with 248 in 1945—and along comes a meaningless second All-Star Game. Irresponsible telecasting and player-juggling between the minors and majors have meant slow death for the minor leagues. Cumulative result: the players become technicians—happy, solvent automatons—and they admit it.

Professional football has handled itself well, though its huge popularity is only a recent thing. Players' salaries are not quite as good as those in major league baseball, but the season is measurably shorter and there are now two leagues (and a third in Canada) to vie for a man's services. This is to the player's (and public's) benefit. The player draft has been handled sensibly, and bonuses have not skyrocketed out of proportion. Even so, the money drive has made some pro football managements forget the lower-income fan, who was the game's principal supporter in the formative years but is now shunted aside by season ticket sales (in New York, Detroit and many other cities) that eliminate the best 40,000 seats from the range of the small man's pocketbook. Nor is pro football above gimmicky sideshows: the Playoff Bowl takes its place alongside the second baseball All-Star Game, though neither is as blatantly commercial as the half dozen or so meaningless college bowl games that have been appended to the season in the last few years.

## VORACIOUS SUICIDE

Professional boxing could not resist strangling itself. It tried to swallow three TV fights a week. There were not enough good fighters to sustain public interest. TV audiences became weary of the same old faces. Meanwhile, the small fight clubs —St. Nicholas and Eastern Parkway arenas in New York and Marigold Arena in Chicago—began to founder, and with them went a good portion of the lifeblood of boxing: the young talent. Of no help were the monopolizing influence of the International Boxing Club and the hoodlum influence of Carbo. As the result of almost universal concern and pressure, the sport now appears to be in reasonably good order, but there is still a disregard of the boxers' safety, and whenever there is a close fight someone is sure to holler fix. Public faith has been shaken.

The finances of pro basketball and pro hockey are now dependent on an interminable league schedule—the hockey season begins in October and ends in April. Pro basketball teams play a minimum of 80 games apiece—and then, as if all that did not mean a thing, they engage in a series of playoffs involving a total of six of the nine teams. "That's not basketball," said a weary Bob Cousy of the Boston Celtics after logging 60,000 miles and playing himself into exhaustion in 1961. "That's vaudeville."

Professional golfers, also enjoying a new boom of interest, do little for their brotherhood by abandoning the tour to take part in big-money but trumped-up "specials." Stars like Arnold Palmer and Gary Player, among many others, have admitted to splitting purses before playoff matches, thereby lessening the professional significance of the match. The end result is a cheated fan.

The horse racing industry, possibly the most self-consciously honest because of its great attraction to the fast-buck crowd, is so well guarded by security measures and is such a cheerful tax supporter of state governments that it has become almost as respectable as living in Darien, Conn. Ex-FBI men are everywhere. So are pastel-colored ticket windows. But the sport's last pretense of esthetic quality—"the betterment of the breed"—is being undermined by an unstinting devotion to The Handle. An Aqueduct, with easier, more mechanical racing and a longer line of ticket windows, thrives, while lovely old Belmont dies on the vine.

There is nothing starry-eyed in believing that the men who manage or take part in the most commercial of sports should combine with their business ambition a dedication to, or at least a real respect for, their sport and all that it stands for. After all, there are millions of ordinary Americans who love their jobs and respect their professions. One would like to think that in the top echelons—which is where the top pro sportsmen belong—the proportion of Americans feeling that way is high.

This magazine will always be on the side of those who remember that a sport does not cease to be a sport when it also becomes a business. It is good to hear Paul Hornung say he would "play for the Packers this year for nothing," but that should not be necessary.

When one mixes young men already made cynical by their college experiences with others whose sole concern is to make money, trouble is to be expected. The change in viewpoint must begin with the people at the top, both in college and in professional circles. When Dr. F. C. (Phog) Allen went to an official of the University of Kansas to urge that college presidents take the lead in cleaning up sports, he says the official replied, "We've got too damned many other things to do that are more important." If this gutless attitude continues to prevail, the "excess" that ruined athletics in Greece will ruin them here. But it does not have to happen.

# Crooked Gambling Devices

## TESTIMONY OF PAUL KARNOV AND HARDY GRAY ACCOMPANIED BY COUNSEL, ROGER Q. WHITE

The CHAIRMAN. Will the two witnesses be sworn, please.

Do you and each of you solemnly swear that the testimony you are about to give before this subcommittee will be the truth, the whole truth, and nothing but the truth, so help you God?

Mr. KARNOV. I do.

Mr. GRAY. I do.

• • •

The CHAIRMAN. The witness on my left, will you state your name, your place of residence, and your business or occupation, please?

Mr. KARNOV. My name is Paul Karnov. I live at 2913 Scott Lynne, Park Ridge, Ill. I am president of H. E. Mason Co.

Adapted from *Gambling and Organized Crime,* Hearings before the Permanent Subcommittee on Investigations of the Committee on Government Operations, United States Senate, Eighty-seventh Congress, First Session, August, 1961, pp. 37–64. The chairman is Senator John L. McCellan, Arkansas. Mr. Jerome S. Adlerman is General Counsel for the Subcommittee.

The CHAIRMAN. Thank you very much. Will the other witness now please identify yourself, and your name and place of residence, and your business or occupation?

Mr. GRAY. My name is Hardy Gray. I live at 312 West Dickens, Chicago, Ill. I am secretary-treasurer of H. E. Mason Co., Chicago.

The CHAIRMAN. Now gentlemen, you have counsel, have you, and do each of you have counsel?

Mr. KARNOV. We do.

The CHAIRMAN. You may now identify yourself for the record.

Mr. WHITE. My name is Roger Q. White, and I am an attorney of Chicago, Ill.

The CHAIRMAN. Give your office address, please.

Mr. WHITE. 141 West Jackson Boulevard, Chicago.

The CHAIRMAN. Do you wish to make some request on behalf of your client?

Mr. WHITE. I have advised them that under your rule 9, they are entitled to request that the television and movie taking be suspended during their testimony on grounds of distraction, harassment, and physical discomfort, and they have asked me to make such a request on their behalf.

The CHAIRMAN. Very well, the request will be granted upon the condition, of course, that they cooperate with the committee. We cooperate with witnesses who cooperate with us.

Mr. WHITE. Thank you very much.

The CHAIRMAN. If they cooperate with us in giving their testimony, as far as I know there is no objection. Unless there is objection on the part of some member of the committee, the request will be granted.

We will proceed.

Mr. ADLERMAN. Mr. Karnov——

The CHAIRMAN. May I suggest to the cameraman, please, that during the course of the witnesses' testimony, unless I give you further permission to do so, you will not place the cameras on the witnesses while they are testifying.

Mr. ADLERMAN. Mr. Karnov, are you connected with the Mason Co.?

Mr. KARNOV. Yes, I am.

Mr. ADLERMAN. And is that also known as the K. C. Card Co., of Chicago?

Mr. KARNOV. That is a trade name, sir, that we use.

• • •

The CHAIRMAN. Is it incorporated?

Mr. KARNOV. Yes, sir.

The CHAIRMAN. It is incorporated, the Mason Co., and therefore uses the trade name of K. C. Card Co.?

Mr. KARNOV. That is correct.

Mr. ADLERMAN. How long have you been connected with this company?

Mr. KARNOV. Off and on for about 12 years, but I have just become owner, since 1957, half owner.

Mr. ADLERMAN. Who is the man that owned the company before that?

Mr. KARNOV. A Mr. Harrington E. Drake.

Mr. ADLERMAN. And you purchased the company along with Mr. Gray?

Mr. KARNOV. Yes, sir.

Mr. ADLERMAN. In 1957?

Mr. KARNOV. Yes, sir; in 1957.

Mr. ADLERMAN. Are you the sole proprietors of this company?

Mr. KARNOV. Yes, we are.

Mr. ADLERMAN. Do you have any other person who has a financial interest in this company, besides yourself?

Mr. KARNOV. No, sir; no one.

Mr. ADLERMAN. Who were on your board of directors?

Mr. KARNOV. Mr. Arthur Marvin, and my wife; those are the only two directors.

Mr. ADLERMAN. Who owns the stock of the corporation?

Mr. KARNOV. Mr. Gray owns 50 percent of the stock and I own the other 50 percent.

Mr. ADLERMAN. What is the nature of your business, Mr. Karnov?

Mr. KARNOV. We are manufacturers of perfect dice and other gaming equipment.

The CHAIRMAN. What kind of dice?

Mr. KARNOV. Perfect dice.

The CHAIRMAN. What do you mean by perfect dice?

Mr. KARNOV. As perfect as machinery and human hands can make them.

Mr. ADLERMAN. I show you this catalog, Mr. Karnov. Is this the catalog put out and sold by your company, or rather distributed by your company?

Mr. KARNOV. Yes, it is.

Mr. ADLERMAN. How many copies of this do you distribute a year?

Mr. KARNOV. If we have two mailings, about 40,000.

Mr. ADLERMAN. In this catalog—do you have a copy of the catalog?

Mr. KARNOV. I don't, sir.

The CHAIRMAN. The catalog may be presented to the witness for certain identifications. The witness will please examine the booklet presented to him and identify it. Is that the catalog that you are testifying about?

Mr. KARNOV. That is right.

The CHAIRMAN. That is put out by your company?

Mr. KARNOV. Yes, sir.

The CHAIRMAN. In the trade name of the K.C. Card Co.?

Mr. KARNOV. That is correct.

The CHAIRMAN. Very well, it may be made exhibit No. 3 to your testimony.

Mr. ADLERMAN. Just taking your catalog for the first 23 pages, what proportion of this 23 pages refers to perfect dice?

Mr. KARNOV. I believe only about three pages, sir.

Mr. ADLERMAN. And the rest of it are so-called "gaff" dice?

Mr. KARNOV. I believe that is the terminology used in the trade, sir.

The CHAIRMAN. Let us get this straight. Perfect dice, as you call them, are legitimate dice?

Mr. KARNOV. Yes, sir.

The CHAIRMAN. And the other dice are what kind?

Mr. KARNOV. They are usually called trick dice or gaff dice, sir.

The CHAIRMAN. And the more common expression is crooked dice, is that right?

Mr. KARNOV. I presume so.

The CHAIRMAN. Proceed.

Mr. ADLERMAN. Let us take the balance of the book. You have a book here which has some 70 or 80 pages, is that right?

Mr. KARNOV. Approximately, yes, sir, I believe so.

Mr. ADLERMAN. What proportion of this 80-page catalog refers to perfect dice or legitimate gaming equipment?

Mr. KARNOV. I believe about half of it, Mr. Adlerman.

Mr. ADLERMAN. About half of it?

Mr. KARNOV. I think so, yes, sir. I have never gone through item by item.

Mr. ADLERMAN. Let us take from page 24 to page 25.

The CHAIRMAN. Now, up to page 23, you had two pages of legitimate equipment, is that right?

Mr. KARNOV. Yes, sir.

The CHAIRMAN. And the rest of it was advertising what we have just termed crooked equipment, is that right?

Mr. KARNOV. May I go through these pages, sir?

The CHAIRMAN. Yes, you may glance at them.

Mr. KARNOV. Sir, I would say approximately 36 pages are devoted entirely to legitimate gaming supplies.

Mr. ADLERMAN. Of the 88 pages, is that right?

Mr. KARNOV. That is without an item-by-item check, and just skimming through the book.

Mr. ADLERMAN. I think probably you are giving yourself a little bit the better of the bargain, but I will accept that.

Mr. KARNOV. Well, thank you.

Mr. ADLERMAN. What is the gross amount of business that you do annually? In 1958 how much was the gross business? Can I refresh your recollection?

Mr. KARNOV. I wish you would. I would appreciate it.

Mr. ADLERMAN. Did you do about $390,000 worth of business in 1958?

Mr. KARNOV. Approximately, I believe.

Mr. ADLERMAN. And in 1959, it dropped down to $368,000?

Mr. KARNOV. About that, yes, sir.

Mr. ADLERMAN. And in 1960, it was back to $389,000?

Mr. KARNOV. It may be true, sir. I am not positive of those figures. I haven't looked at the books lately.

Mr. ADLERMAN. Well, these are the figures that we got from your books. Would you question those figures?

Mr. KARNOV. Your figures are probably correct; yes, sir.

Mr. ADLERMAN. In other words, you do approximately, or almost $400,000 worth of business a year, slightly under that?

Mr. KARNOV. Yes, sir.

Mr. ADLERMAN. And over a 3-year total, you did about $1 million worth of business in gambling equipment since you bought the company?

Mr. KARNOV. Sir, may I qualify my answer on that. You say about $1 million worth in gambling equipment. Everything we sell is not necessarily connected with gambling. We sell trade checks, and we sell poker chips, and we sell chips to the Alcoholics Anonymous.

The CHAIRMAN. Aren't poker chips a little bit of gambling equipment?

Mr. KARNOV. Yes, sir; I will grant you that, but as I say, everything in this book is not 100 percent connected with gambling.

The CHAIRMAN. I understand. What is there in the book that is not used in connection with any gambling operations? Can you think of anything?

(At this point Senator Mundt entered the hearing room.)

Mr. KARNOV. Well, we use our poker chips for the AA, which is the Alcoholics Anonymous, that is never used for gambling by them.

The CHAIRMAN. How do they keep a fellow from drinking?

Mr. KARNOV. I don't know that, sir. It is a sobriety token that they use.

The CHAIRMAN. A sobriety token?

Mr. KARNOV. Yes, sir, and we monogram a thing like "AA" on one side of the check, and the other side shows the amount of time that the party who gets one of these tokens has been on the wagon. In other words, if he has been a nondrinker for, say, 6 months, we put a "6–M" on that, and he walks around with this token, and I don't know what the purpose of it is, and we have never inquired of Alcoholics Anonymous.

Mr. ADLERMAN. How many of those have you sold in a year?

Mr. KARNOV. I really don't know, sir, and we don't keep account of it.

Mr. ADLERMAN. Have you sold as much as $100 worth?

Mr. KARNOV. I think so.

Mr. ADLERMAN. More than that?

Mr. KARNOV. Well, I couldn't say.

The CHAIRMAN. What does a poker chip cost?

Mr. KARNOV. You can buy them for as little as $2 a hundred, sir, and as high as $16 a hundred.

The CHAIRMAN. When you get a little monogram put on it, it costs a little more, doesn't it?

Mr. KARNOV. Yes, sir.

Mr. ADLERMAN. Do you think it was more than $200 worth?

Mr. KARNOV. Probably not, sir.

Mr. ADLERMAN. So that $200 out of the $1 million worth of business you have done in a year, was not connected with gambling equipment?

Mr. KARNOV. All right, I will grant that.

The CHAIRMAN. It doesn't mean that necessarily. I guess that you have some cards and dice that are perfectly legitimate, have you?

Mr. KARNOV. Yes, sir, a good portion of them.

The CHAIRMAN. The legitimate cards and dice are used in gambling, too?

Mr. KARNOV. Yes, sir.

The CHAIRMAN. In fact, most people who gamble with them think that they are using legitimate cards, is that right?

Mr. KARNOV. That is correct.

The CHAIRMAN. Very well.

Mr. ADLERMAN. As a matter of fact, you do make perfect dice for some of the casinos in Nevada?

Mr. KARNOV. Yes, sir, we do.

Mr. ADLERMAN. And that represents about 10 percent of your business, is that right?

Mr. KARNOV. No, sir. It represents about 40 percent of our

business. If you are referring to the State of Nevada alone, I would say it is about 30 percent. But we also sell legitimate dice to casinos in Puerto Rico and other clubs throughout the world.

Mr. ADLERMAN. Now, you say that out of $100,000 worth of business a year, or $400,000 worth of business a year, about one-third of that is legitimate dice?

Mr. KARNOV. If you are limiting it to dice alone, I would say approximately; yes, sir. If you are talking about chips and other items that are considered legitimate, I would say that it would be more than half.

Mr. ADLERMAN. Now, who are your biggest customers?

Mr. KARNOV. Our largest customers are all located in Nevada.

Mr. ADLERMAN. How many dice do you sell in Nevada?

Mr. KARNOV. We have one customer that receives 500 pair every week.

Mr. ADLERMAN. And how much does he pay you for that?

Mr. KARNOV. He pays $1.25 a pair.

Mr. ADLERMAN. That is——

Mr. KARNOV. $637.50 a week, with the tax.

Mr. ADLERMAN. That is your biggest customer?

Mr. KARNOV. That is one of our biggest customers: yes.

Mr. ADLERMAN. Who else is a big customer?

Mr. KARNOV. The Palace Club in Reno.

Mr. ADLERMAN. Let's try to figure out how much you sell by way of legitimate dice.

Mr. KARNOV. Sir, I don't have the figures in front of me. It would be impossible for me to guess.

Mr. ADLERMAN. You sell $600 worth to one casino?

Mr. KARNOV. Every week.

The CHAIRMAN. $600 worth of dice a week?

Mr. KARNOV. $625 worth every week.

The CHAIRMAN. Of dice a week to one casino?

Mr. KARNOV. To one casino; yes, sir.

The CHAIRMAN. I don't know much about this business. Do they wear them out or lose them?

Mr. KARNOV. I don't know, sir.

The CHAIRMAN. All right.

Mr. ADLERMAN. Outside of the legitimate perfect dice, what is the bulk of your business?

Mr. KARNOV. We sell a lot of marked cards, we sell trick dice, we sell poker chips, we sell table layouts, and things of that nature; punchboards.

Mr. ADLERMAN. You were requested to bring some of that equipment in. Have you brought it in?

Mr. KARNOV. Yes; we brought it in. I think Mr. Dunne has it.

The CHAIRMAN. Let me ask you this. Before we start with this equipment let me get my bearings here a little. Do you manufacture this equipment?

Mr. KARNOV. The only thing we manufacture, sir, are dice. We job everything else.

The CHAIRMAN. You do what?

Mr. KARNOV. We job everything else. We buy it from some-one else and resell it. The only manufacturing we do is the dice.

The CHAIRMAN. You do manufacture the dice?

Mr. KARNOV. We do manufacture the dice.

The CHAIRMAN. Where do you get the cards?

Mr. KARNOV. We buy the cards—we also mark the cards. I should qualify that. We mark the cards.

The CHAIRMAN. What you mean is you buy regular cards that are legitimate?

Mr. KARNOV. Right.

The CHAIRMAN. And you mark them scientifically or other-wise so they can be so identified by those who know how to identify them and use them?

Mr. KARNOV. Precisely, yes, sir.

Mr. ADLERMAN. How many employees do you have, Mr. Karnov?

Mr. KARNOV. We have 29 employees.

Mr. ADLERMAN. How do you break those employees down? What are their occupations?

Mr. KARNOV. We have five people who work on cards.

Mr. ADLERMAN. You have five girls?

Mr. KARNOV. Yes, sir.

Mr. ADLERMAN. Are they mostly of Japanese extraction?

Mr. KARNOV. Two of them are.

The CHAIRMAN. They work on cards?

Mr. KARNOV. Yes, sir.

The CHAIRMAN. What do they do?

Mr. KARNOV. They mark them. They mark them by hand.

The CHAIRMAN. Are they marked for ornamental purposes or for business purposes?

Mr. KARNOV. No, sir, they are not marked for ornamental purposes. They are marked just like the magic cards that are sold in novelty shops and so forth. They are marked so that you can read them.

The CHAIRMAN. They are marked so he who knows the alphabet of marking can read them?

Mr. KARNOV. Precisely.

Mr. ADLERMAN. And what are the other employees out of the 29 doing?

Mr. KARNOV. I have three girls in the office. We have an office manager. We have two people in the shipping room. The balance of them work in the dice shop.

Mr. ADLERMAN. In other words, you have 11 people employed in shipping, clerical help, and marking cards, five marking cards?

Mr. KARNOV. Right.

Mr. ADLERMAN. You still have 16 to account for. What do they do?

Mr. KARNOV. They work in the dice shop, manufacturing the dice.

• • •

Mr. ADLERMAN. What type of dice work do they do, outside of perfect dice?

• • •

Mr. KARNOV. We make trick dice, we load dice, we bevel them, we cut them. We make different types of spots on them, heart spots, club spots, diamond spots, and so forth.

Mr. ADLERMAN. I notice that in your catalog you have what they call horses.

Mr. KARNOV. Yes, sir.

Mr. ADLERMAN. Those are tops and bottoms. I think that is on page 18 of the catalog.

Mr. KARNOV. Yes, sir.

Mr. ADLERMAN. What are horses?

Mr. KARNOV. They are double numbered dice, sir.

Mr. ADLERMAN. In other words, they are mismatched dice?

Mr. KARNOV. That is correct.

Mr. ADLERMAN. And they are so mismatched that they only throw certain types of numbers?

Mr. KARNOV. If they are made for certain numbers they will only show certain numbers.

Mr. ADLERMAN. They are what they call 4 and 11 tops?

Mr. KARNOV. Yes, sir.

Mr. ADLERMAN. And then you have 1, 3, 5 tops and so on down the line?

Mr. KARNOV. Yes, sir.

Mr. ADLERMAN. Any combination that you would like, you have mismatched numbers, is that right?

Mr. KARNOV. Right.

Mr. ADLERMAN. Is that used for any purpose other than gambling?

Mr. KARNOV. I really don't know, sir, to be frank with you.

Mr. ADLERMAN. You are not being very frank with us, are you?

Mr. KARNOV. Yes, I am, sir. I don't know who buys these things. You asked me if they are used for any other purpose than gambling. I don't know. I don't know if there is another purpose.

Mr. ADLERMAN. Is there any question in your mind that they are used for anything else but gambling?

Mr. KARNOV. No.

The CHAIRMAN. Primarily, that is what they are for?

Mr. KARNOV. Primarily, that is what dice are for; that is right.

Mr. ADLERMAN. You also have, and I will refer to page 27 of your catalog—I am skipping around quite a bit because I don't want to take too much time—a radio cue prompter. Have you one of those devices here?

Mr. KARNOV. I believe so, sir.

Mr. ADLERMAN. Could we see that?

• • •

The CHAIRMAN. I guess we are going to look at all of that so while you are there, why not open it all up and lay it on the table. Move it down to the other end of the table and get it all in one place.

Mr. ADLERMAN. While they are opening this thing up, I would like to read the description of what they call the radio cue prompter. It says:

Not to be confused with many inferior units now on the market. This item is the ultimate in precision electronics and enables two people to cue each other, such as actors on a stage, mental reading, etc. Using these two miniature units and a dot-dash system, you can carry on a conversation with your partner in any game. No wires, all self-contained, card pack size. Full instructions with every order. Guaranteed the best. Longer distance than many. $350.

The CHAIRMAN. Let's see that little device now.

Mr. ADLERMAN. Will you describe how that works, Mr. Karnov, or would Mr. Gray describe how they work?

The CHAIRMAN. What are they called, the instruments you have in your hand?

Mr. GRAY. We call them a radio cue prompter.

The CHAIRMAN. What are they designed to do? What purpose do they serve?

Mr. GRAY. They are designed to, by the method of dot and dash system, to make signals between people without any actual contact.

The CHAIRMAN. Suppose you and I are sitting across the table as partners in a card game, how would we operate it? I have one of those on me, I suppose, and you have one on you, is that the way?

Mr. GRAY. Yes, sir.

The CHAIRMAN. We are partners in a card game. You have one and I have one. How could we get along with it? What do we do?

Mr. GRAY. One is a sender and the other is a receiver.

The CHAIRMAN. Will it work both ways?

Mr. GRAY. No, sir.

The CHAIRMAN. It only works one way?

Mr. Gray. Yes, sir.

The CHAIRMAN. One does the sending and the other is the receiver?

Mr. GRAY. Yes, sir.

The CHAIRMAN. How does it send? Does it talk?

Mr. GRAY. No, sir. It sends a small electric shock.

Mr. ADLERMAN. It sends an impulse.

Mr. GRAY. It is like an impulse; yes, sir.

The CHAIRMAN. You mean the fellow who is wearing the receiver can feel something?

Mr. ADLERMAN. Where are they usually strapped on a person?

Mr. GRAY. They could be strapped on the arm or the leg.

Mr. ADLERMAN. And one of the electrodes is strapped to the leg and the other man—how does that operate?

Would you put one on, Mr. Dunne? Let him be the receiver.

The CHAIRMAN. We may be advertising your business; I am not sure. Go ahead.

* * *

Mr. GRAY. He could get a good shock from this if he has sweaty hands.

You won't feel it through your clothes, though. You have to put it on your skin. I will move away a little. Are you ready?

Mr. DUNNE. Yes.

(Demonstration.)

Mr. DUNNE. I think it works all right, Mr. Chairman.

The CHAIRMAN. I suppose you can tone it down a bit, can't you, in a game?

Mr. GRAY. Yes, sir; it does have adjustments on it.

The CHAIRMAN. It is like a hearing aid. You can turn it up or down to suit the necessity of the moment.

Mr. GRAY. Yes, sir.

Mr. ADLERMAN. The purpose of that device is to signal your partner as to what cards you have or in some other manner inform him what you want him to do in a game; is that right? That is one way of operating it?

Mr. GRAY. Yes, sir.

Mr. ADLERMAN. Do you have there a one-way mirror?

Mr. KARNOV. Yes, sir.

Mr. ADLERMAN. And this has a fluorescent light on it?

Mr. KARNOV. That is right.

Mr. ADLERMAN. This could be put into the door of a closet or the door of another room?

Mr. KARNOV. That is right.

Mr. ADLERMAN. And the person on the inside of the closet will not be seen by the people outside? It only will be reflected as a mirror?

Mr. KARNOV. That is right.

Mr. ADLERMAN. Would you hold it up?

The CHAIRMAN. What do you mean by a one-way mirror? All I ever saw was one way.

Mr. KARNOV. This is the type of mirror which is called a two-way mirror, actually, but if you have a light on one side of this two-way mirror, you can only see a reflection from this side. The person being on the opposite side, being in a darker section of a room, would be able to see through this glass, which is commercially available, and see who is on the other side.

The CHAIRMAN. In other words, if I am playing cards and I am sitting so there is a closet behind me and you have that mirror on the closet a fellow can stand in the closet and see my hand and if you have one of these things he can signal to his partner who is in the crooked game with him and let him know that I have two aces and, if he can beat it, to bet, to raise.

Mr. KARNOV. That is right, sir.

The CHAIRMAN. That is the way that works?

Mr. KARNOV. Yes, sir.

The CHAIRMAN. What do those little battery things cost?

Mr. GRAY. $350.

The CHAIRMAN. I don't know much about electronics but I have seen things with a whole lot in them that cost less.

Mr. ADLERMAN. Who makes that for you?

Mr. KARNOV. Communications Electronics, Lyndon, Ky.

Mr. ADLERMAN. That is Mr. William Dodson?

Mr. KARNOV. Yes, sir.

•  •  •

The CHAIRMAN. Is Mr. Dodson present?

Have some of the staff check on him and we will find out if he is in town.

Go ahead.

Mr. ADLERMAN. Do you also sell and distribute various types of equipment to anybody who wants to do it, or can do it themselves, that is, to strip the cards, mark the cards, or other things of that sort?

•   •   •

Mr. ADLERMAN. Invisible ink and materials of that type, is that correct?

Mr. KARNOV. Yes, sir.

Mr. ADLERMAN. Card cutters, markers, and so on and so forth?

Mr. KARNOV. Yes, sir.

Mr. ADLERMAN. And you have devices where you can just pinch the card and to a skillful man he can feel it, is that right?

Mr. KARNOV. Yes, sir.

Mr. ADLERMAN. These are all used by gamblers, are they not?

Mr. KARNOV. Mostly, I believe so; yes, sir.

Mr. ADLERMAN. Amongst other things, do you also sell contact lenses?

Mr. KARNOV. Yes, we do.

Mr. ADLERMAN. And have you sold about 400 contact lenses in the past year?

Mr. KARNOV. No, sir.

Mr. ADLERMAN. Do you sell as many as 350 a year?

Mr. KARNOV. I don't believe we have ever sold that many, sir. I think the most we ever sold was about 275 or 280, somewhere in that area.

The CHAIRMAN. What are they?

Mr. KARNOV. They are a round contact lens of a red color.

The CHAIRMAN. Have you brought some of them with you?

Mr. ADLERMAN. Is this the type of glass?

Mr. KARNOV. That is the color used; yes, sir.

Mr. ADLERMAN. This is the type of glass that goes into the contact lens?

Mr. KARNOV. Into the contact.

Mr. ADLERMAN. Are these the types of cards that you gave us to show how they are used?

Mr. KARNOV. Yes, sir.

The CHAIRMAN. I present you with what appears to me to be what you have been talking about as contact lenses. They are in a little case. One is marked "R" and one is marked "L." I guess that means right and left for the eyes, is that correct?

Mr. KARNOV. That is correct, sir.

The CHAIRMAN. Will you identify that, please, sir?

(The articles were handed to the witness.)

Mr. KARNOV. That is correct.

The CHAIRMAN. Are they made on prescription?

Mr. KARNOV. Yes, they are.

The CHAIRMAN. You get a doctor to examine and find what you need in the way of glasses?

Mr. KARNOV. That is right, sir.

The CHAIRMAN. And then the coloring is the thing that enables you to see the cards?

Mr. KARNOV. That is correct.

The CHAIRMAN. The invisible marking of the card, is that right?

Mr. KARNOV. That is correct.

* * *

The CHAIRMAN. What would a lens like that cost?

Mr. KARNOV. We sell them for $160, sir.

The CHAIRMAN. You sell them for $160 a pair, for two eyes. If a fellow had one eye, would he get it half price?

Mr. KARNOV. Yes, sir.

* * *

Senator MUNDT. If they are made out of red glass, they ought to stand out like a wart on a pickle; anybody could see them.

Mr. KARNOV. Well, I don't know, sir. I imagine they would show up pretty badly. They are very small, sir, as you can see.

Mr. ADLERMAN. When they are worn, if you had brown eyes, they would show as red eyes.

Senator MUNDT. All you would have to look for is a red-eyed gambler.

The CHAIRMAN. They will not change the color of your eye, will they?

Mr. KARNOV. No, sir; they will change the color of your eyes, because they are red.

The CHAIRMAN. It invites a fellow to come on, thinking you have been up the night before and are kind of worn out. With these red glasses you are ready to take him for a sucker, and all the time he thinks he is taking you; is that right?

Mr. KARNOV. It could well be.

The CHAIRMAN. I guess so. It fits into a pattern.

Senator CURTIS. May I ask, does a customer go to his own doctor for the eye examination?

Mr. KARNOV. Usually; yes, sir.

Senator CURTIS. What is he instructed to tell the doctor?

Mr. KARNOV. He is instructed to get a correct reading for contact lenses. A prescription for contact lenses.

Mr. ADLERMAN. I would like to call your attention, Senator, to pages 40 and 41, which contain the advertisement on this. In the advertisement on page 40, in the second paragraph, it says:

So small they are invisible. Cannot be seen even under the very closest inspection. Guaranteed. We have done tremendous research in color—

and so forth.

Then they advise you to look at the instructions on page 41, and there they say:

When ordering contact lenses, it is necessary for you to send us an ophthalmometer reading of your eyes, plus your regular spectacle prescription. We must have this reading to properly grind your lenses. If your vision is 20/20 without glasses, be sure to indicate this on your order.

Then it goes on to say:

When you go to a doctor insist that he give you an ophthalmometer reading because without it, we cannot do a perfect job of fitting your lenses * * *. If you cannot obtain a satisfactory reading in your city or nearby, and are able to come to Chicago, we can arrange to have your eyes measured. You will also have the opportunity to see this work. There is no obligation to buy even after your eyes are measured.

NOTE.—Full amount must be sent with all orders for contact lenses.

Then there is the contact lens ink applicator, and so forth, all of the different devices needed to be used with the contact lenses.

Then on page 40, they sell you the marked contact lens cards, the cards that you read with these. They sell 6 decks for $45 and 12 decks for $85, and if you want certain suit markings, add $2 per deck to the above prices.

The CHAIRMAN. On these contact lenses, you don't actually make the lens?

Mr. KARNOV. No, sir.

The CHAIRMAN. Have you some manufacturer working with you that makes the lens?

Mr. KARNOV. Well, we did have; yes, sir.

The CHAIRMAN. What do you get, just the profit off the cards you sell?

Mr. KARNOV. Well, we make a profit off of the lenses and off the cards, sir.

The CHAIRMAN. What do the lens sell for, $160?

Mr. KARNOV. $160; yes, sir.

The CHAIRMAN. What does the ordinary lens cost?

Mr. KARNOV. The ordinary lens, sir?

The CHAIRMAN. Yes.

Mr. KARNOV. Do you mean a clear lens, a white lens?

The CHAIRMAN. Yes.

Mr. KARNOV. I don't know. We don't buy those. We haven't sold any of those.

The CHAIRMAN. I see. What is the profit in this to your company?

Mr. KARNOV. $100. We pay $60 from the manufacturer.

The CHAIRMAN. What I wanted to ascertain is this: Is the $60 really above the normal price for a normal lens? I don't know.

Mr. KARNOV. I don't know, sir, frankly, I really don't.

The CHAIRMAN. Does the manufacturer know when they are providing these lenses that they are such that they may be used for this purpose?

Mr. KARNOV. We believe so, sir. They know what business we are in.

The Chairman. And they know you don't order ordinary lenses for even the most deserving, nearly blind person?

Mr. KARNOV. We would be glad to if a man wanted to.

The CHAIRMAN. I mean this kind?

Mr. KARNOV. No, not this kind.

Senator MUNDT. How big a volume do you do in a business of this type?

Mr. KARNOV. As I say, we sold about 280 pair last year.

Senator MUNDT. Is it a comparatively new development?

Mr. KARNOV. It is a new item; yes, sir.

Senator CURTIS. What States do they go into?

Mr. KARNOV. Almost all States. I couldn't pinpoint which ones they went into or didn't go into.

Senator MUNDT. What is the nature of your customers? Are they usually gambling houses or dealers in a gambling house?

Mr. KARNOV. No, sir. Most of our business is to individuals and we don't know, frankly, if they are gamblers, social gamblers or the fellow next door having fun. We don't know. All we get is a name, nothing else.

Senator CURTIS. Where do you get the list to send your 4,000 catalogs?

Mr. KARNOV. This is a list, sir, the majority of which was in the business when we purchased it. We also do magazine advertising. We purchase lists from list companies. And we send out catalogs after we purchase these lists.

Senator CURTIS. When you purchase from a list company, what kind of a list do you purchase? What do you ask for?

Mr. KARNOV. Well, the last list we purchased, within the last 6 months, we bought from a fishing and hunting magazine. These were all fishermen. We have purchased, in years gone by, turf lists, people who buy turf magazines, horse-racing magazines, and so forth. We also get a lot of names through catalog advertising in the magazines.

Mr. ADLERMAN. There is a large part of your catalogs that go to the armed services?

Mr. KARNOV. I don't believe so. A portion of them do. I don't know how many.

The CHAIRMAN. Do you advertise in armed services magazines?

Mr. KARNOV. Yes, we do.

The CHAIRMAN. You advertise in them?

Mr. ADLERMAN. Isn't it true that there is a substantial amount of this sold to servicemen?

Mr. KARNOV. It is a good amount, but I couldn't tell you how much.

The CHAIRMAN. Isn't it true that servicemen account for a substantial amount of your business?

Mr. KARNOV. I couldn't tell you, sir. We have never kept a separate listing that these were servicemen and these were not.

* * *

Mr. ADLERMAN. Did you bring the magnetic equipment?

Mr. KARNOV. Yes, we did.

Mr. ADLERMAN. Would you describe that equipment?

Mr. KARNOV. This is a magnet belt.

Mr. ADLERMAN. Would you bring that up so we can look at it?

Mr. KARNOV. Keep away from anything steel because that is a permanent magnet. It will attract.

The CHAIRMAN. What is this heavy weight in this?

Mr. KARNOV. That is a piece of alnico five magnet material, sir.

The CHAIRMAN. This is a belt. Who is supposed to wear this belt, the operator?

Mr. KARNOV. The operator; yes, sir.

The CHAIRMAN. Operator of what?

Mr. KARNOV. A dice game.

The CHAIRMAN. How about a roulette wheel?

Mr. KARNOV. No; dice.

The CHAIRMAN. This is for dice games?

Mr. KARNOV. Right; yes, sir.

Mr. ADLERMAN. What will that do in a dice game?

Mr. KARNOV. That will attract a pair of magnetic dice, and if the dice are made for, say, four and three, they will show four and three if they come within that field.

Mr. ADLERMAN. When you are playing at the table, do you wear that as an apron?

Mr. KARNOV. I guess that is the way it could be worn, Mr. Adlerman.

Mr. ADLERMAN. Or is it worn underneath the clothes?

Mr. KARNOV. Usually underneath the clothing.

Mr. ADLERMAN. And if you are wearing that, how do you throw your dice?

Mr. KARNOV. You would have to have a partner to throw toward you.

Mr. ADLERMAN. In other words, you have to have two people?

Mr. KARNOV. Yes.

Mr. ADLERMAN. One man stands at the backboard or near the board where the dice hits and the other throws it?

Mr. KARNOV. To make sure it gets within that field.

Mr. ADLERMAN. When his man is not throwing the dice, he walks away from the table; is that right?

Mr. KARNOV. Right.

Mr. ADLERMAN. That way they can control the magnetic dice?

Mr. KARNOV. Right.

The CHAIRMAN. When he walks back to the table, he may walk to a different place at the table?

Mr. KARNOV. Yes, sir.

The CHAIRMAN. So the fellow throwing the dice knows him and he tries to throw it so they will come within the range of control?

Mr. KARNOV. Of that field; yes, sir.

The CHAIRMAN. Is that right?

Mr. KARNOV. That is correct.

Mr. ADLERMAN. You also have some other magnetic equipment that you haven't brought down because it is too heavy?

Mr. KARNOV. We do sell it; yes, sir.

The CHAIRMAN. What is it for?

•   •   •

Mr. KARNOV. It is a magnet that is installed in tables.

Mr. ADLERMAN. Underneath the tables?

Mr. KARNOV. Right; yes, sir.

Mr. ADLERMAN. It is right underneath the top, like a plate?

Mr. KARNOV. Yes, sir.

The CHAIRMAN. Right underneath the surface where the dice roll?

Mr. KARNOV. Yes, sir.

Mr. ADLERMAN. Is that energized by an electric current?

Mr. KARNOV. Yes; it is.

Mr. ADLERMAN. Do they have remote controls?

Mr. KARNOV. Yes; they have.

Mr. ADLERMAN. These remote controls can be wireless or wired?

Mr. KARNOV. Wireless or wired; yes, sir.

The CHAIRMAN. What does the control do?

Mr. KARNOV. It throws the switch which activates this magnet. In other words, until you throw a switch, nothing happens.

The CHAIRMAN. In other words, everything is legitimate until you throw the switch?

Mr. KARNOV. Yes, sir.

Mr. ADLERMAN. You have what is called a giant magnet, GM No. 500 in your catalog, on page 21.

Mr. KARNOV. Yes, sir.

Mr. ADLERMAN. A description is:

The largest, most powerful magnet made. Heavy duty, rugged construction throughout. Only 1¾ inches thick. Controls an area 28 by 40 inches with perfect control over entire surface. Complete with rectifier wired for double polarity, double switch control, your choice of one pair any combination dice. Requires three wet cell storage (auto) batteries in addition to rectifier for smooth operation. Full instructions included with this king of magnets. Complete $1,200.

Mr. KARNOV. That is right.

Mr. ADLERMAN. Is that a type that you can also use a remote control on?

Mr. KARNOV. Yes, sir.

Mr. ADLERMAN. How much is the remote control for it?

Mr. KARNOV. $650.

Mr. ADLERMAN. And the entire equipment,. with the dice and everything else, does that run about $2,000?

Mr. KARNOV. About $1,850; yes, sir.

The CHAIRMAN. If a fellow is walking into a gambling casino where they have a dice table, just walking in there, would he have any way of observing or knowing that it was so equipped? Could he detect it, unless he actually thought it was there and started out looking for it?

Mr. KARNOV. Well, it would be very difficult if they had it well hidden, I presume.

The CHAIRMAN. It would be unlikely that he would know anything about it?

Mr. KARNOV. That is correct.

The CHAIRMAN. So if they have one of those things and a fellow goes in to play, he is just a sucker, isn't he?

Mr. KARNOV. He would be.

Senator MUNDT. How big a volume do you do in this kind of business?

Mr. KARNOV. I think we have sold two or three of them since they were offered to us, in 3 years.

• • •

Mr. ADLERMAN. Did you purchase 20,000 revenue stamps last year?

Mr. KARNOV. Approximately 20,000 stamps; yes, sir.

Mr. ADLERMAN. You only purchase them for the purpose of marking cards?

Mr. KARNOV. That is right.

Mr. ADLERMAN. When you buy a deck of cards, you buy legitimate decks from legitimate companies?

Mr. KARNOV. That is right.

Mr. ADLERMAN. And there are several different types of decks. There are Bicycle, Fan, Diamond back, and so forth?

Mr. KARNOV. Right.

Mr. ADLERMAN. And each one has to be marked with a certain technique, is that correct?

Mr. KARNOV. That is correct.

Mr. ADLERMAN. These five girls that work there, they work on different types of markings?

Mr. KARNOV. Yes, sir.

Mr. ADLERMAN. What is the type preferred by the professional hustler?

Mr. KARNOV. Well, usually those that are marked all the way down, a Bee back, Bicycle back, mostly.

Mr. ADLERMAN. Diamond back and Bee back?

Mr. KARNOV. Diamond back and Bee back.

Mr. ADLERMAN. That is the card used in most of the professional gambling games?

Mr. KARNOV. I believe so.

Mr. ADLERMAN. The Bicycle decks are not used so frequently?

Mr. KARNOV. Not as much, no.

Mr. ADLERMAN. Not amongst the professional gamblers?

Mr. KARNOV. Well, I don't believe so, sir.

Mr. ADLERMAN. And some of these marked cards are rather expensive, are they not?

Mr. KARNOV. They run $4 a deck, $3, $3.50, depending on marking.

Mr. ADLERMAN. I am talking about some of the assorted cards.

Mr. KARNOV. They run $5.50 a deck; yes, sir.

Mr. ADLERMAN. Aren't there some cards where you have a selection, where you have to go through thousands of cards?

Mr. KARNOV. We don't make those, Mr. Adlerman.

Mr. ADLERMAN. Do you buy those and resell them?

Mr. KARNOV. No. We don't sell them.

Mr. ADLERMAN. What is the most expensive marked cards that you sell?

Mr. KARNOV. The contact lens card, $8 a deck. That is the most expensive deck we sell.

Mr. ADLERMAN. On the gaffed dice, what is the most expensive set you sell?

Mr. KARNOV. Magnetic dice, transparent, $60 a pair.

The CHAIRMAN. $60 a pair, for two?

Mr. KARNOV. Yes, sir.

The CHAIRMAN. And what do they have in them?

Mr. KARNOV. Metal. They have metal in the spots, to attract them to a magnet.

The CHAIRMAN. They roll to it?

Mr. KARNOV. Into the magnetic field; yes, sir.

The CHAIRMAN. In other words, to operate this, you have to have the dice to go with it?

Mr. KARNOV. You have to have the dice to go with it, right.

The CHAIRMAN. It would have no effect on normal dice?

Mr. KARNOV. No, sir.

Mr. ADLERMAN. Did you bring the holdout machine with you?

Mr. KARNOV. Yes.

The CHAIRMAN. What is that one?

Mr. KARNOV. This is known as a holdout machine. It will hold out playing cards.

The CHAIRMAN. You have this up your sleeve?

Mr. KARNOV. That is right.

The CHAIRMAN. So you can switch the whole deck right quick?

Mr. KARNOV. No, you couldn't switch a deck. That only holds about five cards, sir.

The CHAIRMAN. Only holds about four or five?

Mr. KARNOV. Four or five, that is right.

The CHAIRMAN. The idea is to get you a card there that you need?

Mr. KARNOV. That is right.

Mr. ADLERMAN. You also have cold-decking machines?

Mr. KARNOV. We have, but I don't believe we have sold one of those in about 4 years.

The CHAIRMAN. This is what you call the third arm in a poker game?

Mr. KARNOV. That is right.

The CHAIRMAN. You only put two or three cards in it, is that right?

Senator CURTIS. Do you hold a patent on that machine?

Mr. KARNOV. No. That is made by everybody and his brother.

The CHAIRMAN. You just ease it down and reach and get your card up your sleeve, is that right?

Mr. KARNOV. Right.

The CHAIRMAN. Well, I don't guess I will have time to learn how to work it.

Proceed. First, let me ask you—well, go ahead. We will get it all in first. What do these things sell for?

Mr. KARNOV. $75, sir.

The CHAIRMAN. What? That little bit. There must be a patent on it.

Mr. KARNOV. I don't know. We buy them from another source.

The CHAIRMAN. Somebody gets a pretty good royalty on that. There is not much material in there, only about a quarter's worth altogether.

• • •

Mr. ADLERMAN. Mr. Karnov, do you also sell other types of things, such as cellophane wrappers for people to make their own cards and then rewrap them in cellophane wrappers so they look like the original pack?

Mr. KARNOV. Yes, sir.

Mr. ADLERMAN. I think you went before into the idea of marking, and so forth?

Mr. KARNOV. Yes, sir.

Mr. ADLERMAN. So there are many people who are professional hustlers that prefer to do their own marking of cards and their own—well, to make their own equipment, is that right?

Mr. KARNOV. Right.

The CHAIRMAN. How is that? You sell them the equipment to replace the card after it has been marked?

Mr. ADLERMAN. A cellophane wrapper.

Mr. KARNOV. To rewrap the package, we sell them a piece of cellophane to rewrap the package.

The CHAIRMAN. Do they have to put on a new stamp?

Mr. KARNOV. We do. I don't know if anybody else does.

The CHAIRMAN. That is after they rewrap it. They are supposed to put on a new stamp. How do they get the original stamp off?

Mr. KARNOV. I don't know. We tear ours in two, wash them off, and put our own stamp back on, a new one.

Mr. ADLERMAN. When you reseal them, you put it on like a company tear seal, like the original, is that right?

Mr. KARNOV. The ones we put on are a white band, sir, with no printing on it. The original company seal has printing on it.

Mr. ADLERMAN. You will replace them with a pink tab, if requested?

Mr. KARNOV. We can't.

Mr. ADLERMAN. Can you slip the pack out without tearing that?

Mr. KARNOV. I don't know how to do it, sir. I could never do it.

The CHAIRMAN. What was that, to slip the pack out?

Mr. ADLERMAN. We understand that some of the companies can slip a pack out without tearing the seal and then reseal it again without apparently having opened the seal. Here is a marked deck that still has the little tear seal.

•  •  •

Senator MUNDT. How many companies are there in a similar business to yours, do you know? Have you any idea?

Mr. KARNOV. I would venture a guess, sir. I have never made a count of it. I would say approximately 20.

Senator MUNDT. Are you the biggest of the 20?

Mr. KARNOV. I doubt very much. I don't know what the other people sell in the way of volume but we doubt very much if we are the largest.

Senator MUNDT. Being in the business, you pretty well know who your biggest competitors are.

Mr. KARNOV. I don't know, sir. There is no way for us to tell who is competing against us. We know they are in a similar business, but we don't know what their volume is. In other words, I can't go to a customer and say "Did you buy from 'so and so' and how much?"

There is no way for us to determine that.

Senator MUNDT. But you get some idea by the extensive cataloging and sales activities?

Mr. KARNOV. Well, we get some idea from advertising that we see in places where we advertise. We do have competition. We are not alone in our field.

Senator Mundt. Do you think there are bigger companies than yours in the business?

Mr. Karnov. I don't know, sir, frankly.

Senator Mundt. You don't know of any?

Mr. Karnov. I don't know if they are bigger.

Senator Mundt. Do you make roulette wheels, too, and sell them?

Mr. Karnov. No, sir; we do not.

Senator Mundt. Did you ever?

Mr. Karnov. Not while we owned the firm. I think the firm used to make roulette wheels, 25 years ago.

Senator Mundt. From your knowledge of the business, are there people making crooked roulette wheels, too?

Mr. Karnov. I don't think so, sir. The percentages are there without the necessary changes to be made. The percentage in roulette is so good I don't think they need anything, mathematically speaking.

Senator Ervin. I would like to ask you a little about nomenclature. I notice on page 16 you have something that speaks of floats. It says:

> Can be burned and nothing will show.

Mr. Karnov. That is right.

Senator Ervin. What is the object of that?

Mr. Karnov. Well, the dice are made by removing some of the material. In other words, you counterbalance them. Therefore, there is nothing added to them in the way of metal or material.

• • •

Senator Ervin. What does this expression to be "burned" mean?

Mr. Karnov. Well, if the dice are weighted or loaded, there must be a weighted material put into them which, if you burn the dice, will show up as a glob of metal; whereas if you have a float, the only thing you have done with a float is to remove some of the material. You have put nothing else into it. Therefore, they can be burned and nothing will show except some ashes.

Senator Ervin. I notice that these advertisements of combination dice say that certain dice are fair and others are filled.

Mr. KARNOV. That is right.

Senator ERVIN. And they are sold in various combinations so that when the dice which are filled—that is, we would call them loaded dice, I presume?

Mr. KARNOV. Loaded; yes, sir.

Senator ERVIN. They show certain combinations, either a winning combination or a losing combination?

Mr. KARNOV. Or a losing combination, right.

Senator ERVIN. That means that the man who has possession of the dice will make a substitution?

Mr. KARNOV. They usually substitute whatever the way the play is going.

Senator ERVIN. I am struck by the language on the top of page 17, about percentage dice. The object of percentage dice is to give the house, so that the house will get a winning percentage?

Mr. KARNOV. If you will go further down on that page, sir, you will find they show two kinds. They show missers and passers, which would be either for the house or the player, you see.

Senator ERVIN. For the missers, you have miss house. Some of the dice are called miss house.

Mr. KARNOV. That is right. They are considered losing dice. The passers are those that make the points.

Senator ERVIN. I was struck by the description on the top of page 17, shaped percentage dice.

All our shaped percentage dice are accurately machine cut and represent a degree of perfection that will please the most critical.

Who is the most critical to be pleased?

Mr. KARNOV. Our customers, sir.

Senator ERVIN. And they are the ones that use them for their game?

Mr. KARNOV. For the additional percentage, that is correct.

Senator ERVIN. But it would not please the others?

Mr. KARNOV. Probably not.

Senator ERVIN. That is all, Mr. Chairman.

The CHAIRMAN. I would like to ask you how many different kinds of crooked dice do you manufacture?

Mr. KARNOV. All those that are shown in our catalog, Senator. I don't know how many kinds there are.

The CHAIRMAN. How much does it add up to?

Mr. KARNOV. In what, sir?

The CHAIRMAN. Well, the different kinds, like models. You have 100 models or 10 models or whatever.

Mr. KARNOV. Probably around 15 or 20 different types.

The CHAIRMAN. That would be 15 or 20 different types of non-legitimate dice that you manufacture?

Mr. KARNOV. That is correct; yes, sir.

The CHAIRMAN. How many different kinds of markings or patterns of marked cards do you produce?

Mr. KARNOV. I will have to count those.

The CHAIRMAN. Is it a good many of those, too?

Mr. KARNOV. Quite a few; yes, sir.

The CHAIRMAN. Of course, the marking, I guess, depends upon the pattern of the card, the picture pattern of the card; does it not?

Mr. KARNOV. That is right.

The CHAIRMAN. You might even take the old Bicycle cards and you might have a half dozen different ways of marking the Bicycle cards?

Mr. KARNOV. That is right, in different positions on the cards.

The CHAIRMAN. On different picture cards you would have to use different markings?

Mr. KARNOV. That is right.

The CHAIRMAN. So it is hard to estimate how many different markings you might have?

Mr. KARNOV. That is right.

The CHAIRMAN. Marking is not the only thing. You have something else you do to the cards, don't you?

Mr. KARNOV. Yes, we cut them. We have what are known as strippers.

The CHAIRMAN. Strippers?

Mr. KARNOV. Yes.

The CHAIRMAN. You strip out the card you want?

Mr. KARNOV. That is right. In other words, this is what you do. I have four kings here in my hand. I pull them right out of the deck, and anybody can do it because they are cut in such a manner that you can do it. They are used by magicians. They are used for theatrical props, also.

The CHAIRMAN. As well as gambling?

Mr. KARNOV. As well as gambling.

The CHAIRMAN. And entertainment as well as gambling.

Mr. KARNOV. That is right. In other words, "I am going to pull four kings," and I have four kings.

The CHAIRMAN. While you have that deck of cards, if you hand that deck of cards to someone else, doing it as a magician, couldn't they do the same thing?

Mr. KARNOV. Not unless they knew what to do. If someone else grabbed the deck like this, they wouldn't know what to do with it.

The CHAIRMAN. You can cut those so that you can strip four aces or two aces?

Mr. KARNOV. Yes, sir, any combination.

• • •

The CHAIRMAN. One deck of cards is stripped for one single combination?

Mr. KARNOV. One combination; that is right.

The CHAIRMAN. Well, I guess if you were gambling you would only want to use that occasionally, wouldn't you?

Mr. KARNOV. I presume they would just want it for one particular game.

The CHAIRMAN. One particular hand would be about enough, wouldn't it?

Mr. KARNOV. That is right, if you had enough money bet.

The CHAIRMAN. If he stripped that thing three or four times in one game and had a full house of aces up, he is liable to get shot if he persisted in it too long, wouldn't you think?

Mr. KARNOV. Probably, if someone was there with a gun.

Senator CURTIS. What volume of your sales go outside of the State of Illinois?

Mr. KARNOV. I would say about 90 percent.

The CHAIRMAN. How do you ship your merchandise?

Mr. KARNOV. By parcel post, railway express, common carriers.

Senator CURTIS. And when you advertise, what do you advertise that you sell, thick cards, trick dice for party games, and things of that sort?

Mr. KARNOV. No. We advertise that we sell cards and dice— cards that can be read from the backs and trick dice, tops and bottoms, shapes and flats and so forth. In other words, we advertise our product as we show it in the catalogs. We also advertise the fact that they can be used at parties and gatherings.

The CHAIRMAN. I have here the Police Gazette, the July 1961 issue. I see some advertising in here, I believe by your company, K. C. Card Co.: "Win with cards." Do you advertise there?

Mr. KARNOV. Yes, sir; that is our advertisement.

The CHAIRMAN. That publication may be filed as exhibit 4.

• • •

Senator MUNDT. Senator Ervin was asking you about the nomenclature used, and I notice in connection with your electromagnets, table magnets, and so forth, you talk about rectifiers. Do you also manufacture the kind of rectifiers that they used to use out in Deadwood, S. Dak.? That was that 6-gun that they put on the poker table.

Mr. KARNOV. No, sir.

Senator MUNDT. You don't manufacture that type of rectifier?

Mr. KARNOV. No, sir. We only manufacture dice and marked cards. We purchase and resell everything else shown in our catalog.

Senator MUNDT. What is this rectifier that you talk about?

Mr. KARNOV. A rectifier is an electrical instrument which changes a.c. currents into d.c. currents, because no magnet will operate on a.c. current. It must be changed to d.c. current. That is the rectifier we are describing in the catalog.

The CHAIRMAN. I have just one thought here. You have been very cooperative and I want to thank you for it.

Mr. KARNOV. We try to be, sir.

The CHAIRMAN. You have been very cooperative and I think it is very helpful to us to understand some of the difficulties of the problems involved in this particular field when we go to considering legislation.

But I wonder, is there any such thing as a code in this profession, a code of ethics or anything?

Mr. KARNOV. Do you mean in our business, sir?

The CHAIRMAN. Yes.

Mr. KARNOV. Or in the gambling fraternity?

The CHAIRMAN. Both. Let's start with your business first.

Mr. KARNOV. Well, I don't know, as far as the code of ethics is concerned in our business, exactly what you mean, sir. A code of ethics in relation to what?

The CHAIRMAN. It seems to me like a great deal of this equipment, particularly where you sit down and purposely go into the business of marking cards, and manufacturing dice that are not fair or not designed to perform as normal perfection dice would perform, that there is an element of fraud involved.

Would you say that a fellow playing with a marked deck of cards, knowing they were marked and being able to read the markings on them, and the fellow he was playing with, gambling with, did not know, would you say he was getting his money legitimately on the basis of honor and integrity, rather than just on a game of chance?

Mr. KARNOV. Well, I don't think he is, sir.

The CHAIRMAN. The point I am making is, in your understanding, do you regard it as such that crooked dice or marked cards that are solely for the purpose of giving an advantage to one player over another?

•  •  •

Mr. KARNOV. You are asking my opinion as to whether I am a cheat; is that it?

The CHAIRMAN. I am trying to rationalize: how can a fellow go out and manufacture, advertise, and sell equipment so constructed and so manufactured and make it and mark it and load it and shape it so that it becomes crooked equipment and deceives and misleads and cheats and defrauds somebody who has put his confidence in it as honest. I don't see how he can escape being a party to the fraud that is being perpetrated.

Mr. KARNOV. But we don't hide it. We advertise it as being exactly what it is.

The CHAIRMAN. I don't question that, but the other fellow who doesn't know what it is, is victimized by it. You are not able to be at the card table and say to the fellow on the other side, "This fellow over here has a marked deck of cards that we fixed for him." You are not able to be there to protect him, are you?

Mr. KARNOV. No, sir.

The CHAIRMAN. The other fellow knows what he is getting when he buys this. You are honest with him. You tell him what it will do.

Mr. KARNOV. That is right.

The CHAIRMAN. To that extent, your code of ethics would require you, and I am sure you conform with it, not to advertise that it will do something that it won't do.

Mr. KARNOV. That is correct.

The CHAIRMAN. You try to be honest with your customer.

Mr. KARNOV. Right.

The CHAIRMAN. But the very purpose of making this crooked equipment is so that some one gambler can cheat another; is that correct?

Mr. KARNOV. If you say so, sir.

The CHAIRMAN. That is the real purpose of it?

Mr. KARNOV. That is the real purpose of it.

The CHAIRMAN. So the fellow who gambles without knowing that he is not the one who has the advantage, he is the sucker?

Mr. KARNOV. He is going to lose money.

The CHAIRMAN. He is going to lose money?

Mr. KARNOV. Yes, sir.

Senator MUNDT. How long have you been operating this company? Three years?

Mr. KARNOV. Since February 1, 1957.

Senator MUNDT. And in those four or four and a half years,

how many times have you had law enforcement officials, State, Federal, or local, come in and look at your books to determine the destination to which your material is sent?

Mr. KARNOV. Only once, to my knowledge, sir.

Senator MUNDT. You are talking about this committee now?

Mr. KARNOV. This committee, yes, sir.

Senator MUNDT. That is the only time it has been done?

Mr. KARNOV. Yes, sir.

Senator MUNDT. There would be legal processes, I am sure, by which a law enforcement official could have access to your books?

Mr. KARNOV. Our books are open to anybody who wants to look at them, sir. They always have been.

Senator MUNDT. So it wouldn't take a highly imaginative law enforcement official to come in and look at your books and find out who that fellow was who paid $100 for a magnetic table, so he would know that that fellow was running a crooked gambling house.

Mr. KARNOV. That is right. The books are there. Anybody can look at them.

Senator MUNDT. So the failure to find out what is being done with your mechanisms and who are using this is the failure of the law enforcement officers in part to pursue with due diligence to look at your books, because this catalog is pretty widely circulated. Some law enforcement official earning his pay, would have access to it, would he not?

Mr. KARNOV. Anybody would have access to it.

Senator MUNDT. It seems to me that the finger should be pointed primarily at the law enforcement officials who have access to the information, seeing it advertised in the Police Gazette and in service magazines. Seeing this catalog and others they simply don't exercise enough energy to walk over and look at the books and see what gambling houses are buying the equipment, because they could have a great big finger pointed directly at somebody engaged in crooked gambling; is that right?

Mr. KARNOV. That is right.

Senator MUNDT. Thank you.

Senator ERVIN. So far as you know, there is no law in the world that prohibits anything you are doing?

Mr. KARNOV. No, sir.

Senator ERVIN. Your enterprise is recognized by the law as being a perfectly legal and legitimate calling?

Mr. KARNOV. Yes, sir.

The CHAIRMAN. What effect do you think it would have on your business if you did have a Federal law prohibiting the manufacturing or changing or developing of devices, cards, dice, other equipment such as this, to be used in gambling, to prohibit its shipment in interstate commerce? Would that have any impact on your business?

Mr. KARNOV. Yes. We would probably go out of business tomorrow.

The CHAIRMAN. If all such manufacturers were put out of business tomorrow, it would, to a great extent—to some extent, at least—put the gamblers back on an even keel, each having about an equal chance with the other?

Mr. KARNOV. That is right. You know, the State of Illinois——

The CHAIRMAN. In other words, take away from those who had the good fortune of making contact with you and being smart enough to purchase crooked cards and knowing how to use them, it would put them back on about an even keel with the other fellow, if you and all your competitors were put out of business?

Mr. KARNOV. We are practically out of business because the State of Illinois just passed a new criminal code which makes it illegal for the manufacture of gaming supplies.

The CHAIRMAN. Cards, as such, may not be gaming supplies. That is, the manufacture.

Mr. KARNOV. I don't know, sir. There is no definition.

Mr. ADLERMAN. There is nothing to prevent you from moving across the State line to another State?

Mr. KARNOV. Except money. It takes money to move.

The CHAIRMAN. I guess $100 profit for a little pair of glasses for the eye would help.

Mr. KARNOV. That would help a little.

Mr. ADLERMAN. You made a profit of $75,000 a year?

Mr. KARNOV. No.

Mr. ADLERMAN. I thought you grossed $35,000 apiece?

Mr. KARNOV. Yes, sir.

Mr. ADLERMAN. In other words, you are making a profit of $75,000 a year?

Mr. KARNOV. No, it is not that. We have our auditor here. He can explain the figures to you.

Mr. ADLERMAN. What is the profit on a gross of $385,000?

Mr. KARNOV. $16,000 last year.

Senator CURTIS. After salaries?

Mr. KARNOV. After salaries.

Mr. ADLERMAN. And you draw around $75,000 between you?

Mr. KARNOV. That is right.

Mr. ADLERMAN. In other words, actually, your profit with your drawing comes to something like $86,000?

Mr. KARNOV. About that.

The CHAIRMAN. About one-third is profit, for every dollar you take in?

Mr. KARNOV. 86 into 350? I don't know. I guess it is pretty close to that.

Mr. ADLERMAN. No further questions.

The CHAIRMAN. Very well.

You have been candid. I want to express the appreciation of the subcommittee to you for it.

Mr. KARNOV. We are happy to help any time, sir.

The CHAIRMAN. We have a problem here that we have to consider and look into. If all the witnesses that come before us were as candid, as honest and truthful as you have been, it would make the work of this committee much easier and much more pleasant.

Thank you very much. You may stand aside for the present. Will you need them further?

Mr. ADLERMAN. I don't think so.

Would you leave your equipment and we will arrange to return it.

Mr. KARNOV. Surely.

The CHAIRMAN. Thank you.

# Christians and the Gambling Mania

*LYCURGUS M. STARKEY, JR.*[1]

The boys in the office work up a football pool. The P.T.A. operates a cakewalk at the school bazaar. A bookie takes $2 bets at the local newsstand. The candy store operates punch boards and pinball machines for the kids. Mother plunks down $1 for bridge game prizes. Dad continues to play the horses in spite of approaching bankruptcy.

Some wager privately, some wager legally, some wager illegally, some wager addictively. A majority of adult Americans can be counted among the chance-takers who each year toss close to $50 billion into the quicksands of gambling. In some states this means that more is spent in gambling than for groceries. Some estimates indicate that Americans spend more on gambling than on national defense.

## ARGUMENTS OF THE APOLOGISTS

In any discussion of the issue, one becomes familiar with a number of semiplausible arguments for gambling:

Argument number one: *Gambling is merely amusement.* Conscientious people who use this argument must not be aware that public gambling provides the treasure chest of the underworld. As Attorney General Robert F. Kennedy wrote in an article entitled "The Baleful Influence of Gambling" in the *Atlantic* for April 1962:

> No one knows exactly how much money is involved in gambling in the United States. What we do know is that the American people are spending more on gambling than on medical care or

Reprinted by permission of the Christian Century Foundation from *The Christian Century* LXXX (February 27, 1963), 267–270.

education; that, in so doing, they are putting up the money for the corruption of public officials and the vicious activities of the dope peddlers, loan sharks, bootleggers, white-slave traders and slick confidence men. . . . Investigation this past year by the FBI, the Internal Revenue Service, the Post Office Department, and all other federal investigative units has disclosed without any shadow of a doubt that corruption and racketeering, financed largely by gambling, are weakening the vitality and strength of this nation.[2]

Obviously a distinction needs to be made between public gambling and occasional private wagering. But can a conscientious citizen justify his gambling as a personal amusement in the face of such evidence as this? Organized gambling invites corruption, and the high stakes involved encourage unhealthy competition. So-called "petty" gambling can lead to psychological decay and a desire for ever larger stakes.

Furthermore, the Christian knows that he is a steward of all the time, talent and treasure entrusted to him by God. Can he honestly use his gifts in gambling when his winnings are gained at the expense of another's losing, and where the "house" is ultimately the only winner?

Argument number two: *All of life is a gamble*—the stock market, farming, raising a family, even (according to some theologians) faith; therefore, why is the wagering of money in a game of chance any less moral than the investing of time, money and effort in the chancy game of life?

Life does have its normal risks which one must accept with faith and courage. But those normal risks are in no sense morally equivalent to the risks taken in a game of chance. Gambling offers artificial risks in the hope of excessive gain, gain far beyond what the investment of time, money or skill justifies. And the chance taken is unrelated to creative effort such as that called for from the farmer or the stockbroker who invests his mental and physical resources. At the gambling table money changes hands according to the luck of the persons involved; results depend not on effort or ingenuity but on the turn of the wheel, the throw of the dice, the odds on a race or the drawing of a number.

The Christian knows that ultimately life is not a gamble,

a risk, a game of chance. Rather, life is lived in the providential care and keeping of the Lord of history, whose self-giving love has been disclosed in Jesus Christ. Understanding the universe as a purposeful, consistent creation, the Christian will take the odds of life and transform them into response to the will of God.

## AN ACQUIRED TASTE

Argument number three: *Gambling is instinctive with human beings.* Those who advance this argument ask why we should fight against an activity that human nature seems to lead man to indulge in. Let us rather *control* gambling by strict legislation and governmental supervision, they say; then taxes on gambling can go to the state and be returned to the people in the form of needed services.

To this ancient plea for legalized vice—the granting of respectability through recognition—the reply is that gambling is *not* instinctive in man. The Massachusetts crime commission has shown that bookmaking, a racket important to the underworld today, did not exist as a crime problem worthy of mention until pari-mutuels were legalized. Legalized pari-mutuel betting has led to growth not only of legal at-track betting but also of illegal off-track betting. Writes award-winning reporter Fred J. Cook: "Gambling is an acquired habit, and nothing shows this more clearly than the manner in which it was stimulated and grew in Massachusetts under the opening wedge of the pari-mutuel system." As the Massachusetts commission bluntly said: "There has not always been gambling with organized racketeers on a scale which amounts to a state of lawlessness in an entire society, and there need not be."

Gambling elevates money and material gain to a place of priority in life; it encourages dependence on chance rather than on the providence of God. The gambler uses the individual as a tool for his own profit; a common term for the customer is "sucker." God created man for an excellence which has no place for intentional profiteering in human misery or for dependence on the whim and caprice of chance. And for men who have fallen to the level where such ways of life have become theirs, God has come in Christ and remains in the Holy Spirit to lift them to a higher level.

Argument number four: *Gambling should be legalized as a means of providing revenue for the state.* There are those who paint such places as Las Vegas, Lake Tahoe, Hot Springs or Charles county, Maryland, as golden paradises with built-in solutions for the economic plight of hard-pressed business and government. In reply, one might cite the comment of a Los Angeles police chief on the proposal to legalize bookmaking in New York city: "Any society that bases its financial structure on the weaknesses of its people doesn't deserve to survive."

The state has not only ethical but also economic responsibility for the well-being of its citizenry. Speaking in the United States Senate Alexander Wiley of Wisconsin advised the new state of Alaska not to legalize gambling as an economic panacea. The idea that gambling will be a revenue raiser is an illusion, he said; every dollar raised from such sources means $5 spent in "higher police costs, higher court costs, higher penitentiary costs and higher relief costs." The fact that Nevada's crime rate is double and its suicide rate triple the national average would seem to support the former senator's warning.

Additional economic aspects of the legalized gambling picture are the high rate of embezzlement by persons seeking funds to bet or to replace sums lost in that manner, the reluctance of industry to locate in areas where gambling is rampant, and the invitation to corruption gambling offers to public officials. Virgil Peterson of the Chicago crime commission has pointed out that the Louisiana Lottery Company controlled Louisiana politically for 20 years in the late 19th century, a situation that eventually led the people of that state to outlaw the lottery. The appeal to legalize gambling as a means toward the financial support of the state inevitably turns out to be a deceit and a sham.

Argument number five: *Gambling is an effective means for the financial support of churches and private charities.* Among those who use this argument are some who would not favor gambling on any other basis but who feel that in this case the end justifies the means. They argue that since people are inclined to give money to charity anyway (a dubious assumption) we might as well make the process palatable by offering the possibility of a prize. Besides, they insist, when gambling is controlled by a church or a charity one may be sure that the underworld is not involved, and that all profits will be honestly directed to their intended use.

If there are ethical questions for the state in the matter of gambling as a means of support, surely the same questions are pertinent for that community which claims to be the people of God. How can the church, even in the name of supporting the Christian mission, justify an enterprise which contributes to social, economic and psychological deterioration of people? The church which uses gambling to fill its own coffers is left in a very compromised position. Not only does she appear to encourage the weakness of people for her own financial advantage, but she becomes a part of that irresponsible overworld that condones the criminal underworld's associations with legal and illegal gambling.

The case of a compromised Cardinal Cushing of Boston is an example. Some time ago a "C.B.S. Reports" program presented a documentary film titled "Biography of a Bookie Joint." Hidden cameras recorded visits to a Boston bookie joint by several members of the city police department in uniform, thus showing the close relationship between gambling and graft, the paid silence of the crooked cop. Cardinal Cushing's response was to demand that C.B.S. apologize to the city of Boston. This was shortly after the cardinal had declared to an audience at a local police ball: "In my theology, gambling itself is not a sin any more than to take a glass of beer or of hard liquor is a sin." Perhaps the cardinal is one of those who consider graft paid by the underworld a peccadillo, holding that it would not exist if gambling were legal. The *Reporter* concluded its estimate of the cardinal's compromise with words of judgment on those churches whose moral witness has been blurred by willingness to let Christian ends justify the dubious financial means: "Apparently it is left for mass communications, those reporters who serve it best, and playwrights, to awaken the public conscience."

## ROOTS OF THE DISEASE

Beneath these arguments so frequently advanced to justify a pastime known to be destructive lie deeper reasons for the existence of the current gambling mania in the United States.

No longer merely a sport for kings and wealthy playboys, gambling with its lure of something for nothing has permeated other economic and social levels. Among some low economic groups, particularly among urban Negroes, the "numbers racket" has come to seem the one desperate hope men have to pull themselves out of unbearable living conditions. Yet the numbers game is certainly not limited to the nickel-and-dime operation of the "down and out" in the city slums; according to reports in the New York press the "up and in" on Wall Street have taken to the numbers game as well.

Spread across the social and economic spectrum of the nation, gambling is symptomatic of a deep distress in society. For many people of high estate and low, the unreal dream world of something-for-nothing provides an escape from neurotic anxiety. For the neurotic person gambling can become addictive, as is testified to by the appearance of Gamblers Anonymous groups on the order of the familiar Alcoholics Anonymous. Beset by his personality problems, the neurotic looks to the gaming table as solution or escape or compensation, perhaps even as punishment to salve a guilty conscience. In his world of unreality all problems are to be solved by the fall of a card or the turn of a wheel. He can be diverted from gambling neither by common sense argument nor by moral appeal. I quote from *Science Digest:* "Every neurotic gambler in the casino or on the race track knows the odds are against him. But the thrill of gambling, the feeling of omnipotence, and the unconscious self-punishment overpower him."

The prevalence of gambling points to a breakdown of the Puritan ethic of work which held that in one's daily calling

honest, industry, thrift and service to God and man should
be stressed. In many sectors of our common life this ethic
has been replaced by the something-for-nothing philosophy.
Automation, increased production, more leisure time, the spe-
cialization and secularization of our economy—all have led to
a crisis in vocation. With uncertainty concerning the value
of work and the significance of leisure time widespread, it
is not surprising that gambling has found such ready acceptance by so many people.

## ROLES THE CHRISTIAN CAN PLAY

In the search for prescriptions that will bring sanity and
sanctity to efforts to deal with the menace posed by the gambling mania, the churches can play a useful role. Above all,
they can support strong enforcement of the gambling laws.
In most states gambling is clearly illegal. In recent months
Senator Estes Kefauver and Attorney General Robert F. Kennedy have led the fight for strict controls to assist the states
in their war on the syndicated interstate criminal enterprise
represented by gambling. In the face of proof that extensive
graft and pay-off exist in some local law enforcement circles,
strong federal laws and action are sorely needed. Under the
new laws prohibiting interstate transportation of gambling
paraphernalia, information and promotional material, many of
the wire services and bookie joints have closed down. In the
first 13 months after the laws were passed the Federal Bureau
of Investigation looked into 4,990 possible violations. As a
result, 943 cases were forwarded to the department of justice
for further study. So far 115 persons have been indicted and
26 convicted. Meanwhile there is need for responsible support
of law enforcement agencies by an awakened citizenry. And in
a related area, churchmen could well support the initiation
of higher qualifications for appointment to police forces, as
well as increases in pay which would make graft offers less
attractive. They should encourage such moves in spite of the
higher taxes those increases would mean.

The churches can work against legalization of gambling.

Over a decade ago Thomas E. Dewey as governor of New York state denounced a plea for legalization of gambling presented to the state legislature by New York city:

The entire history of legalized gambling in this country and abroad shows that it has brought nothing but poverty, crime and corruption, demoralization of moral and ethical standards, and ultimately lower living standards and misery for all the people.

As to "glamorous" Las Vegas, reporter Fred J. Cook has written: "The sinister truth is that Nevada's legalization of gambling was one of the greatest boons ever bestowed on the American underworld by a grateful government. . . . The net result has been to make 'fun-loving' Las Vegas virtually the capital of American crime." Churchmen need not be apologetic or timid about fighting such an adversary—though they may find veterans' organizations, charity groups and other churchmen on the adversary's side.

The church must lead its own people through education and commitment to newness and wholeness of life in the Spirit. This is by all odds the most important role it can play in the search for effective prescriptions. In the church, the community of the Spirit, such personal and social habits as gambling should be openly discussed without intimidation by either the sophisticated libertine or the self-righteous pharisee. When youth and adults are acquainted with the facts, they should be allowed the freedom of the Spirit to make their commitment in terms of their personal appropriation of the love of Christ. The possessor of a new life in Christ supported by the resources of God's gracious spirit will become increasingly dissatisfied with the crutches offered by contemporary paganism. The church's pre-eminent task is to be the agency of such healing, a healing that leads one to find his adequacy in God and his enjoyment in the welfare of others.

Within the maturing life of the redemptive community that is the church, many an individual may arrive at a resolution to submit his life to no other priority or providence than that found in the God and Father of our Lord Jesus Christ. His love of neighbor will then stand against every practice which hinders the growth of the human spirit toward the likeness of Christ or which breaks down the structures of justice in society. The Christian will himself refrain from gambling and from publicly endorsing it in any form, realizing that gambling is detrimental to the purpose of life as revealed in Jesus Christ.

# Gambling and Police Corruption

## *J U D G E   J O H N   M .   M U R T A G H*

Last February 29 was my first day in office as chief justice of the Court of Special Sessions of the City of New York. I spent the day presiding in the Gamblers Court, a court that is truly an enigma to anyone concerned with judicial administration. The calendar was crowded—there are some 20,000 arrests of gamblers annually in New York. The atmosphere in the court was permeated by the odor of corruption that inevitably envelops police enforcement of gambling laws. The defendants were represented by a small coterie of lawyers. Racket lawyers are endemic to a Gamblers Court. Many suspect that they are mouthpieces for gambling syndicates. Others suggest that they are mere hirelings for the bondsman, who is the general factotum guiding the gambler through the maze of judicial procedures. It is a challenge for the judge to escape being entwined in the web of these nefarious influences and feeling a certain futility regarding the proceeding.

That first day was a revelation for gamblers. Bookmakers and policy collectors went to jail for terms of up to six months with no alternative of a fine—this in a court where gamblers with ten or fifteen prior convictions traditionally have been fined and the penalty paid by a member of the syndicate standing by.

For the six succeeding months, I continued to deal sternly with gamblers appearing in the court. Repeaters were jailed as standard practice. More substantial jail terms were meted out than had been imposed in the previous decade. In the interim, the legislature vested exclusive jurisdiction of gambling cases in the Magistrates' Courts, effective September first. The judges of the Magistrates' Courts promptly adopted the new policy and are rather uniformly imposing jail sentences on gamblers with prior convictions. Judicial concern has greatly reduced the number of jacket lawyers. The activities of the bondsmen are being subjected to a continuing scrutiny. The judiciary seeks to escape the labyrinth of corruption.

On April 7, Robert Beaman, a thirty-six-year old Harlem policy collectory, was sentenced by me to a $100 fine or ten days in jail; he paid the fine. His relatively light sentence was based on a police record, known as a "yellow sheet," showing that he was a first offender. Shortly after the sentence had been imposed, a sharp-eyed stenographer stated that he had reason to believe that Beaman had a previous record. A recheck on the gambler's yellow sheet showed fifteen prior convictions. It developed that a half-dozen other gamblers had similarly avoided the harshness of the new policy. There are unconfirmed reports that the gamblers were paying between $2500 and $3500 to have their police records altered.

Suspicion centers on the Bureau of Criminal Identification, one of the most heavily guarded units of the police department. After a defendant is fingerprinted, the prints are brought to the Bureau of Criminal Identification. There they are matched with filed records, and a yellow sheet is prepared.

According to the authorities, the fake yellow sheets were on official forms and bore a true imprint of the seal kept in the Bureau of Criminal Identification. This would indicate that the fakes were prepared by someone with access to Bureau of Criminal Identification equipment, but the actual switching could have been done later, possibly in the court building.

What is sought to be determined is how the yellow sheets were abstracted from the offices of the Bureau of Criminal Identification so that the forgeries could be committed. The official records in the offices of the Bureau of Criminal Identification were not altered.

The record fixing reflects the acute desperation felt by gamblers and their hirelings as they sense the end of an era of turnstile justice and routine fines. The entire matter is under investigation by New York County's district attorney, Frank S. Hogan, and already has resulted in three indictments, including that of a lawyer.

On April 19, shortly after the initial expose, New York City's police commissioner, Stephen P. Kennedy, referred to gambling as "the most corrupting influence since prohibition." On August 2, Commissioner Kennedy marked the completion of five years in office. The press commented favorably on his administration and the fact that his tenure has been almost completely free of the traditional scandals that have confounded most of his predecessors. Nonetheless, the commissioner was frank to confess that he is not convinced that police corruption has been ended and to state that at any moment scandal may be exposed. Not without reason, many regard Commissioner Kennedy as the ablest police commissioner New York City has ever had. It is perhaps because of his ability and experience and his knowledge of police history that he does not make the error of deluding himself about the issue of police corruption.

Modern police forces, such as that in New York City, are little more than a century old. It was only at about the time of the Civil War that cities really began to feel the need for paid professional guardians. Yet, virtually from the beginning, corruption has characterized the police in their efforts to enforce laws against gambling.

As early as 1874 the New York state legislature conducted the first investigation into the administration of New York City's police department. Notwithstanding the youth of the department, the investigation revealed widespread corruption on the part of police officers having to do with the enforcement of laws against gambling. One of the colorful personalities on whom the investigation focused was Captain Alexander S. Williams. Captain Williams was known as "Clubber" Williams, his nickname deriving from the fact that he made excessive use of his night stick.

Despite minor periodic exposes, police corruption continued open and unashamed until 1892, when a new brand of reformer came upon the scene. He was the Reverend Dr. Charles H. Parkhurst, sober-looking, dark-eyed, fifty-year-old pastor of the wealthy and conservative Madison Square Presbyterian Church. One Sunday morning in February he entered his pulpit and proceeded to denounce policemen who were in league with gamblers and prostitutes, and Tammany politicians who countenanced such conditions. He told of a gambling house operating in the Tenderloin and boldly accused the police of receiving bribery for its protection.

Dr. Parkhurst was immediately denounced by the police, the politicians, and the press. His sermon was described as "vulgar," "unchristian," "violently vituperative." Other members of the clergy suggested that, since wickedness seemed to hold such attraction for the holy man, he ought henceforth to talk about Sodom and Gomorrah. Charles A. Dana, editor of the *Sun,* thought he should be driven from his pulpit. On February 23, nine days after he had spoken out, Dr. Parkhurst was hailed before the Grand Jury and told to produce proof of the charges he had made. Since his evidence was vague and general, he was rebuked for his "irresponsible accusations."

A weaker man would have retired to lick his wounds, but not Dr. Parkhurst. Instead, he determined to secure the kind of firsthand knowledge at which no jury could scoff. He hired a canny, hard-faced mustachioed private detective named Charles W. Gardner to show him the city's night life. Dr. Parkhurst dressed in a pair of loud flannel trousers, a brown slouch hat pulled low over the right eye, and a bright scarlet neckerchief, and together with Gardner he made the rounds of the most sordid spots in New York City, such as the Five Points, the Bowery, and Satan's Circus.

On Sunday, March 13, two days after they had completed the tour, Dr. Parkhurst chose as his text the eighth verse of the twelfth Psalm: "The wicked walk on every side, when the vilest men are exalted." Everyone, parishioners and the overflow crowd of visitors, knew to whom he had reference.

The Grand Jury, forced to recognize the validity of the new Parkhurst accusations, requested that the four commissioners of the mayor's police board and the top police brass come in and talk about the connection between the city's vice and gambling and its policemen. Although the Grand Jury could not gather enough evidence for a single indictment, it did find that: "The police are either incompetent to do what is frequently done by private individuals with imperfect facilities for such work, or else there exist reasons and motives for such inaction which are illegal and corrupt. The general inefficiency of the Department is so great that it is our belief that the latter suggestion is the explanation of the particular inactivity."

This finding aroused the state legislature, which appointed a committee headed by State Senator Clarence E. Lexow to examine the minister's charges. John D. Goff was named counsel to the committee. Goff called the police superintendent, inspectors, and captains as witnesses before the committee. Widespread police corruption was unearthed. The superintendent was Thomas F. Byrnes, known as the "Great Detective." He had accumulated some $350,000 in real estate and securities during the thirty-two years he had served on the force. Arrogantly he declared that he had "obtained more years of convictions against criminals than the detective forces of Scotland Yard, Paris, and Jersey City all put together," and then surprised everyone with the admission that the department was rotten from top to bottom.

Max F. Schmittberger, a police captain, testified that he collected large sums from the gambling houses, brothels, and saloons of his district. He had to pay $200 a month to his immediate superior, "Clubber" Williams, who was by this time Inspector Alexander S. Williams. Schmittberger, by his testimony, not only avoided a conviction but was retained in the department by the then chairman of the police board, Theodore Roosevelt.

During the investigation, William L. Strong, a liberal

banker, was elected mayor on a fusion reform ticket. But on November 2, 1897, only two years after the investigation, a Tammany candidate, Robert A. Van Wyck, defeated Strong, and men and women snake-danced through the streets singing, "Well, well, well, reform has gone to hell."

While police alliance with gamblers was generally believed to be widespread during the years following the Lexow investigation, it was not until 1912 that another major scandal broke out. Rhinelander Waldo was police commissioner. Schmittberger was chief inspector of the department. Lieutenant Charles F. Becker was the officer in charge of the commissioner's vice squad—traditionally regarded as the most remunerative spot in the department for a dishonest cop. The commissioner had ordered Becker to make an effort to suppress the gambling houses that were in evidence throughout the city. On April 17, the Becker squad conducted a raid on an establishment on 45th Street owned by Herman Rosenthal, much to the annoyance of the gambler. What disturbed Rosenthal particularly was the fact that Becker had been levying tribute for years and even held a chattel mortgage on the raided premises.

Rosenthal called on the police commissioner and on Mayor William J. Gaynor and offered to produce proof that Becker was involved in the protection of organized gambling. When he was rebuffed, he sought out Charles S. Whitman, the district attorney of New York County.

Even before he saw the district attorney, Rosenthal was negotiating with the New York *World* to publish an affidavit in which he exposed Becker's role in organized gambling. Finally, on Saturday, July 13, the New York *World* announced that it would print Rosenthal's affidavit in its Sunday edition, which it did.

Whitman then issued subpoenas to Rosenthal and other prominent gamblers to testify before the Grand Jury. On Tuesday morning at 2 A.M., as Rosenthal emerged from the Hotel Metropole in Times Square, Gyp the Blood, a burglar, Lefty Louis, a pickpocket, Dago Frank, a burglar, and Whitey Lewis, a thief, put four slugs into his body and escaped in a cab that was waiting for them.

Seldom has New York been so aroused. Suspicion immediately focused on Lieutenant Becker. The district attorney pursued the investigation relentlessly and brought about the indictment of Lieutenant Becker and the four actual killers for murder in the first degree. There ensued two trials that were undoubtedly more publicized than any others in New York's history. Public opinion was sharply divided. Whitman presented evidence in the first trial before John D. Goff, who was now a judge of the Court of General Sessions. The jury found the lieutenant guilty of murder in the first degree. The wide acclaim that resulted from the successful prosecution spiraled Whitman to the governor's chair. The conviction was, however, reversed by the Court of Appeals.

A second trial was conducted before Supreme Court Justice Samuel Seabury and again resulted in a conviction of murder in the first degree. Becker was sentenced to death and died in the electric chair.

Meantime, Samuel Seabury became a renowned judge of the Court of Appeals of the State of New York and later one of the most distinguished members of the New York bar. Scandal once again broke out in 1931, and Seabury was appointed counsel to a legislative investigation. While this was a broad investigation of municipal government, the police department was one of the main targets. Corruption was discovered, as usual, to center in the vice squads dealing with gambling and prostitution. One patrolman, James Quinlivan, was found to have deposited $31,000 in five years, and his frugal wife to have banked $57,744.67. A plain-clothes officer, Robert E. Morris, had saved more than $50,000. When called upon for an explanation, Morris stated that he had won $10,000 in gambling and that his Uncle George had given him some $40,000. Unfortunately, Uncle George was dead and could not verify his nephew's statement.

The Seabury investigation was the most sweeping exposé in New York's history. It involved even city hall and brought about the resignation of the then mayor, James J. Walker. It resulted in another fusion reform administration, the administration of Fiorello H. La Guardia. La Guardia's term of office, from 1934 through 1945, is generally regarded as an era of unparalleled integrity in New York's municipal history. Nonetheless, corruption continued to flourish in connection with the police effort to curb gambling.

In the early 1940s, an investigation conducted by Special Prosecutor John Harlan Amen in Brooklyn revealed that gambling was widespread and led to the dismissal and forced resignation of scores of police officers, many of whom held high rank. A highlight of this investigation was photographs of police officers openly taking bribes from known gamblers.

In 1943, the New York City Department of Investigation raided a store in Harlem. For three years prior to the raid, the proprietor of the store had been conducting a policy (numbers) game as an incident to the operation of a grocery business. A ledger, which became known as the "little black book," was seized during the raid. The little black book contained entries of bribes paid to police officers. Each entry had the date, the name of the officer or officers, and a symbol to denote the payment, which varied in amount according to the rank of the police officer. The names of 111 officers of various ranks assigned to the police commands having jurisdiction over the store appeared in the ledger. These included more than 90 per cent of the officers in principal police commands. There perhaps has never been a more graphic revelation of the universality of police corruption arising from the enforcement of gambling laws.

And in 1950 the city was once again rocked by police scandal arising from the enforcement of gambling laws. The testimony of a bookmaker, Harry Gross, led to the indictment, conviction, dismissal, and resignation of scores of police officers of all ranks—easily the greatest shake-up in the city's police history. The investigation did much to discredit the administration of William O'Dwyer, a distinguished mayor who, contrary to popular impression, had personally worked more diligently than any of his predecessors to curb the corrupting influence of gambling on the police department.

My professional career has been almost entirely in the criminal law, as prosecutor, as chief magistrate, and a chief justice of the Court of Special Sessions. My experience with the enforcement of gambling and related laws has made me increasingly critical of the criminal process. I find myself substantially in agreement with President William Howard Taft, who characterized the criminal law as a disgrace to American civilization. I have had to ask myself the basic question: What is—or what should be—the criminal law?

The primary purpose of a code or a system of criminal law is to protect you and me in the security of our lives and property. But if you view the police effort in any of our major cities, you will gain the impression that the protection of human life and property is but a minor and incidental part of the police function.

Criminal law should deal primarily with such matters as murder, robbery, assault, arson, theft, burglary—crimes that threaten the security of our lives and property. Insofar as criminal law deals with other antisocial conduct, the police emphasis should be on prevention rather than detection and arrest.

As for gambling, I believe that existing anti-gambling laws are not only futile but mistaken in basic philosophy. I believe in the moral law. I believe that there is an objective norm of morality. But I do not believe that gambling is a violation of the moral law. Certainly the double standard that makes a bet at a race track morally and legally superior to one placed on a street corner is dubious, to say the least. Even if we grant that gambling is immoral, that it is a violation of the moral law, I question the wisdom of dealing with the problem by criminal or prohibitory legislation.

Gambling is essentially the poor person's means of satisfying a normal human instinct. It puts a spark in his daily existence—an important item when you think of the boredom and the lack of home life of the underprivileged. In a recent policy trial, the prosecutor sought to discredit a defense witness. To a question as to whether she ever played policy, the witness replied with commendable frankness: "Why, sure, man; everyone in Harlem play the numbers." The policy racket is reputed to be a billion dollar a year business. It has been estimated that the American public spends 20 billion dollars a year—most of it illegally—on horse races, football pools, slot machines, and the policy game.

I decry a Las Vegas, but I believe in the legalization of gambling under public control. Bring gambling out in the open. Give the public a chance to satisfy its desire. Then, by appropriate regulatory legislation, extend it in one direction or another, or confine it, as developments warrant.

My policy of strict enforcement of gambling laws does not reflect sympathy with existing laws but rather an attempt to cleanse the court of involvement in corruption and to bring the merits of these laws under broader public scrutiny, paving the way to their ultimate repeal.

In England, too, there is a long history of frustrated gambling legislation, dating back to the reign of King Henry VIII, in 1541. But even more than in the United States, the law in England has never conformed to the dictates of society and has not succeeded in changing a traditionally tolerant attitude toward gamblers. Betting has always enjoyed a kind of social status in British society. After next May, Britain's new Betting and Gaming Bill will permit across-the-counter cash bets on horses in licensed shops, shops in which racing information and odds will be posted on blackboards but in which music, television, and drinking will be prohibited as enticements to loitering. The vote for the bill in the House of Commons was 311 to 49. The decisiveness of the vote is an indication of the public acceptance of gambling in England. In the course of the debate in the House of Commons, J. Chester Ede, a former Labor home secretary, brought an appropriate response when he declared: "I do not believe gambling is a sin. I don't believe it is a crime. I believe it is a folly—and I speak from experience."

And after the laughter subsided, he added: "There is only one day I can recollect when I came home from Epsom Downs feeling that at last I had outwitted the tote."

The new bill even has the approval of Dr. Geoffrey Fisher, the Archbishop of Canterbury, who feels that it may become a way to control a "great social evil."

Yet a similar proposal advanced by New York's present mayor, Robert F. Wagner, at the last two sessions of the state legislature has received little support. The mayor envisages a series of licensed betting parlors, with a "service"

charge on bets. He frankly urges the idea as a revenue-pro-
ducing device. I unqualifiedly endorse the mayor's proposal
for the legalization of off-track betting, not alone in New
York but throughout the nation.

I also endorse a government-operated lottery, such as that
proposed by Congressman Paul A. Fino. The proposed lottery
is very similar to the Irish Sweepstakes, the Mexican National
Lottery, and the much newer French National Lottery. These
have been operated by government agencies, without any
breath of scandal. The major portion of the money taken in
is paid out in prizes; the remainder is used on public health
projects. Would not such a lottery provide some comparatively harmless sublimation for the game player's instinct?
If the federal government does not want to enter the field,
I see no reason why the city or the state should not.

The underworld is thriving on our hypocrisy and stupidity.
So long as we persist in our efforts to end gambling by prohibitory legislation, we promote police corruption. Police hon-
esty can never be a relative matter. Police corruption erodes
the average citizen's respect for the law and makes him cynical about all law enforcement. We cannot continue to tolerate
a partnership that invites corruption. And, yes, we owe it to
the judiciary to end the existing judicial farce.

# GLOSSARY

**Ace**—The 1 spot on a die.

**Across-the-Board**—Race bettor's term for placing a win, place, and show bet.

**Action**—The betting.

**Bankroll Man**—The man who finances a gambling scheme.

**Bevels or Beveled Shapes**—Crooked dice having one or more sides slightly rounded rather than flat so that the dice tend to roll off the rounded surface more than the flat.

**Blanket Roll**—In craps, a controlled 2-dice roll made on a soft surface, usually a blanket.

**Blockout Work**—A method of marking cards in which parts of the design are blocked out with white ink, or some configuration in the design is slightly exaggerated.

**Bootlegging**—Usually refers to getting the information from inside the track to a point outside the track by a radio or runner or some other device. However, where the physical structure of the track permits it, the common method of obtaining such information is by the device called the peek.

**Breaks or Breakage to a Nickel or Dime**—The rounding out or dropping of the last cent digit or fraction thereof to a 5 or 0 on each $2 mutuel race ticket. The racetracks in New York State break to a dime.

**Brick**—A crooked die that has been cut so that it is not a true cube.

**Bug**—(1) A steel gimmick placed in the mechanism of a slot machine which prevents certain combinations from hitting. (2) A clip which can be attached to the underside of a card table to hold cards secretly removed from the deck. "To Bug": To gimmick as above.

**Busters**—In craps, a pair of "tops" (misspotted dice). Tops are made in various combinations which make only certain numbers and are called busters because one combination will bust up another combination.

**Bustout Man**—A dice mechanic whose specialty is switching crooked dice (usually "busters") in and out of the game.

**Cackle the Dice**—To pretend to shake the dice by making them rattle when actually they are held by a special finger grip that prevents them from turning freely in the hand.

**Calculators**—Mathematicians, or odds men, who work in the calculations rooms at racetracks and do the work that cannot be done by the track's totalizator.

**Card Mechanic**—A person who manipulates cards for cheating purposes.

**Check Cop**—An adhesive paste which a cheat places on his palm. When

This glossary of gambling terminology and related terms was prepared by the staff of the Permanent Subcommittee on Investigations of the Committee on Government Operations, United States Senate, 87th Congress, First Session, 1961 for *Gambling and Organized Crime*.

he puts his hand on a stack of checks (chips) or coins, the top one adheres to his palm, and he cops (steals) it.

**Cold Deck**—A deck of cards which has secretly been arranged by a card cheat in a certain order for the purpose of switching later for the deck in play. Also called cooler.

**Comeback Money**—Money bet away from the track with bookies which they then rebet at the track to try to change the odds on a certain horse.

**Cover**—(1) To accept a wager. (2) To place a bet on a gambling layout.

**Cut-Edge Dice**—Crooked dice with some edges cut at a 60-degree angle and others at a 45-degree angle. They tend to fall in the direction of the 60-degree cut more often than the 45-degree cut.

**Cutout Card Markings**—To make these, a minute area of ink on the back design is chemically bleached or scraped with a knife, adding a white area that wasn't there originally.

**Drop**—Usually a bookmaking operation, but may also signify a more localized distributor to the bookmakers.

**Edge Work or Edge Markings**—A deck of cards marked with a slight bevel or "belly" drawn on certain points of each card between the design and the edge of the card. A bevel mark high up indicates an ace, lower down a king, etc.

**Electric Dice**—Crooked dice loaded with steel slugs and used over an electric magnet hidden in or under a counter or dice table.

**First Flop Dice**—Heavily loaded dice used with a slick cup. So called because the loads are so heavy that a skilled dice cheat can throw five of a kind. Also called Dead Number dice.

**Five-Cent or Nickel Line**—A bookie's baseball or sports price line that has a differential of one-quarter point between his lay and take odds. The bookie quotes odds of 5⅛ to 5, pick 'em.

**Flat Passers**—Crooked dice which have the 6-1 sides cut down on one die and the 3-4 sides cut down on the other so that 4, 5, 9, and 10 appear more often.

**Flats**—Crooked dice which have been shaved so that they are slightly brick-shaped. Also called Bricks.

**Forty-Cent Line**—A bookie's baseball or sport's price line that has a differential of 2 points between his lay and take odds. The bookie quotes odds of 6 to 5, pick 'em.

**Gaff, G, or Gimmick**—Any secret device or method which accomplishes or aids in cheating.

**Gaffed Dice**—Doctored or crooked dice.

**Handbook**—A street bookie who takes horse bets.

**Handicapper**—(1) Track official employee who assigns weights to certain horses in a race. (2) A writer working for a newspaper or racing sheet who tries to select probable race winners.

**Handle**—The total amount of money that repeatedly changes hands in a betting scheme before it is actually won or lost.

**Holdout Man**—A card cheat who specializes in palming, holding out of play, and reintroducing valuable cards into a game by means of palming.

**Hot Horse**—A horse who, in a series of races, has not been allowed to try to win, so that his performance is not good. On a day certain when conditions are right, he will be allowed to run and is expected to win. The price will be long on him so the bookmakers are warned against him. Such horses are controlled by gambling stables.

**Humps**—See "Strippers."

**Inside Work**—Any gaff—"Loads," for example—placed inside a die or pair of dice.

**Jar Game**—A form of punchboard in which numbered paper tickets, individually folded and sealed, are drawn from a jar.

**Keyed Punchboards**—Punchboards sold with a secret key (list) that gives the cheat the location of the big prize awards.

**Light Work**—Doctored cards marked with very fine lines.

**Line Work**—On doctored cards, additional small spots, curlicues or lines added to the back design of playing cards so that they can be read from the back by the cheat.

**Loads**—Loaded dice. See also "Inside Work."

**Low Belly Strippers**—A crooked deck of cards in which the edges of the high cards are concave rather than straight, making it possible for the cheat to cut a low card at will.

**Luminous Readers**—Marked cards that can be read only through tinted glasses.

**Misses**—(1) Crooked dice that are gaffed to make more 7's than point numbers. (2) Crooked dice that are gaffed to make more missouts than passes.

**Morning Line**—A handicapper's or pricemaker's morning guess as to the probable odds on horses that are to run in the afternoon races.

**Order Horse**—A horse that has been entered in a race with no purpose of winning. So long as he is not to win, no further information is necessary. On the day that he is to win, the information goes out and the "order horse" becomes a "hot horse."

**Outside Work**—Anything done to gaff dice on their surfaces.

**Passers**—Crooked dice which are so gaffed that they tend to make more passes than fair dice.

**Past Posting**—The trick of betting with a bookie on the results of a race which is already known to the bettor because his information is more prompt than the bookmaker's.

**Peek**—A setup whereby an operator from a position outside the track can observe the totalizer board by telescope or other means and thus give out the results promptly and properly.

**Percentage (P.C.)**—An advantage obtained by offering less than the true odds or by the use of crooked dice or controlled shots. Also called Edge or Vigorish.

**Percentage Dice**—Crooked dice which over a period of time supply a percentage in the cheater's favor.

**Pitcher and Catcher**—Refers to a "bootlegging" operation whereby the "pitcher," an operator from inside the track (a wigwagger), transmits the race results to the "catcher," a confederate outside the track, who relays the information to those in the business of selling prompt information of use in gambling on horse races.

**Price Line or Line**—A sports bookie's lay and take odds on a sports event. "I'll lay 7 to 5 that Navy beats Army or take 8 to 5 that Army beats Navy": This is his price line.

**Pricemakers' Percentage Table**—A table which transposes the odds "to 1" into percentages.

**Revised Line**—A racing sheet which prints the latest revised odds. Also called Late Line.

**Scratch Sheet**—A publication containing the program of the day's races at all tracks, the names and post positions of the horses, the names of the jockeys and probable odds. It is the "worksheet" for offtrack horse betting among bookies. There are many types of scratch sheets such as Armstrong, National, etc. Bettors refer to horses' names, but bookies refer to them as "Armstrong No. 1," etc.

**Script**—Refers to providing a running description of the race. This is never essential to the bookmaker, but it transports some of the atmosphere of the track to the horse room or betting establishment and stimulates the interest of the player.

**Shapes**—Dice whose shapes have been altered in some way so that they are no longer perfect cubes.

**Shiner**—A small mirror which reflects the face of the top card of the deck as it is dealt. Usually concealed in rings, matchboxes, pipes, coins, etc.

**Six-Ace Flats**—Crooked dice which give a favorable percentage to a wrong bettor.

**Slick Dice Cup**—A cup which is gaffed with a polished inner surface.

**Strippers**—A deck of cards whose edges have been trimmed, making some cards either narrower or shorter than others.

**Ten-Cent or Dime Line**—A bookie's baseball or sports price line that has a differential of one-half point between his lay and take odds. The bookie quotes odds of 5¼ to 5, pick 'em.

**The Ticket**—A list of the horses as they finished in the race in positions 1, 2, and 3; i.e. the win horse, the place horse, and the show horse, plus the prices they paid for these positions.

**Tip Book**—A variation of the punchboard made to resemble a paper match folder and containing sealed and numbered paper tickets.

**Tops and Bottoms**—Gaffed dice which bear only 3 different numbers on each die. Also called Tops, Busters, T's, and Mis-spots.

**Twenty-Cent Line**—A bookie's baseball or sports price line that has a differential of 1 point between his lay and take odds. The bookie quotes odds of .5½ to 5, pick 'em.

**Vigorish, Viggerish, or Vig**—The percentage under which the bookie works or his edge on bets, or the percentage taken by a banking-game operator. It may be either overt or hidden by the mechanics or mathematics of the game.

**WATS**—The abbreviation for wide area telephone service. This is a telephone company service whereby the customer is given a flat rate for long-distance telephone calls to limited areas at specific times of the day. This service is wanted by the bookies because of the special rates and also because the telephone company does not keep records of the long-distance calls for this service.

**Whip Shot**—A controlled dice shot in which the two dice are spun from the hand and strike the table surface with a flat spinning motion so that the controlled numbers are on top when the dice stop.

**Wigwaggers**—This usually refers to some "bootlegging" operation where a person obtains the race results from inside the track and transmits it to a point outside, such as by walking, signaling, or flashing the information to someone outside the track for relay to others.

**Work**—(1) Crooked cards, or dice. (2) The gaff itself.

# NOTES

# "Policy": Poor Man's Roulette
## St. Clair Drake and Horace Cayton

1 The origin of the term "policy" is obscure, but at least as early as the Nineties it was applied to lottery games in which the gambler "purchased" a number and received a duplicate receipt, the original being forwarded to the headquarters of the "pool." Gosnell, in his *Negro Politicians*, states that this type of lottery was so prevalent in New York City around the turn of the century that an anti-policy law was passed by the state in 1901. Illinois passed a similar law in 1905 in an effort to break up the game in Chicago.

In the early policy games the winning numbers were selected by drawing numbered slips from a bowl. In the late Twenties, some enterprising New Yorkers hit upon the idea of taking bets on the probable last three numbers of the daily Federal Reserve Clearing House report. This variant form of "policy"—known as the "numbers game"—was very popular on the Eastern seaboard because it placed the game "on the level." No racketeer could tamper with the Clearing House figures, and anyone could read them in the newspaper. During an attempt to smash the racket, newspapers were asked to print these reports in round numbers. The resourceful racketeers then shifted to other published numbers. Throughout this period, "policy" numbers in Chicago were selected by the traditional lottery drawings. Clearing House numbers were never popular in Midwest Metropolis.

2 There are two other two-number plays: "Sides" and "Caps." A policy slip is printed in either one or two vertical rows of twelve numbers each. These twelve numbers, when divided into threes, result in sections known as "Caps." Two numbers directly beside each other and within a "cap" constitute a winning "cap." On the other hand, any two numbers in a two-legged book, beside each other but not in "caps," are known as "sides" and return $8 for a dime. A winning "cap" yields $20.

3 Before the present policy syndicate had made satisfactory arrangements with the city fathers, the drawings were conducted surreptitiously in old garages, in the front rooms of apartments, in trucks, or in the open fields and woods in the suburbs of the city. During the last ten years, when the "heat was on" several times temporarily, the drawings have been made in a truck equipped with a lottery wheel and printing press.

4 One prominent policy syndicate member told an interviewer about a period when the "heat was on"—i.e., when an attempt was being made by the police to suppress the game: "In the spring of 1929, the heat was turned on the policy game and stations as well as wheels were raided. Small fines were assessed in some cases. They were paid by operators, and business was continued the next day. The heat stayed on until about 1933, but this did not stop the wheels from operating.

They continued to run and pay bonds for the writers. After the death of Mayor Cermak, the syndicate was formed and policy has run under this protection since." The heat was turned on temporarily during the winter of 1940, creating considerable excitement in Bronzeville.

## Observations on Gambling in a Lower-Class Setting
### Irving Kenneth Zola

° This report is part of a study entitled "Relocation and Mental Health: Adaptation Under Stress," conducted by the Center For Community Studies in the Department of Psychiatry of the Massachusetts General Hospital and the Harvard Medical School. The research is supported by the NIMH, grant # 3M 9137-C3. The author wishes to acknowledge Edward Ryan and Leonora K. Zola for their repeated readings and criticisms, and Frances Morrill, Stanton Wheeler, and George H. Wolkon for their valuable suggestions.

1 Edmund Bergler, *The Psychology of Gambling*, New York: Hill and Wang, 1957; and "The Gambler—A Misunderstood Neurotic," *Journal of Criminal Psychopathology*, 4 (1943), pp. 379–393.

2 James Hunter and Arthur Bruner, "Emotional Outlets of Gamblers," *Journal of Abnormal and Social Psychology*, 23 (1928), pp. 38–39; and Robert P. Morris, "An Exploratory Study of Some Personality Characteristics of Gamblers," *Journal of Clinical Psychology*, 13 (1957), pp. 191–193.

3 Edward C. Devereux, Jr., "Gambling and the Social Structure—A Sociological Study of Lotteries and Horse Racing in Contemporary America," Unpublished doctoral dissertation, Harvard University, 1949.

4 Herbert A. Bloch, "The Sociology of Gambling," *American Journal of Sociology*, 57 (1951), pp. 215–222; and "The Gambling Business: An American Paradox," *Crime and Delinquency*, 8 (1962), pp. 355–364.

5 Devereux, *op. cit.*

6 Devereux, *op. cit.*

7 Gustav G. Carlson, "Number Gambling—A Study of a Culture Complex," Unpublished doctoral dissertation, University of Michigan, 1939; and Devereux, *op. cit.*

8 Devereux, *op. cit.*

9 Walter B. Miller, "Lower Class Cultures as a Generating Milieu of Gang Delinquency," *Journal of Social Issues*, 14 (1958), pp. 5–19.

10 *Ibid.*

11 Albert K. Cohen, *Delinquent Boys*, Glencoe, Illinois: Free Press, 1955; and Robert K. Merton, *Social Theory and Social Structure*, Rev. and Enl. Ed., Glencoe, Illinois: Free Press, 1957, Chaps. IV and V.

12 Robert A. Dentler and Kai T. Erikson, "The Functions of Deviance in Groups," *Social Problems*, 7 (1959), pp. 98–107.

13 Lewis A. Coser, "Some Functions of Deviant Behavior and Normative Flexibility," *American Journal of Sociology*, 68 (1962), pp. 172–181; and Kai T. Erikson, "Notes on the Sociology of Deviance," *Social Problems*, 9 (1962), pp. 307–314.

14 Robert D. Herman, "Gambling Institutions: The Race Track,"

Unpublished manuscript presented at the 1963 Meeting of The Pacific Sociological Association.

## The Adoration of the Nag
### Leo Rosten

† According to a Gallup poll, 29 percent of the adult American population have participated in church lotteries—a greater number, incidentally, than the 23 percent who have played slot machines, the 21 percent who have played cards for money, the 19 percent who have bet on elections, the 13 percent who have held sweepstakes tickets, the 10 percent who have bet on horse races (*sic!*), or the 9 percent who have fallen for the charms of the numbers game. (The percentages would be even greater today; the Gallup poll was taken in 1938.) Pinball, punchboards, and slot machines take in from a half to three-quarters of a *billion* dollars annually—as much as the total business in all the shoe stores of the nation.

* Joseph M. Schenck had $403,000 invested in the Compañia Mexicaña del Agua Caliente's vast hotel, casino, clubhouse, dog track, and golf course; he sold his holdings for $50,000 after the Mexican government outlawed gambling.

## Sport of Kings, Bums, and Businessmen
### John McDonald

* Hervey took his name from the great horse Salvator, an immensely popular three-year-old champion of 1889.
* Incidentally, there are no descendants in U.S. racing of the Belmont, Keene, and Jerome families, who dominated the sport just after the Civil War, when it became popular in the North. However, a branch of the Jeromes is active in British racing: Leonard Jerome had a daughter, Jennie, who married Lord Randolph Churchill, and had a son, Sir Winston, who has had a stable in England since 1949.

## The Jackpot: Gambling in the Soviet Bloc

1 The more intimate and sophisticated games of chance and skill—roulette, backgammon, card and dice games—which were once a standard feature of casinos and clubs have all but disappeared. Bulgaria's new Black Sea resorts, however, have gambling casinos, and there has been talk, after the war and again after 1956, of opening a casino for tourists on Margaret Island in Budapest.
2 There are now two—"Sazka" and "Sportka."
3 August 16, 1960 drawing, as published in *Izvestia na Presidiuma* (Sofia), August 19, 1960.
4 Average monthly industrial wage: 600 leva.

# Gambling as Work: A Sociological Study of the Race Track
## Robert D. Herman

[1] *The American Racing Manual* (Triangle Publications, Inc., 1964). In 1963, wagering increased 6.7 percent over 1962.

[2] Attendance at horse races increased 8 percent while the U.S. population 21 years of age and older increased 1.1 percent. *Statistical Abstract of the United States, 1963* (Washington, D.C.,: U.S. Department of Commerce).

[3] John Scarne, *Scarne's Complete Guide to Gambling* (New York: Simon & Schuster, 1961), p. 32. A more moderate estimate was reported by Robert Kennedy to Congress that $7 billion was gambled in the U.S. in 1960. See, *Hearings*, Subcommittee on the Judiciary, House of Reps., 87th Congress, Washington, 1961, "Legislation Relating to Organized Crime," p. 24.

[4] The "Big A" had an average daily attendance of 33,120 in 1964 with an average daily handle of $3,236,086. Hollywood Park (Los Angeles) had an average daily attendance of 34,081 that year and an average daily handle of $2,885,795.

[5] Nevada Gaming Commission, *Legalized Gambling in Nevada* (Carson City, Nevada: Gaming Policy Board, 1963).

[6] Except for articles in this volume by Zola and Frazier, the following are the most important publications by sociologists on gambling in the last two decades: The best treatment of horse racing is Edward C. Devereux, Jr., "Gambling and the Social Structure—A Sociological Study of Lotteries and Horse Racing in Contemporary America," (unpublished Ph.D. dissertation, Harvard University, 1949). As this book goes to press, a second doctoral dissertation on the sociology of horse racing is being prepared by Marvin Scott, University of California, Berkeley. Soccer pools are studied by Nechama Tec, *Gambling in Sweden* (Totawa, N.J.: The Bedminster Press, 1964). Herbert A. Bloch has contributed two essays: "The Sociology of Gambling," *American Journal of Sociology*, 57 (1951), pp. 215–222; and Chapter 23 of *Crime in America*, edited by Bloch (Philosophical Library, New York, 1961). A few sociologists have, of course, examined issues related to gambling, especially racketeering, organized crime, and gambling among ethnic minorities.

[7] In "hunch betting," a horse is selected on arbitrary grounds having nothing to do with the horse's ability. Hunch players usually agree that their actions are not objectively based, but other complex motives may be involved. For a discussion of "psychological probability," see John Cohen, *Chance, Skill and Luck: The Psychology of Guessing and Gambling* (Baltimore, Md.: Penguin Books, 1960).

The term "handicapper" formerly referred to the person, now called the racing secretary, who assigns racing conditions and weights carried by horses. The term now has been extended to include anyone who makes a calculated attempt to determine the winning probabilities of horses in a given race. Many city newspapers publish "selections" which are of some aid to novice bettors. For monthly ratings of major public handicappers, see the magazine, *Turf and Sports Digest* (Baltimore, Md.: Montee Publishing Co., Inc.).

[8] Marvin Scott gives special attention to the fact that the act of a trainer's giving final instructions to the jockey occurs in full view of the crowd—but out of earshot. *Op. cit.*

[9] Among the most highly regarded *Form*-oriented books is Robert S. Dowst, *The Odds, The Player, The Horses* (New York: Dodd Mead & Co., 1959). Two examples of crowd-oriented texts are Burton P. Fabricand, *Horse Sense* (David McKay Co., 1965); E. R. DaSilva and Roy M. Dorcus, *Science in Betting* (New York: Harper & Row, 1961).

[10] Fabricand, *op. cit.* This book purports to have been based on analyses of races performed by a high-speed digital computer. One is reminded of an analysis of blackjack ("21") gambling also based on computer analysis. See E. O. Thorp, *Beat the Dealer* (New York: Vintage Books, 1966).

[11] Scarne, *op. cit.,* p. 57.

[12] For further discussion of the daily pattern of betting at race tracks, see William H. McGlothlin, "Stability of Choices among Uncertain Alternatives," *American Journal of Psychology,* 69 (1956), p. 406.

Of the total handle, an unknown proportion consists of bets made by nonattendees who send money to the track by two main channels. Often attendees are given money by friends to bet on horses previously selected; bookmakers occasionally send "layoff" money by way of professional couriers. In layoff betting, the bookmaker places a bet with another bookmaker or at the track at which a race is to be run so as to hedge his losses to his customers should their heavy favorite in that race win. Layoff networks are illegal, and they are periodically the objects of Congressional scrutiny. See *Gambling and Organized Crime,* Hearings before the Permanent Subcommittee on Investigations of the Committee on Governmental Operations, United States Senate, 87th Congress, 1961.

[13] Derived from R. C. Evenson and C. C. Jones, *The Way They Run* (Los Angeles, Cal.: Techno-Graphic Publications, 1964), p. 55. The average win payoffs of first, second, third, and fourth choices were (for $2 wagered): $5.75, $8.90, $11.80, and $15.83.

[14] Literally any race could serve as an example of a violation of the general rule, but to take a prominent instance, the 1965 Kentucky Derby: the fourth choice won, and the favorite placed tenth. Fabricand, a mathematician, is so taken with the correlation between wagering and winning, that he devotes an entire chapter of his "textbook" to extolling the public's wisdom. Fabricand, *op. cit.,* Chapter IV.

[15] Bloch, "The Sociology of Gambling," *op. cit.,* pp. 217–218.

[16] Tec, *op. cit.,* p. 108.

[17] *Ibid.*

[18] Irving Kenneth Zola, "Observations on Gambling in a Lower-Class Setting," reprinted in this volume from *Social Problems,* 10 (1963), p. 360.

[19] Some experimental attempts have been made to investigate the "utility of money" apart from the "utility of gambling." See Halsey L. Royden, Patrick Suppes, and Karol Walsh, "A Model for the Experimental Measurement of the Utility of Gambling," *Behavioral Science* 4 (1959), pp. 11–18.

[20] Gregory Stone has written that some sport modes, "mark transformations of the play form into work—professional and otherwise sub-

sidized athletes. . . . Second, there are sports that are transformations
of work form into play." These latter are engaged in by "amateurs."
See Gregory P. Stone and Marvin J. Taves, "Camping in the Wilder-
ness," in Éric Larrabee and Rolf Meyersohn (eds.), *Mass Leisure*
(Glencoe, Illinois: The Free Press, 1958), p. 296.

[21] That such standards are obsolete is suggested by John Kenneth
Galbraith, *The Affluent Society*, (Boston: Houghton Mifflin Co., 1958).

[22] For a prediction of the ways in which automation may be
separating middle managers from the traditional decision-making satisfactions of supervision, see Harold J. Leavitt and Thomas L. Whistler,
"Management in the 1980's," *Harvard Business Review*, Vol. 36
(Nov./Dec., 1958), p. 46. For evidence that their predictions are
correct, see Jack B. Weiner, "Cutbacks in Middle Management," *Dun's
Review and Modern Industry*, Vol. 84 (July, 1964).

[23] 1963 data reported in Evenson and Jones, *op. cit.*, p. 55.

[24] Lee Rainwater, Richard P. Coleman, Gerald Handel, *Workingman's Wife* (New York: MacFadden-Bartell, Inc., 1962), Chapter III,
"Inner Life and the Outer World." "In comparison with the middle-
class wife, *reality is, in its ordinary presentation to her, flat, unvarnished
and not highly differentiated.*" p. 52.

[25] Betty Friedan (*The Feminine Mystique*, New York: W. W.
Norton & Co., 1957), has described middle-class women as suffering
from many of the same deprivations as those of their lower-class sisters.
If she is correct, their similar gambling behavior could be accounted
for by the same factors.

[26] Mirra Komarovsky, "Functional Analysis of Sex Roles," *American
Sociological Review*, XV (August, 1950), 508–516.

[27] Thorstein Veblen, *The Theory of the Leisure Class* (New York:
Macmillan Co., 1899), p. 36.

## The Gambler and His Love
### Iago Galdston, M.D.

[1] Read at the 116th annual meeting of The American Psychiatric
Association, Atlantic City, N.J., May 9–13, 1960.

[2] The New York Academy of Medicine, 2 East 103 St., New
York 29, N.Y.

## Inspirational Group Therapy:
## A Study of Gamblers Anonymous
### Alvin Scodel, Ph.D.

[1] Department of Psychology, Ohio State University.

[2] The writer joined the group while working at Mt. Zion Psychiatric
Clinic, San Francisco, on a United States Public Health Service Stipend.
All the members knew his occupational affiliation, and he made no
attempt to hide the fact that he was primarily interested in how such
groups work rather than any personal therapy. Still, it is relevant to

note that while the writer hardly regards himself as a compulsive gambler, his history is sufficiently replete with instances of gambling behavior (about which he was necessarily candid) that he had few misgivings concerning his presence in the group. In fact, this history dictated the choice of inspirational groups.

There are no taboos against publicizing the activities of the group so long as anonymity of the members is maintained.

3 A provocative critique of theories of mass man is provided in the first chapter of Daniel Bell's *The End of Ideology,* Free Press, Glencoe, Ill., 1960.

4 Lindner, R. *Rebel Without A Cause.* Grune & Stratton. New York, 1944.

5 Bell, D., Ed. *The Radical Right.* Doubleday, Garden City, N.Y., 1963.

6 Toqueville, A. de: *Democracy in America.* Vol. II. Knopf. New York, 1945.

7 Freud, S. Dostoevsky and Parricide. In *Collected Papers,* Vol. V. Hogarth Press, London, 1950.

8 Greenson, R. On Gambling. *Am. Imago,* 4: 61, 1947.

9 Bergler, E., *The Psychology of Gambling.* Hill & Wang, New York, 1957.

## Christians and the Gambling Man
### Lycurgus M. Starkey, Jr.

1 *Mr. Starkey is a member of the faculty of the Saint Paul School of Theology* (*Methodist*), *Kansas City, Missouri.*

2 Quoted by permission of the attorney general.

# Index